MEME

Family Genealogies of the following families:

Nicholas Schroeder from Hallschlag, Trier, Germany

John Phillip Schmidt from Würtemburg, Germany

Augustus Seifert from Walterhausen, Bavaria, Germany

John Bauman from Saxony, Germany

Augustus Hahn from Hanover, Hessen, Germany

by Karen Emery Dwyer

Author's Notes

1. There are no living people mentioned in this book except for my immediate family from who I have permission.

2. Very often, a name, especially in the census records, would be misspelled. It was spelled as it was pronounced.   You will see in this book various spellings of the same name as I spelled the name the way I found it in the research record.

3. Siblings and descendants often spelled their last names differently than their parents for many different reasons. In most cases, this was done to Americanize their name.

4. Ancestors that are in bold print are my direct line.

5. In some cases, because the borders in Europe were changing, the ancestor's place of birth changed from census to census. For example: If an immigrant was born close to the German border near Poland, in one census it might be listed that he was born in Germany and in the next census, it might be listed he was born in Poland.

ISBN 1442127139

EAN-13 9781442127135

© Copyright 2009 Karen Emery Dwyer
6226 Willet Court
Lakewood Ranch, Florida 34202
karensdwyer@yahoo.com

Cover by the author

Printed in the United States of America by CreateSpace, a DBA of On-Demand Publishing LLC, part of the Amazon group of companies.

Acknowledgements

Thank you to my many cousins who shared names and dates of their family's births, marriages, deaths and most of all pictures. Thankfully we were able to find each other and share our information.

A special thanks to my mother, Gertrude Bowman Emery Weyneth (Meme), who thought she was no help at all, but was a wealth of information. She was able to point me in the right direction and help me so much in piecing together the family tree. She was able to help me with some family stories which are scattered throughout this book. Because of this, I found it appropriate to name this book after her.

This family research has been very gratifying to me and has allowed me to meet many cousins that I never knew I had.

Karen Emery Dwyer
2009

A Word about the Genealogical Number System

The numbering system used in this book is the Simple Register Report format, the format accepted by the New England Historic Genealogical Society, one of the oldest genealogical societies in the country. The format dates back to 1870 and is used to establish "pedigrees".

This book consists of five chapters of Genealogical Summaries. Numbers are assigned to the people covered in the genealogy.

The progenitor is given the number 1. Each child is then numbered in order with lower-case Roman numerals (i, ii, iii, iv, v, etc.) and those whose lines are carried on are also given an Arabic number. For instance, No. 1 may have had seven children (i through vii), but only one of these had descendants, say iv. No. iv is then also given the Arabic number 2 and his children, in turn, are numbered from i on, with, perhaps, Nos. i, iv and vi given the additional identification of 3, 4 and 5.

For example, in Chapter Two:

6. Mary Johanna Schmidt[3] (John Jacob Schmidt[2], John Philip Schmidt[1]) was born 8 November 1864 in West Leyden, New York.

Mary Johanna Schmidt and George Sifer had the following children:

27.   i.   Susanna Etta Sifer Bowman was born 17 July 1893 in Ava, New York
       ii.   George John Sifer was born 18 April 1900 in Utica, New York

The bold numbers are Mary and Susanna's unique Arabic numbers in the system.
John Phillip Schmidt [1] with unique number [1] is the progenitor who immigrated to America. The number **27** for Susanna indicates she had children. Whereas George has the ii, which indicates he did not have children.

Table of Contents

The Relationship between the Schroeders, Schmidts and Seiferts

(Author's Mother's Maternal Side)

The Schroeders	The Schmidts
(Chapter One)	(Chapter Two)

Matthew Schroeder's Daughter: John Philip Schmidt's Son:

Catherine…………… Married………….. John Jacob Schmidt

The Seiferts

(Chapter Three)

Their daughter   Augustus Isaac Seifert's Son

Mary Johanna Schmidt …..........Married………… George Sifer

The relationships between the Baumans and the Hahns and how they connect to the Schroeders, Schmidts and Seiferts.

(Author's Mother's Paternal Side)

The Bauman's   ## The Hahn's

(Chapter Four)   (Chapter Five)

John Bauman's son   Augustus Hahn's daughter

George............ married.....................Rose Hahn

Their son

George Francis Bowman.......... Married............. Susanna Etta Sifer

The daughter of Mary Johanna Schmidt and George Sifer.

The Schroeders settled in the Town of Ava, New York.

Ava was formed from the Town of Boonville on May 12, 1846. Ava lies 12 miles north of Rome and is five miles long and about ten miles wide. The land is quite level and well watered by streams that enter the Mohawk River on the east and Fish Creek on the west making good locations for saw mills cutting heavy timber for market. Dairy farming was another big occupation in this area. Following the Revolutionary War, the inhabitants were early pioneers from Connecticut and Massachusetts. They were soon followed by Germans eager to leave Germany in the 1800's. By 1860 the population of Ava was 1260. Many cheese factories opened up along with saw mills. An early history of Oneida County states that the schools in the Town of Ava were generously sustained. The funds raised to maintain high educational standards exceeded the majority of the towns in the county. The early schools were often located in buildings that served other purposes, such as local meeting halls.[1]

Post card of Ava, New York circa 1900. Postcard given to me by a friend and used with permission.

---

[1] A Brief History of Ava by James Pitcher

The Schmidts and Seiferts settled in West Leyden, New York.

The Town of Lewis was formed form the towns of Leyden and West Turin on November 11, 1852. The village of West Leyden had the only post office in the Town of Lewis. West Leyden was first settled in the summer of 1798 and about 1831 ten German families settled in this town. At the time of the 1855 census, 376 of the inhabitants were from Germany. They were divided between the Catholic, Lutheran and Reformed Protestant Dutch denominations. These foreigners were industrious, hardy and frugal people, obedient to the laws and mostly became naturalized citizens as soon as they were allowed. St. Michael's Church at Mohawk Hill, New York, just north of West Leyden was the first Catholic Church in built by Germans. Then in 1859 aboard a small sailing vessel were Prussian Catholics, the Urtz family, who at the height of the storm dropped to their knees and promised God that if He brought them safe to America, they would build a church with their own hands and dedicate it to the Blessed Virgin Mary. By 1881 the German settlers were ready to build their promised church. The Urtz brothers donated land and the church was built from stones taken from nearby fields. They named the church St. Mary's. St. Mary's was located west of West Leyden on the Osceola Road. The church burned to the ground in the spring of 1940.

Photo of West Leyden, New York in 1918. Photo given to me by a friend and used with permission.

<u>The Baumans and Hahns</u> settled in Utica, New York.

Utica was first settled by Europeans in 1773, on the site of Fort Schuyler which was built in 1758 and abandoned after the French and Indian War. The settlement eventually became known as Old Fort Schuyler when a military fort in nearby Fort Stanwix was renamed Fort Schuyler during the American Revolution, and gradually evolved into a village. The perhaps apocryphal account of Utica's naming suggests that around a dozen citizens of the Old Fort Schuyler settlement met at the Bagg's Tavern to discuss the name of the emerging village. Unable to settle on one particular name, the name Utica was drawn from several suggestions, and the village thereafter became associated with Utica, Tunisia, the ancient Carthaginian city. [2]

Post card of the Busy Corner, Utica, New York, ca 1890 to 1900 in the personal collection of the author.

---

[2] http://en.wikipedia.org/wiki/Utica,_New_York   x

Chapter One

Descendants of Nicolas Schroeder

Generation One

1. Nicolas Schroeder[1] was born in 1740 in Hallschlag, Germany and died 7 April 1808 in Hallschlag, Germany. Nicholas married Barbara Plattes *about* 1765. She was born *about* 1743 in Hallschlag, Germany and died 2 February 1780 in Hallschlag, Germany.[1] After Barbara's death he married Gertrude Breuer *about* 1793 in St. Nicholas Church, Hallschlag, Germany. She was born *about* 1750 and died 10 April 1805 in Hallschlag, Germany. It was a common practice in the 1700 and 1800's that if a male child died in infancy, the next male child born was again named after the father to carry on his name.

Nicholas Schroeder and Barbara Plattes had the following children:
      i.   Margaret Schroeder was born 1 December 1766 in Hallschlag, Germany.
      ii.   Barbara Schroeder was born 27 February 1769 in Hallschlag, Germany.
      iii.   Nicholas Schroeder was born 28 April 1771 in Hallschlag, Germany.
      iv.   Nicholas Schroeder was born 3 November 1773 in Hallschlag, Germany.
      v.   Mary Schroeder was born 8 October 1776 in Hallschlag, Germany and died 13 March 1779 in Hallschlag, Germany.

Nicholas Schroeder and Gertrude Breuer had the following child:
2.   i.   **Nicolas Schroeder** was born 7 December 1794 in Hallschlag, Germany and died 6 August 1862 in Ava, New York.[2]

---

[1] All the above information was taken from the FHC Film #432733 from St. Nikolaus Church, Hallschlag, Germany
[2] St. Michael's Cemetery, Mohawk Hill, New York

Generation Two

2. Nicolas Schroeder[2] (Nicolas[1]) was born in December 1794 in Hallschlag, Germany[3] and died 6 August 1862 in Ava, New York.[4] Nicolas was baptized in St. Nikolaus Church, Hallschlag, Germany. He married Anne Leif 1 August 1813 in Hallschlag.[5] She was born in 1787 and died before 1850.[6] Hallschlag is a small town in the Trier region of Germany. The Schroeder family, which consisted of Nicolas, and his wife Anne, their sons, Nicolas and Peter, their daughters, Margaret and Barbara, and his oldest son, Matthew along with Matthew's wife, Sally and daughter Anna left for America in 1842. They sailed on the ship "The Harvest" which left Antwerp, Belgium, captained by

Henry Spalding, and carried a full load of passengers originally from Prussia. They arrived in New York City 3 August 1842. The family moved up the Hudson River to Albany and then westward on the Erie Canal to Utica, New York. They stayed in Utica for a short time and then eventually settled in Ava, New York. Matthew's wife, Maria Salome Sasges (Sally), gave birth to her second child, Nicholas, in Utica as his baptismal record was found at St. Joseph's Church, Utica, New York. Nicolas became a naturalized citizen 10 May 1852 in Oneida County, New York.[7] Nicolas was living with his son, Nicolas, in Ava, New York in the 1850 and 1860 Town of Ava, New York Census.

Gravestone of Nicholas Schroeder in St. Michael's Cemetery, Mohawk Hill, New York "died Aug 6, 1862" Photo taken by the author.

---

[3] Family History Center, Film 432733, St. Nikolaus Church, Hallschlag, Germany Baptismal records
[4] St. Michael's Cemetery, Mohawk Hill, New York
[5] Family History Center, Film 432733, St. Nikolaus Church, Hallschlag, Germany Marriage records
[6] North Country Families by Herbert Schrader
[7] Naturalization records Oneida County, New York.

Anne Leif Schroeder was not listed in the census with her husband.   She must have died between the time they arrived in New York City and 1850. I have not been able to find a date or place of death for her. Nicolas Schroeder's name was spelled Nickolas Rither in the 1850 Town of Ava, New York Census.

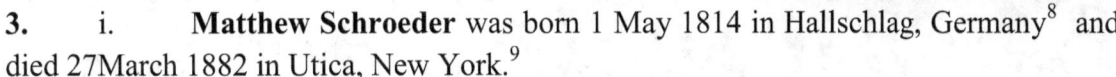

St. Nikolaus Church, Hallschlag, Germany
This is the church where all the
Schroeder Family members were baptized.
Photo taken by the author in September 2009.

Nicolas Schroeder and Anne Leif had the following children:

3.   i.   **Matthew Schroeder** was born 1 May 1814 in Hallschlag, Germany[8] and died 27March 1882 in Utica, New York.[9]

ii.   Joannes Nicolas Schroeder was born in Hallschlag, Germany. I was unable to find his baptismal record. However I did find his death record. He died in March 1824 in Hallschlag, Germany.[10]

4.   iii.   Nicholas Schroeder Jr was born July 1816 in Hallschlag, Germany.[11]

iv.   Barbara Schroeder was born November 1818 in Hallschlag, Germany. She was baptized November 27, 1818 in St. Nikolaus Church, Hallschlag, Germany.[12] Perhaps Barbara died young as another child was born in 1829 that was also named Barbara.

5.   v.   Peter Joseph (Joannes Nicholas) Schroeder was born in 1822 in Hallschlag, Germany.[13]

6.   vi.   Margaret Schroeder was born 1 January 1823 in Hallschlag, Germany.[14] She died 1 November 1911 at 69 Miller Street, Rochester, New York.[15]

v.   Susanna Schroeder was born in August 1829 in Hallschlag, Germany. She died in Hallschlag, Germany in August 1830. I believe Susanna was a twin to Barbara

---

[8] Family History Center, Film 432733, St. Nikolaus Church, Hallschlag, Germany Baptismal records
[9] St. Joseph's Church Records, Utica, New York
[10] Family History Center, Film 432734, St. Nikolaus Church, Hallschlag, Germany Baptismal records
[11] Family History Center, Film 432733, St. Nikolaus Church, Hallschlag, Germany Baptismal records
[12] Family History Center, Film 432733, St. Nikolaus Church, Hallschlag, Germany Baptismal records
[13] Family History Center, Film 432733, St. Nikolaus Church, Hallschlag, Germany Baptismal records
[14] Family History Center, Film 432733, St. Nikolaus Church, Hallschlag, Germany Baptismal records
[15] North Country Families by Herbert Schrader

who was baptized on the same day at St. Nikolaus Church, Hallschlag, Germany. A death record for Susanna was found.[16]

      vi.   Barbara Schroeder was born August 1829 in Hallschlag, Germany.[17] She was baptized in August 1829 in St. Nikolaus Church, Hallschlag, Germany. I believe Barbara was a twin to Susanna who was baptized on the same day.[18] I was unable to find Barbara in the 1850 census with her family. Perhaps she had either married by that time or she had died.

Generation Three

3. Matthew Schroeder[3] (Nicolas[2], Nicolas[1]) was born 1 May 1814 in Hallschlag, Germany. He was baptized May 23, 1814 at St. Nikolaus Church, Hallschlag, Germany.

Gravestone of Matthew Schroeder found in St. Joseph's Cemetery, Utica, New York indicated Matthew's date of birth as May 1, 1814 and the date of death as March 27, 1882. Photo was taken by the author.

The baptismal record showed Matthew baptized as Jonas Joseph.[19] His marriage record also gave the name of Johann Joseph. He died 27 March 1882 in Utica, New York.[20] He married Maria Salome Sasges 20 November 1839 in St. Nikolaus Catholic Church, Hallschlag, Germany,[21] the daughter of Mathias Sasges and Anna Bauer. She was born about 1823 in Madrid, Spain[22] and died May 26, 1875 in Utica, New York.[23] Matthew became a naturalized citizen 10 May 1852 in Oneida County, New York.[24]

---

[16] Family History Center, Film 432734, St. Nikolaus Church, Hallschlag, Germany death records page 46
[17] 1855 Town of Ava Census, Ava, New York
[18] Family History Center, Film 432734, St. Nikolaus Church, Hallschlag, Germany Baptismal records
[19] Family History Center, Film 432733, St. Nikolaus Church, Hallschlag, Germany Baptismal records
[20] St. Joseph's Church Records, Utica, New York
[21] Family History Center, Film 432734, St. Nikolaus Church, Hallschlag, Germany marriage records page 96
[22] 1865 Town of Lewis Census, Town of Lewis, New York
[23] St. Joseph's Church Records, Utica, New York
[24] Naturalization records Oneida County, New York

Matthew and his family were found in the 1850 and 1855 Census in the Town of Ava, New York. His name in the 1855 census was listed as Martin Schrater. The 1855 Census stated he owned 75 acres of land; 25 acres were improved and 50 acres were unimproved. The cash value of the farm was $900. The census listed that eight acres were plowed and he had harvested 150 bushels of potatoes in the past year. He had two cows, one horse and one pig and had sold 200 pounds of butter. This census stated he had lived in Ava, New York for 12 years. In the 1860 Town of Ava Census, Matthew was listed as Martin Schrieder. The 1865 Lewis County Census says Matthew had been married only once, he was a naturalized citizen and he owned land. In the 1880 Utica, New York Census, Matthew lived with his daughter, Mary, in Deerfield, New York. The family story of Maria Salome Sasges, wife of Matthew Schroeder, is told that Maria was a gypsy from Madrid, Spain. She traveled to Germany and danced for the German soldiers. There she met Matthew as he was serving in the German Army. I did not find any other families listed with the name Sasges in the St. Nikolaus Church records in Hallschag, Germany, so perhaps this is true.

Matthew Schroeder and Maria Salome Sasges (Sally) had the following children:

7.   i.   Ann Schroder was born 13 January 1841 in Hallschlag, Germany.[25] She was baptized January 1841 at St. Nikolaus Church, Hallschlag, Germany[26] and she died 11 March 1920 in Chadwicks, New York.[27]

8.   ii.   Nicholas Schrater was born October 29, 1842 in Utica, New York. He was baptized November 1, 1842 in St. Joseph's Church, Utica, New York[28] and died in 1889.[29]

    iii.   Margaret Schroeder was born August 1844 in Ava, New York.[30] She was baptized with the name Margaretha in St. Michael's Church, Mohawk Hill, New York. Her Godparents were her Uncle Peter Schroeder and Aunt Margaret Schroeder.[31] Margaret was listed in the 1855 Census, but not in the 1860 census, so perhaps she either died young or married early.

9.   iv.   Barbara Schroeder was born 24 October 1845 in Ava Corners, Ava, New York and died 16 February 1908 in Utica, New York.[32]

---

[25] North Country Families by Herbert Schrader
[26] Family History Center, Film 432734, St. Nikolaus Church, Hallschlag, Germany Baptismal records
[27] Obituary Utica Newspaper March 12, 1920
[28] St. Joseph's Church Records, Utica, New York
[29] North Country Families by Herbert Schrader
[30] North Country Families by Herbert Schrader
[31] FHC film of St. Michael's Church Records, Mohawk Hill, New York
[32] Obituary Saturday Evening Globe, Utica, New York February 22, 1908

10.   v.   **Catherine Schroeder** was born 30 August 1847 in Ava, New York[33] and died in March 1871 in West Leyden, New York.[34]

11.   vi.   Hubert Schroeder was born 30 June 1849 in Oneida County, New York and died 13 May 1875 in Utica, New York.[35]

12.   vii.   Peter Schrader was born 17 December 1850 in Ava, New York and died 28 July 1922 at 1695 Lincoln Avenue, Utica, New York. [36]

13.   viii.   Francis Schrader was born 22 April 1852 in Ava, New York and died 9 November 1925 in Utica, New York.[37]

14.   ix.   Anna Maria Schroeder was born 14 June 1853 in Oneida County, New York and died 7 July 1934.[38]

x.   Elizabeth Schroeder was born 11 April 1855[39] in Oneida County, New York and died before 1908. She was baptized in St. Michael's Church, Mohawk Hill, New York. Her Godparents were Casper Mattee and Elisabetha Hess.[40]

xi.   Joetta (Gertrude) Schroeder was born 21 May 1856 in Oneida County, New York[41] and died 20 February 1871 in Utica, New York.[42] Joetta was baptized at St. Michael's Church, Mohawk Hill, New York. Her Godparents were Simon Urz and Gertrude Paulis.[43]

15.   xii.   Richard Otto Schrader was born 25 July 1858 in Ava, New York and died 30 April 1943 in Utica, New York.[44]

4.   Nicholas Schroeder Jr.[3] (Nicolas[2], Nicolas[1]) was born in July 1816 in Hallschlag, Germany.[45] Nicholas was baptized at St. Nikolaus Church in Hallschlag, Germany July 29, 1816.[46]   He married Margaret Mathew about 1850. She was born in 1832 in Germany.[47] In the 1850 Ava Census, his name was spelled Nikolas Rither.

---

[33] Oneida County Gen Web page list of births from 1847 to 1851
[34] John J. Schmidt's Civil War papers
[35] North Country Families by Herbert Schrader
[36] Obituary Utica Newspaper July 29, 1922
[37] Obituary Utica Newspaper November 10, 1925
[38] North Country Families by Herbert Schrader
[39] North Country Families by Herbert Schrader
[40] FHC film of St. Michael's Church Records, Mohawk Hill, New York
[41] North Country Families by Herbert Schrader
[42] St. Joseph's Church Records, Utica, New York
[43] FHC film of St. Michael's Church Records, Mohawk Hill, New York
[44] Obituary Utica Newspaper May 1, 1943
[45] Declaration of Intent signed July 27, 1848, Oneida County, New York
[46] Family History Center, Film 432733, St. Nikolaus Church, Hallschlag, Germany Baptismal records
[47] 1860 Town of Ava Census, Ava, New York

Nicholas Schroeder Jr. and Margaret Mathew had the following children:

      i.   Catharine Schroeder was born 30 October 1850 in Ava, New York. Catherine was baptized at St. Michael's Church, Mohawk Hill, New York and her Godparents were Nicholas Schrader and Katherine Schrader.[48]

      ii.   Caroline Schroeder was born 1851 in New York State. [49]

      iii.   Matthew Schroeder was born 17 March 1852 in Ava, New York. Matthew was baptized at St. Michael's Church, Mohawk Hill, New York and his Godparents were Mathias Schroeder and Gertrude Heilig.[50]

      ix.   Maria Schroeder was born 19 August 1859 in Ava, New York. Maria was baptized at St. Michael's Church, Mohawk Hill, New York and her Godparents were Nicholas Schroeder and Maria Sentief. [51]

      v.   Rosina Schroeder was born 2 June 1861 in Ava, New York. Rosina was baptized at St. Michael's Church, Mohawk Hill, New York and her Godparents were Daniel Heil and Rosina Mathew.[52]

5. Peter Joseph (Joannes Nicholas) Schroeder[3] (Nicolas[2], Nicolas[1]) was born in 1822 in Hallschlag, Germany and was baptized in St. Nicholas Church, Hallschlag, Germany 26 December 1822.[53] He married Mary *about* 1852. She was born in 1833.

Peter Joseph (Joannes Nicholas) Schroeder and Mary had the following children:

      i.   Joseph Schroeder was born 1853 in Ava, New York.[54]

      ii.   Edward Schroeder was born May 1855 in Ava, New York.[55]

6. Margaret Schroeder[3] (Nicolas[2], Nicolas[1]) was born 1 January 1823 in Hallschlag, Germany[56] and died 1 November 1911 at 69 Miller St., Rochester, New York.[57] She married Francis Sentiff in 1845, the son of Sebastian and Margaret Sentiff. He was born in 1809 and died 12 November 1861.[58] Margaret lived in Webster, New York in the 1870 Rochester, New York Census and was listed as a widow. In the 1900 Rochester

---

[48] FHC film of St. Michael's Church Records, Mohawk Hill, New York
[49] 1860 Town of Ava Census, Ava, New York
[50] FHC film of St. Michael's Church Records, Mohawk Hill, New York
[51] FHC film of St. Michael's Church Records, Mohawk Hill, New York
[52] FHC film of St. Michael's Church Records, Mohawk Hill, New York
[53] Family History Center, Film 432733, St. Nikolaus Church, Hallschlag, Germany Baptismal records
[54] 1855 Town of Ava Census, Ava, New York
[55] North Country Families by Herbert Schrader
[56] Family History Center, Film 432733, St. Nikolaus Church, Hallschlag, Germany Baptismal records
[57] North Country Families by Herbert Schrader
[58] North Country Families by Herbert Schrader

Census, she lived with her daughter, Anna, in Rochester, New York and was listed as unable to read.

Margaret Schroeder and Francis Sentiff had the following children:

16.   i.   Marie Salome Sentiff was born 11 August 1846 in Ava, New York.[59]

17.   ii.   Joseph Sentiff was born 05 October 1847 in Ava, New York[60] and died 17 March 1924 in Rochester, New York.[61]

18.   iii.   Barbara Sentiff was born 27 March 1849 in Ava, New York[62] and died 7 January 1936 in Rochester, NY. [63]

 19.   iv.   Margaret Sentiff was born 25 October 1853 in Ava, New York[64] and died before 1923. She was married in 1883 in St. Peter's Church, Deerfield, New York[65]

 20.   v.   Anna Sentiff was born 29 September 1855 in Ava, New York[66] and died after 1911. She was married 26 September 1883 in St. Michael's Church, Rochester, New York.[67]

         vi.   John Sentiff was born 13 January 1858 in Ava, New York.[68] John was baptized in St. Michael's Church, Mohawk Hill, New York and his Godparents were John Sentiff and John Eller and Margaretha (Muthig) He died 5 July 1906 in Rochester, New York.[69]

Generation Four

7. Ann Schroeder[4] (Matthew Schroeder[3], Nicolas[2], Nicolas[1]) was born 13 January 1841 in Hallschlag, Germany.[70] She died 11 March 1920 in Chadwicks, New York.[71] She married Simon Urtz 16 October 1860 in Lewis County, New York, the son of John Urtz and Anna M. Baulig. He was born 29 April 1832 in Muhlheim Prussen Coblenzon Reihn, Germany[72] and died 19 June 1900 in Chadwicks, New York.[73] Anna spent her early

---

[59] FHC film of St. Michael's Church Records, Mohawk Hill, New York
[60] FHC film of St. Michael's Church Records, Mohawk Hill, New York
[61] Family information from TomAcquaviva
[62] FHC film of St. Michael's Church Records, Mohawk Hill, New York
[63] Death announcement Rochester, New York newspaper January 9, 1936
[64] FHC film of St. Michael's Church Records, Mohawk Hill, New York
[65] Family information from TomAcquaviva
[66] FHC film of St. Michael's Church Records, Mohawk Hill, New York
[67] Family information from TomAcquaviva
[68] FHC film of St. Michael's Church Records, Mohawk Hill, New York
[69] Family information from TomAcquaviva
[70] North Country Families by Herbert Schrader
[71] Obituary Utica Newspaper March 12, 1920
[72] Family information from Vincent Urtz

years in Lewis County before moving to Chadwicks, New York. She was a member of St. Joseph's Church, Utica, New York. She delivered 22 children, most of which lived to adulthood. In my estimation, she must have been quite a person. Her husband, Simon Urtz, emigrated from Antwerp, Belgium in the spring of 1853 along with his brother John and sister-in-law Elizabeth. The vessel they took was at sea 59 days. While they were on the crossing, John and Elizabeth lost their first son, John, who was buried at sea. They all settled in West Leyden, New York then called Prussian Settlement and built a log cabin. Three months later another brother, Jacob came over. On November 24, 1854 on the ship "Omar Pasha", the rest of Simon's family including his mother and father, brothers Anthony, and Peter and his sister Elizabeth and her husband, John Pelzer, and their two children. This ship was at sea for 90 days. During the trip, the mast of the ship was nearly washed away. This group of people promised themselves, and their god, that if they were ever safely joined to their loved ones in America, they would show their gratitude by building a church in their new homeland. True to their promise, in 1861, seven years after arriving, "using stones from the fields" and land donated by the Urz Brothers, they completed the Prussian Settlement Church. While living in Lewis County, New York, Simon's occupation was farming. Simon's naturalization papers indicated his birth allegiance to the King of Prussia. Simon had lived in Chadwicks, New York for 17 years with his wife and family prior to his death. Perhaps he moved to Chadwick to work in the mill. He was a member of St. Joseph's Church in Utica, New York.

Anna Schroeder Urtz and family circa 1900. Photo from the collection of Thomas Schafer used with permission.

[73] Obituary Utica Newspaper

Ann Schroeder and Simon Urtz had the following children:

      i.   Peter Urtz was born 4 September 1860 in Lewis County, New York [74] and died 3 October 1918 in Chadwicks, New York.[75] Peter spent his early years in West Leyden and later moved to New York Mills and then to Chadwicks with his parents. He was a carpenter and shoemaker by trade and was a very industrious man. Peter ran grocery store on the corner of Eagle Street and McQuade Avenue, Utica, New York. The building was built by Richard Schrader and his sons. They would be a brother and nephews of Anna Schroeder Urtz.

21.   ii.   Anthony Urtz was born 3 November 1861 in Highmarket, New York [76] and died 1 March 1893.[77].

      iii.   Barbara Urtz was born 25 October 1863 in West Leyden, New York and died 10 February 1935 in Utica, New York.[78] She married John Link 2 February 1882 in St. Michael's Church, Mohawk Hill, New York.[79] John was born 16 May 1852 in Lewis County, New York, the son of George Link and Juliana Seifen. He died December 11, 1891. He is buried in the Prussian Settlement Cemetery, West Leyden, New York.[80] She then married Joseph Welter 23 April 1906 in St. Peter's and Paul's Church, Frankfort, New York.[81] He was born 29 December 1865 in Lintengen, Luxembourg and died 17 July 1921 at 122 Second Street, Utica, New York.[82] Joseph was a baker by trade

and for some years was employed by Mr. Whiteman. Later he worked for Mr. Smithson, but just preceding the time he was taken ill he was employed in a bakery in Mohawk, New York. He was a member of St. Peter and Paul's Church, Frankfort, New York and also a member of the German Club. Barbara had a stroke and lived with her cousin, Mary Sifer, in her later years. Mary is my great grandmother and my mom remembers Barbara as the "Old yady with the cane." Barbara came to Utica in 1878 and was a member of St. Joseph's Church, Utica,

Barbara Urtz and Joseph Welter. Photo in the collection of Thomas Schafer used with permission.

---

[74] North Country Families by Herbert Schrader
[75] Obituary Utica Newspaper October 4, 1918
[76] North Country Families by Herbert Schrader
[77] St. Joseph's Cemetery Tombstone inscription, Utica, New York
[78] Obituary Utica Newspaper February 11, 1935
[79] FHC film of St. Michael's Church Records, Mohawk Hill, New York
[80] Prussian Settlement Cemetery, West Leyden, New York
[81] Wedding announcement Utica Newspaper
[82] Obituary Utica Newspaper July 18, 1921

New York.   Barbara is buried with her parents in St. Joseph's Cemetery, Utica, New York. [83] She did not have children.

22.   iv.   John E. Urtz was born 5 December 1863 in West Leyden, Lewis County New York and died 19 November 1945 at Clinton Road, New Hartford, New York.[84]

23.   v.   Matthew Uertz was born 27 March 1865 in Lewis County, New York[85] and died 3 April 1937 in New Hartford, New York.[86]

Photo of Jacob Urtz from the collection of Thomas Schafer and used with permission.

vi.   Jacob Urtz was born 3 June 1866 in Lewis County, New York[87] and died 28 February 1939 in Chadwicks, New York.[88] Jacob was baptized in St. Michael's Church, Mohawk Hill, New York and his Godparents were Jacob Uertz and Margaretha   Uertz.[89]Jacob moved to Chadwicks in 1884. He had been employed by the Willowvale Bleachery until he became ill a year before he died. He was a member of St. Anthony of Padua Church and its Holy Name Society. He did not have children. The 1910 Census for New Hartford, New York listed Jacob Urtz as a laborer at the Bleachery.

24.   vii.   Margaret D. Urtz was born 27 October 1867 in Lewis County, New York[90] and died 23 November 1950 in Chadwicks, New York.[91]

viii.   Francis Urtz was born 29 April 1869 in Lewis County, New York and died 10 March 1870.[92]

25.   ix.   Anna Maria Urtz was born 16 May 1870 in Highmarket, Lewis County, New York[93] and died 21 May 1947 in Ilion Hospital, Ilion, New York.[94]

---

[83] St. Joseph's Cemetery Tombstone inscription, Utica, New York
[84] Obituary Utica Newspaper November 20, 1945
[85] Obituary Utica Newspaper April 4, 1937
[86] New York State Vital Records
[87] North Country Families by Herbert Schrader
[88] Obituary Utica Newspaper
[89] FHC film of St. Michael's Church Records, Mohawk Hill, New York
[90] North Country Families by Herbert Schrader
[91] Obituary Utica Newspaper November 24, 1950
[92] Family information from Vincent Urtz
[93] North Country Families by Herbert Schrader
[94] Obituary Utica Newspaper May 21, 1947

x.   John Simon Urtz was born May 1871 in Highmarket, New York and died 10 October 1894. [95]

xi.   George Uertz was born 22 October 1872 in Lewis Co, New York[96] and died 8 May 1954 in Los Angeles, California.[97] George was baptized at St. Michael's Church, Mohawk Hill, New York and his Godparents were George Thomann and Susanna Urtz.[98] George lived in Chadwicks, New York as a child and then in Utica, New York.   About 1924 he moved to Long Beach, California where he had lived for 30 years.

Photo of George and Mary Uertz from the collection of Thomas Schafer used with permission.

26.   xii.   Joseph S. Urtz was born 15 March 1874 in Lewis County, New York[99] and died 5 January 1957 in Frankfort, New York.[100]

27.   xiii.   Elizabeth Urtz was born 1 July 1875 in Mohawk Hill, New York and died 21 August 1955 at 359 Oneida Street, Sauquoit, New York.[101]

xiv.   Francis (Frank) Urtz was born 22 October 1876 in Lewis County, New York[102] and died 24 July 1934 in Mohawk, New York.[103] Frank was baptized in St. Michael's Church, Mohawk Hill, New York and his Godparents were Francis Rheinbrecht and Catharina Pelser.[104]

Photo of Frank Urtz from the collection of Thomas Schafer used with permission.

[95] St. Joseph's Cemetery Tombstone inscription, Utica, New York
[96] North Country Families by Herbert Schrader
[97] California death index, Ancestry.com
[98] FHC film of St. Michael's Church Records, Mohawk Hill, New York
[99] North Country Families by Herbert Schrader
[100] Obituary Utica Newspaper January 5, 1957
[101] Obituary Utica Newspaper August 22, 1955
[102] North Country Families by Herbert Schrader
[103] New York State Vital Records
[104] FHC film of St. Michael's Church Records, Mohawk Hill, New York

xv.   Charles M. Urtz was born 10 October 1878 in West Leyden, New York and died 11 March 1951 in Herkimer Memorial Hospital, Herkimer, NY.[105] Charles was baptized in St. Michael's Church, Mohawk Hill, New York under the name Karl. His Godparents were Karl Schmidt and Katherine.[106] Charles was employed for several years by the Gerwig and Laird Coal Company and the Division of Highways of the State Department of Public Works. He was a member of St. Francis deSales Church and its Holy Name Society. He lived on Highland Avenue, Herkimer, New York at the time of his death. He had no children.

Photo of Charles M. Urtz from the collection of Thomas Schafer and used with permission.

xvi.   William Urtz was born 23 February 1879 in Utica, New York[107] and died 16 October 1879.[108] William was baptized in St. Michael's Church, Mohawk Hill, New York and his Godparents were Wlihelm Ernst and Anna Maria Ernst.[109]

xvii.   Mary Urtz was born 1882 and died 25 August 1882.[110].

28.   xviii.   Lawrence Uertz was born 25 June 1882 in Chadwicks, New York and died 26 June 1928 in Ilion, New York.[111]

xix.   Boy Urtz was born 1885 and died the same day in 1885.[112]

xx.   Marie Urtz was born 25 August 1885 and died 20 October 1885.[113]

29.   xxi.   Rose C. Urtz was born 17 March 1887 in Chadwicks, New York[114] and died 27 November 1974 in St. Luke's Hospital, New Hartford, New York.[115]

8. Nicholas Schrater[4] (Matthew Schroeder[3], Nicolas[2], Nicolas[1]) was born about 1842 in Oneida County, New York[116] and died in 1889.[117] He married Mary Jane Hayes 6 April 1869 in Lee Center, New York, the daughter of Richard and Florinda Hayes. She was

---

[105] Obituary Utica Newspaper March 12, 1951
[106] FHC film of St. Michael's Church Records, Mohawk Hill, New York
[107] North Country Families by Herbert Schrader
[108] Family information from Vincent Urtz
[109] FHC film of St. Michael's Church Records, Mohawk Hill, New York
[110] Family information from Michael Terrell
[111] Obituary Utica Newspaper June 27, 1928
[112] Family information from Thomas Schafer
[113] Family information from Vincent Urtz
[114] Social Security Death Index from Ancestry.com
[115] Obituary Utica Newspaper November 28, 1974
[116] 1880 Town of Lewis Census, Lewis County, New York
[117] North Country Families by Herbert Schrader

born in 1846 in Lee Center, New York[118] and died 16 September 1915.[119] He married Laura Perry in 1866. Nicholas served in the Union Army in the Civil War in Company F, 2nd Regiment, New York Heavy Artillery. He signed his surname Schrader when he enlisted but when he was discharged, he signed it Schrater which he continued to use in his post war life. His army records indicated he moved to Boise, Idaho in 1885 and died there. In the 1880 Town of Lewis Census, Lewis County, New York he had living with him in his household Isaac Rivers and Peter Young. [120]

Nicholas Schrater and Mary Jane Hayes had the following children:

     i.   John N. Schrater was born about 1869 in Lewis County, New York[121] and died 8 July 1926.[122]

     ii.   Margery Schrater was born in 1872 in Lewis County, New York.[123]

     iii.   Dellia Schrater was born in 1879 in Lewis County, New York.[124]

     iv.   Frank E. Schrater was born 8 May 1884 in Highmarket, New York[125] and died 10 November 1966 in Cleveland, New York.[126] Frank operated a saw mill for many years. He did not marry.

Nicholas Schrater and Laura Perry never married, but had the following child:

30.   i.   Henry Nicholas Schrader was born 30 November 1866 in New York State and died 11 February 1920. [127]

9. Barbara Schroeder[4] (Matthew Schroeder[3], Nicolas[2], Nicolas[1]) was born 24 October 1845 in Ava, New York.[128] Barbara was baptized in St. Michael's Church, Mohawk Hill, New York and her Godparents were Nicholas and Barbara Schroeder.[129] She died 16 February 1908 in Utica, New York.[130] She married George Thomann Sr. 27 August 1863 in Rome, NY, the son of Peter Thomann. He was born 13 February 1834 in Bavaria, Germany[131] and died 24 October 1911 at Walker Road, Deerfield, New York.[132]

---

[118] North Country Families by Herbert Schrader
[119] Genealogy from Herbert Schrader
[120] 1880 Town of Lewis Census, Lewis County, New York
[121] 1880 Town of Lewis Census, Lewis County, New York
[122] North Country Families by Herbert Schrader
[123] 1880 Town of Lewis Census, Lewis County, New York
[124] 1880 Town of Lewis Census, Lewis County, New York
[125] North Country Families by Herbert Schrader
[126] Obituary Utica Newspaper November 11, 1966
[127] Genealogy from Herbert Schrader
[128] Obituary Utica Newspaper February 17, 1908
[129] FHC film of St. Michael's Church Records, Mohawk Hill, New York
[130] St. Joseph's Church Records, Utica, New York
[131] Family Search Ancestral File v4.19

According to her obituary, Barbara died of a brain hemorrhage as a result of severe case of the grip and had been sick about four weeks. The 1865 Town of Lewis Census said she had had two children, but only one was listed. She lived at 317 Lincoln Ave, Utica, New York at time of her death in 1908. She moved to Utica about 1873 and was a member of St. Joseph's Church, Utica, New York. George lived with his son, Paul, at the time of his death. In 1900 he lived at 338 Whitesboro St., Utica, New York. He was born in Germany and had lived in Utica for 40 years. He worked as a teamster for different lumber concerns including Downer & Kellogg, The Charles C. Kellogg and Sons Co., and Thomas Brothers. He was a member of St. Joseph's Church, Utica, New York.

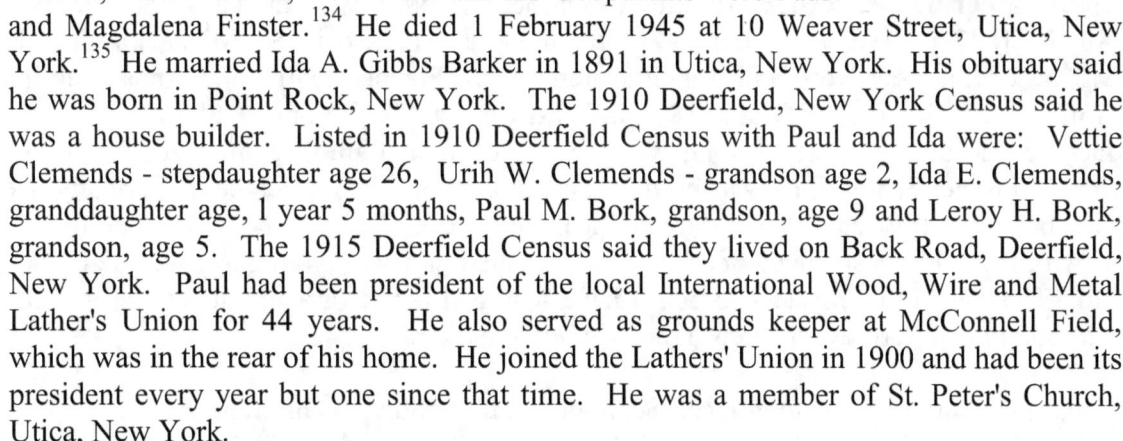

Photo of George Thomann Sr. from the collection of Jane Spence and used with permission.

Barbara Schroeder and George Thomann Sr. had the following children:

    i.   Paul Thomann was born 29 January 1865 in Highmarket, New York.[133] Paul was baptized in St. Michael's Church, Mohawk Hill, New York and his Godparents were Paul and Magdalena Finster.[134] He died 1 February 1945 at 10 Weaver Street, Utica, New York.[135] He married Ida A. Gibbs Barker in 1891 in Utica, New York. His obituary said he was born in Point Rock, New York. The 1910 Deerfield, New York Census said he was a house builder. Listed in 1910 Deerfield Census with Paul and Ida were: Vettie Clemends - stepdaughter age 26, Urih W. Clemends - grandson age 2, Ida E. Clemends, granddaughter age, 1 year 5 months, Paul M. Bork, grandson, age 9 and Leroy H. Bork, grandson, age 5. The 1915 Deerfield Census said they lived on Back Road, Deerfield, New York. Paul had been president of the local International Wood, Wire and Metal Lather's Union for 44 years. He also served as grounds keeper at McConnell Field, which was in the rear of his home. He joined the Lathers' Union in 1900 and had been its president every year but one since that time. He was a member of St. Peter's Church, Utica, New York.

    ii.   Anna A. Thomann was born 4 June 1867 in Highmarket, Lewis County, New York.[136] Anna was baptized in St. Michael's Church, Mohawk Hill, New York. Her Godparents were Anna Urtz and Casper Thaler.[137] Anna married Michael Joyce and lived in West Seneca, New York in 1908. Anna lived in Lackawanna City, New York in the

---

[132] Obituary Utica Newspaper October 25, 1911
[133] Genealogy from Herbert Schrader
[134] FHC film of St. Michael's Church Records, Mohawk Hill, New York
[135] Obituary Utica Newspaper February 1, 1945
[136] Genealogy from Herbert Schrader
[137] FHC film of St. Michael's Church Records, Mohawk Hill, New York

1920 and 1930 census. She lived in Fayetteville, New York in 1943. She did not have children.

Photo of the Thomann family Barbara Schroeder Thomann and George Thomann Sr with their children Peter R., George H., Margaret Scott and Paul Thomann from the collection of Jane Spence and used with permission.

31.   iii.   Margareth J. Thomann was born 26 March 1870 in Highmarket, Lewis County, New York.[138]

32.   iv.   George Henry Thomann Jr. was born 23 January 1874 in Utica, New York and died 18 July 1957 in Utica, New York.[139]

v.   John J. Thomann was born February 1876 in Utica, New York[140] and died 5 April 1903 in Deerfield, New York after a four month illness.[141] John was lather by trade and a member of St. Joseph's Church, Utica, New York.

33.   vi.   Peter R. Thomann was born 31 July 1878 in Utica, New York and died 25 April 1943 in Utica, New York.[142]

10.   Catherine Schroeder[4] (Matthew Schroeder[3], Nicolas[2], Nicolas[1]) was born 30 August 1847 in Ava, New York.[143] Catherine was baptized in St. Michael's Church, Mohawk Hill, New York and her Godparents were Francis Sentiff and Anna Caterina Hoffmann.[144] She died in March 1871 in West Leyden, New York.[145] She married John Jacob Schmidt about 1864. John was the son of John Philip Schmidt and Walburga (Mary) Fischer Schmidt. He was born 18 September 1841 in Würtemberg, Germany. He died 6 August 1891 at 12 Wiley Street Utica, New York.[146] Catherine was found in 1865 Town of Lewis Census, New York. Catherine died at a very young age, only 24 years old. This has been a mystery to me. I have searched for her grave, but suspect that she was buried in West Leyden, New York without a marker.

Catherine Schroeder and John Jacob Schmidt had the following children:

34.   i.   **Mary Johanna Schmidt** was born 8 November 1864 in West Leyden, New York. She was baptized in St. Michael's Church, Mohawk Hill, New York and her

---

[138] Genealogy from Herbert Schrader
[139] Obituary Utica Newspaper July 19, 1957
[140] Genealogy from Herbert Schrader
[141] Obituary Utica Newspaper April 6, 1903
[142] Obituary Utica Newspaper April 26, 1943
[143] Oneida County Gen Web page list of births from 1847 to 1851
[144] FHC film of St. Michael's Church Records, Mohawk Hill, New York
[145] John J. Schmidt's Civil War papers
[146] Obituary Utica Newspaper August 7, 1891

Godparents were Hubertus Schroeder and Marie Magdalena Finster.[147] Mary died 5 January 1958 in Utica, New York.[148]

       ii.   Maria Magdalena Schmidt was born 6 April 1866 in West Leyden, New York. Maria was baptized in St. Michael's Church, Mohawk Hill, New York and her Godparents were Hubertus Schroeder and Marie Magdalena Finster.[149] She died between 1870 and 1875 as she was listed in the 1870 Town of Lewis, New York Census as Lena, but she was not listed in 1875 Town of Lewis Census or 1880 Utica, New York Census.

35.   iii.   Joseph Lee Schmidt was born 6 July 1867 in West Leyden, New York[150] and died 25 July 1945 in Rome Hospital, Rome, New York.[151]

11.   Hubert Schroeder[4] (Matthew Schroeder[3], Nicolas[2], Nicolas[1]) was born 30 June 1849 in Oneida County, New York.[152] Hubert was baptized in St. Michael's Church, Mohawk Hill, New York and his Godparents were Hubert Huber and Maria Hever.[153] He died 13 May 1875 in Utica, New York.[154] He married Elisabeth Agnes Schliker 9 February 1875 in Utica, New York.[155] Hubert died of Typhoid fever. He was a laborer working in the hoop shaving business.

Hubert Schroeder and Elisabeth Agnes Schliker had the following child:

 36.   i.   Herbert John Schrader was born 31 December 1875 in Madison, New York and died June 12, 1941 in Faxton Hospital, Utica, New York.[156]

12.   Peter Shrader[4] (Matthew Schroeder[3], Nicolas[2], Nicolas[1]) was born 17 December 1850 in Ava, New York.[157] Peter was baptized in St. Michael's Church, Mohawk Hill, New York. His Godparents were John Peter Briler and Margaret Schroeder.[158] He died 28 July 1922 at1695 Lincoln Avenue, Utica, New York.[159] He married Julia Monahan in 1876. He later married Anna Shoemaker 5 October 1885 in Utica, New York. She was born 12 January 1860 in Prussia, Germany and died 11 July 1912 at 689 Lincoln Avenue, Utica, New York.[160]Peter had had a stroke 3 years before his death and never fully recovered. He lived at 1695 Lincoln Avenue, Utica, New York at the time of his death. He was a member of St. Joseph's Church, Utica, New York and the Carpenters Union.

---

[147] FHC film of St. Michael's Church Records, Mohawk Hill, New York
[148] Obituary Utica Newspaper January 6, 1958
[149] FHC film of St. Michael's Church Records, Mohawk Hill, New York
[150] FHC film of St. Michael's Church Records, Mohawk Hill, New York
[151] Obituary Utica Newspaper July 26, 1945
[152] Genealogy from Herbert Schrader
[153] FHC film of St. Michael's Church Records, Mohawk Hill, New York
[154] Genealogy from Herbert Schrader
[155] Genealogy from Herbert Schrader
[156] Obituary Utica Newspaper June 13, 1941
[157] Obituary Utica Newspaper July 29, 1922
[158] FHC film of St. Michael's Church Records, Mohawk Hill, New York
[159] Obituary Utica Newspaper July 29, 1922
[160] Obituary Utica Newspaper July 12, 1912

Anna was sick about a year before she died. Anna came to America and to Utica in 1883 at 23 years of age. She was a member of St. Joseph's Church, Utica, New York and its Alter Society. She had a sister and half brother at the time of her death that was still living in Germany.

Peter Schrader and Julia Monahan had the following children:
       i.   Edward Schroeder was born 16 June 1877 in Forestport, New York.[161] Edward was baptized in St. Michael's Church, Mohawk Hill, New York and his Godparents were Simon Urtz and Anna Schroeder Urtz.[162] He died 1922 at 1009 Cleveland Avenue, Utica, New York.[163] He never married.
       ii.   William Peter Schrader was born 16 April 1879 in Highmarket, New York.[164] William was baptized in St. Michael's Church, Mohawk Hill, New York. His Godparents were Peter Urtz and Margaretha Pelzer.[165] He died 13 July 1903 at 318 Elm Street, Utica, New York.[166] William came to Utica, New York when he was about five years of age. He learned the trade of a baker and was employed by George Harris who operated a bakery on Oneida Square in Utica, New York. He later moved to Gloversville, New York and returned to Utica to work for the Standard Harrow Works. He then returned to work for George Harris. He was a member of St. Joseph's Church, Utica, New York and died of consumption. He never married.

Peter Schrader and Anna Shoemaker had the following children:
37.   i.   Charles (Carl) Peter Schrader was born 8 June 1890 in Utica, New York[167] and died 15 November 1950.[168]
38.   ii.   Mary Frances Schrader was born 12 July 1892 in New York State[169] and died 14 July 1964.[170]
       iii.   Sarah Gertrude Schrader was born June 1896 in Utica, New York[171] and died 29 June 1940.[172] Sarah was a milliner who in later life was the manager of the Freemont Millinery Shop in Utica. She never married. The 1900 Utica, New York 11th Ward Census listed her as a saleslady.

---

[161] Genealogy from Herbert Schrader
[162] FHC film of St. Michael's Church Records, Mohawk Hill, New York
[163] Genealogy from Herbert Schrader
[164] Obituary Utica Newspaper July 14, 1903
[165] FHC film of St. Michael's Church Records, Mohawk Hill, New York
[166] Obituary Utica Newspaper July 14, 1903
[167] World War I draft registration from Ancestery.com
[168] Genealogy from Herbert Schrader
[169] Family information from Mary Jane Chynoweth, daughter of Mary Schrader
[170] Obituary Utica Newspaper July 15, 1964
[171] Birth Announcement Utica Observer Dispatch June 30, 1896
[172] Genealogy from Herbert Schrader

13. Francis Shrader[4] (Matthew Schroeder[3], Nicolas[2], Nicolas[1]) was born 22 April 1852 in Ava, New York.[173] Francis was baptized in St. Michael's Church, Mohawk Hill, New York and his Godparents were Francis Ritzel and Margaret Schroeder.[174] He died 9 November 1925 in Utica, New York.[175]   He married Ella F. Palmer 4 July 1876 in Central Hotel, Lee Center, New York by Rev. J. Stanton.[176] Ella was the daughter of Jesse Palmer. She was born 13 January 1856 in Taberg, New York and died 22 November 1897 in Lee Center, New York.[177] Francis moved to West Leyden, New York in 1860 and then to Utica, New York in 1869.   He was a tool sharpener by trade. He rode a bicycle to which he rigged a grinding wheel, going from house to house to apply his services. He would turn his cycle upside down, engage the grinder on the back wheel, pump the rear wheel with the pedal by hand and sharpen the knives or shears. He had been ill for two years prior to his death.

Francis Schrader and Ella F. Palmer had the following children.

39.   i.   Ernest W. Schrader was born August 1879 in New York State[178] and died 1 November 1904 at 112 Schuyler Street, Utica, New York.[179]

40.   ii.   Luella G. Schrader was born 29 August 1882 in Lee, New York and died 13 February 1952 in St. Luke's Memorial Hospital, Utica, New York.[180]

   iii.   Royal L. Schrader was born July 1890 in New York State[181] and died *before* 1925.[182]

41.   iv.   Leo P. Schrader, Sr was born 1 July 1890 in Lee Center, New York[183] and died 24 June 1967.[184]

   v.   Beulah Schrader was born August 1895 in New York State.[185] Beulah married Lynn F. Brown.

14. Anna Maria Schroeder[4] (Matthew Schroeder[3], Nicolas[2], Nicolas[1]) was born 14 June 1853 in Oneida County, New York.[186] Anna Maria was baptized in St. Michael's Church, Mohawk Hill, New York and her Godparents were Albert Bacceoico and Anna Maria

---

[173] Obituary Utica Newspaper November 10, 1925

[174] FHC film of St. Michael's Church Records, Mohawk Hill, New York

[175] Obituary Utica Newspaper November 10, 1925

[176] Wedding Announcement Utica Newspaper

[177] Obituary Utica Newspaper November 23, 1897

[178] 1900 Utica, New York Census

[179] Death Announcement Utica Newspaper November 2, 1904

[180] Obituary Utica Newspaper February 14, 1952

[181] 1900 Utica, New York Census

[182] Father's obituary

[183] Social Security Death Index from Ancestry.com

[184] Genealogy from Herbert Schrader

[185] 1900 Utica, New York Census

[186] 1865 Town of Lewis Census, Lewis County, New York

Wilbert.[187] She died in July 1934.[188] She married Nicholas Mirkes in 1876 in Utica, New York. He was born 3 December 1838 in Prussia, Germany and died 12 August 1901 at 170 North Genesee Street, Utica, New York.[189] Following the death of Nicholas, Anna married Thomas Sinnott 29 May 1902 in Trinity Church Rectory, Utica, New York.[190] She married Michael E. Colwell in 1906, the son of William Colwell and Mary Quillman.

Nicholas Mirkes came to American in 1869 settling in Litchfield, New York. He moved to Utica, New York in 1871. He was a tailor by trade and conducted a tailor shop at 170 North Genesee Street for 22 years. He later worked for Crouse and Brandegee's Clothing Factory. He was a member of St. Peter's Church, Utica, New York. Michael Colwell was born in 1870 in New Hartford, New York and died 29 April 1932 in Utica, New York.[191] He had been employed by The Mott Wheel Company for 15 years and the last 11 years of his life he worked at Utica Products Company. He was a member of St. Joseph's Church, Utica, New York.

She had married Thomas Sinnott and later found out he was already married. She sued him for bigamy in March of 1904.

Anna Maria was born in Ava, New York and lived in Utica, New York most of her life. She moved to New York City in 1932. She was a member of St. Joseph's Church, Utica, New York. She went by Annie Mary or Mary.

Anna Maria Schroeder and Nicholas Mirkes had the following children:

42. i. Mary Catherine Mirkes was born 21 July 1877[192] and died 30 November 1901 at Schuyler Road, Deerfield, New York.[193]

ii. Nettie R. Mirkes was born in 1884 and died 29 April 1938 in New York City, New York.[194] She moved to New York City after the death of her husband in 1931. She married Albert E. Scott.[195]

iii. William Mirkes. No information was uncovered on William.

---

[187] FHC film of St. Michael's Church Records, Mohawk Hill, New York
[188] Genealogy from Herbert Schrader
[189] Obituary Utica Newspaper August 13, 1901
[190] Wedding Announcement Utica Newspaper
[191] Obituary Utica Newspaper April 30, 1932
[192] Forest Hill Cemetery Records, Utica, New York
[193] Obituary Utica Newspaper December 2, 1901
[194] Genealogy from Herbert Schrader
[195] Obituary Utica Newspaper April 30, 1938

Anna Maria Schroeder and Michael E. Colwell had the following child:

  i. Mary Colwell was born in 1896.

15. Richard Otto Shrader[4] (Matthew Schroeder[3], Nicolas[2], Nicolas[1]) was born 25 July 1858 in Ava, New York.[196] Richard was baptized in St. Michael's Church, Mohawk Hill, New York and his Godparents were Richard Ritz and Maria Salome Sentiff.[197] He died 30 April 1943 in Utica, New York.[198] He married Mary Agnes Moak 14 May 1881 in St. Michael's Church, Mohawk Hill, New York. The witnesses to this marriage were Clemens and Mary Finster.[199] Mary Agnes was the daughter of Paul Moak and Mary Hauck. She was born 13 October 1861 in New York State[200] and died 30 October 1950 at 1022 Champlin Avenue Yorkville, New York.[201] Richard lived in Utica most of his life and worked as a building contractor until he retired in 1925. He was a member of St. Mary's Church, Utica, New York and was the last of the Schroeder children to die. In the 1880 West Leyden, New York Census, Richard lived with Samuel and Hittie Gray. In the 1910 Utica, New York Census, the family lived on Brinckerhoff Avenue, Utica, New York. He and his wife were both members of Sacred Heart Church, Utica, New York

Richard Schrader and Mary Agnes Moak had the following children:

  i. Ada Schrader was born 27 April 1882 in Swancott Mills, New York. She died 11 March 1895 in Utica, New York. She was buried in St. Mary's Cemetery, Utica, New York.[202]

  ii. Adam John Schrader was born January 1884 in West Leyden, New York.[203] Adam was baptized in St. Michael's Church, Mohawk Hill, New York and his Godparents were Adam Cordair (Kotary) and Barbara Schroeder.[204] He died 2 June 1953 in Utica, New York of coronary thrombosis.[205] He worked as a self employed carpenter and was a member of St. Joseph's Church, Utica, New York. He never married.

  iii. Agnes Schroeder was born 24 August 1886 in Utica, New York and died 17 October 1969 at 1603 Whitesboro Street, Utica, New York.[206] She married Raymond Aubry in 1919 in Schenectady, New York. He was born 30 March 1894 in Napabee,

---

[196] Obituary Utica Newspaper May 1, 1943
[197] FHC film of St. Michael's Church Records, Mohawk Hill, New York
[198] Obituary Utica Newspaper May 1, 1943
[199] FHC film of St. Michael's Church Records, Mohawk Hill, New York
[200] Genealogy from Herbert Schrader
[201] Obituary Utica Newspaper October 31, 1950
[202] Genealogy from Herbert Schrader
[203] 1900 Utica, New York Census, 12th Ward
[204] FHC film of St. Michael's Church Records, Mohawk Hill, New York
[205] Obituary Utica Newspaper June 3, 1953
[206] Obituary Utica Newspaper October 18, 1969

Ontario, Canada and died 29 August 1964 at 909 Churchill Avenue, Utica, New York.[207] Agnes was a member of Sacred Heart Church, Utica, New York. She did not have children.

43.   iv.   Nicholas Matthew Schrader was born 16 August 1888 in Utica, New York[208] and died 16 February 1935 in Utica, New York.[209]

44.   v.   Howard M. Schrader was born 29 May 1891 in West Leyden, New York and died 19 March 1964 in Faxton Hospital, Utica, New York.[210]

vi.   Herbert J. Schrader was born July 1893 in Utica, New York[211] and died 6 January 1988 in St. Luke's Hospital, Utica, New York.[212] He married Blanche Ann Brady 6 July 1953 in St. Bernard's Church, Waterville, New York.[213] Blanche was born 23 January 1910 in Waterville, New York, the daughter of John Brady and Alice Wilcox. She died 31 October 2008 in the Presbyterian Home, New Hartford, New York. Herbert was educated in Utica, New York Schools. He served as a Private in the US Army in World War I and served in France. Herbert was a self employed carpenter for many years retiring in 1960. He was a member of Sacred Heart Church and its Holy Name Society, the Whitestown American Legion Post #1113 and the Carpenters Local #120.

vii.   Gertrude Schrader was born 26 April 1896 in Utica, New York[214] and died 19 September 1968 in Utica, New York.[215] Gertrude was buried with her brother Herbert in St. Joseph's Cemetery, Utica, New York. She retired from the Utica Knitting Company in 1949 and was a member of Sacred Heart Church, Utica, New York. She was a twin to Margaret and never married.

viii.   Margaret Schrader was born 26 April 1896 in Utica, New York and died 6 May 1896 in Utica, New York.[216] Margaret was a twin to Gertrude.

ix.   Paul Schrader was born March 1900 in New York State.[217]

x.   Raymond Schrader was born 14 March 1900 in Utica, New York and died 5 November 1900 in Utica, New York.[218]

---

[207] Obituary Utica Newspaper August 30, 1964
[208] World War I draft registration from Ancestery.com
[209] Obituary Utica Newspaper February 17, 1935
[210] Obituary Utica Newspaper March 20, 1964
[211] World War I draft registration from Ancestery.com
[212] Genealogy from Herbert Schrader
[213] Obituary Utica Newspaper July 7, 1953
[214] Genealogy from Herbert Schrader
[215] Obituary Utica Newspaper September 20, 1968
[216] Genealogy from Herbert Schrader
[217] 1900 Utica, New York Census, 12th Ward
[218] Genealogy from Herbert Schrader

16. Marie Salome Sentiff[4] (Margaret Schroeder[3], Nicolas[2], Nicolas[1]) was born 11 August 1846 in Ava, New York. Marie was baptized in St. Michael's Church, Mohawk Hill, New York and her Godparents were Nicholas Schroeder and Maria Salome Sassisus.[219] She married John B. Sanderl who was born in 1850.[220]

Marie Salome Sentiff and John B. Sanderl had the following children:
    i.   John B. Sanderl was born November 19, 1875and died June 1964.[221]
    ii.   Minnie Sanderl was born 1877.[222]

17. Joseph Sentiff[4] (Margaret Schroeder[3], Nicolas[2], Nicolas[1]) was born 5 October 1847 in Ava, New York. Joseph was baptized in St. Michael's Church, Mohawk Hill, New York and his Godparents were Joseph Sentiff and Maria Barbara Schroeder[223]. He died 17 March 1924 in Rochester, New York.[224] He married Wilhelmina Richert. She was born in 1857 in Germany and died 30 March 1910 at 4 Kay Place, Rochester, New York.[225]

Photo of Joseph Sentiff from the collection of Tom Acquaviva and used with permission.

Joseph Sentiff and Wilhelmina Richert had the following children:
    i.   Frank Sentiff was born in 1877 and died 18 March 1949 in Rochester, New York.[226] Frank was a patient at the Ogdensburg State Hospital, Ogdensburg, New York at the time his World War I draft registration was filled out and his full birth date was not documented.[227]
45.   ii.   Emory Sentiff was born 10 August 1881 in Rochester, New York and died 8 March 1963 in Rochester, New York.[228]
46.   iii.   Florence Sentiff was born in 1884 and died 26 November 1969 in Rochester, New York.[229]

---

[219] FHC film of St. Michael's Church Records, Mohawk Hill, New York
[220] Family information from Tom Acquaviva
[221] Social Security Death Index from Ancestry.com
[222] Family information from Tom Acquaviva
[223] FHC film of St. Michael's Church Records, Mohawk Hill, New York
[224] Family information from Tom Acquaviva
[225] Family information from Tom Acquaviva
[226] Family information from Tom Acquaviva
[227] World War I draft registration from Ancestry.com
[228] Family information from Tom Acquaviva

iv.   Evelyn Sentiff was born in 1886 in Rochester, New York and died 24 March 1892 in Rochester, New York.[230]

v.   Mary Sentiff was born 20 January 1889 in Rochester, New York and died 26 January 1889 in Rochester, New York.[231]

47.   vi.   Joseph Anthony Sentiff was born 31 July 1891 in Webster, New York[232] and died in Rochester, New York.[233]

vii.   Howard W. Sentiff was born 4 January 1895 in Niagara Falls, New York.[234]

48.   viii.   Harold Sentiff was born 18 November 1897 in Rochester, New York and died 13 August 1968 in Rochester, New York.[235]

ix.   Rose Sentiff was born in 1898.[236]

18. Barbara Sentiff[4] (Margaret Schroeder[3], Nicolas[2], Nicolas[1]) was born 27 March 1849 in Ava, New York. Barbara was baptized in St. Michael's Church, Mohawk Hill, New York and Godparents her were Nicholas Schroeder and Barbara Schroeder.[237] She died 7 January 1936 in Rochester, New York.[238] She married Emory A. Smith.

Barbara Sentiff and Emory A. Smith had the following children:
i.   Estella Smith. Estella married a man named Doyle.
ii.   Female child Smith married Charles Clement.
iii.   Ambrose John Smith was born February 2, 1878.[239] Ambrose married a girl by the name of Marie J. They lived at 132 Dove Street, Rochester, New York in 1918.[240]
iv.   George W. Smith.

19. Margaret Sentiff[4] (Margaret Schroeder[3], Nicolas[2], Nicolas[1]) was born 25 October 1853 in Ava, New York. Margaret was baptized in St. Michael's Church, Mohawk Hill,

---

[229] Family information from Tom Acquaviva
[230] Family information from Tom Acquaviva
[231] Family information from Tom Acquaviva
[232] World War I draft registration from Ancestery.com
[233] Family information from Tom Acquaviva
[234] World War I draft registration from Ancestery.com
[235] Family information from Tom Acquaviva
[236] Family information from Tom Acquaviva
[237] FHC film of St. Michael's Church Records, Mohawk Hill, New York
[238] Death Announcement Rochester, New York newspaper January 9, 1936
[239] World War I draft registration from Ancestery.com
[240] World War I draft registration from Ancestery.com

New York and her Godparents were Matthew Schroeder and Margaret Sentiff.[241] She died before1923. She married Nicholas John Turck in 1883 in St. Peter's Church, Deerfield, New York. He was born 7 July 1852 in Metz, Lorraine, France and died 14 April 1923 in Deerfield, New York.[242] Margaret lived in Rochester, New York before she was married and then moved to Deerfield, New York after the wedding. Nicholas J. Turck came to this country in 1871 and settled in Deerfield, New York where he lived out his life. He was a farmer and made a specialty of keeping bees. He kept bees about 40 years and some years his honey ran into the thousands of pounds.

Margaret Sentiff and Nicholas John Turck had the following children:
49.   i.   Genevieve (Jeannette) Turck was born January 1885.[243]
      ii.   Charles J. Turck was born March 1888.[244].
50.   iii.   Caroline (Carrie) E. Turck was born October 1889 in Deerfield, New York and died 26 February 1981 in Faxton Hospital, Utica, New York.[245].
      iv.   Estella Turck was born December 1899.[246]In the 1920 Utica, New York Census, Estella was living with her sister's family, Genevieve Moran. Her occupation was listed as a machine operator in a knitting mill. Estella lived in Rochester, New York in 1930 and was working as a film inspector.

20.   Anna Sentiff[5] (Margaret Schroeder[4], Nicolas[3], Nicolas[2], Nicolas[1]) was born 29 September 1855 in Ava, New York. Anna was baptized in St. Michael's Church, Mohawk Hill, New York and her Godparents were Valentine Welke and Anna Schroter.[247] She died after 1911. She married George Messmer 26 September 1883 in St. Michael's Church, Rochester, New York.[248] He died before 1900. Anna was listed as a dressmaker in the 1900 Rochester, New York census.

Anna Sentiff and George Messmer had the following children:
      i.   Adelaid Messmer was born May 1886.[249]
      ii.   Irene Messmer was born September 1887.[250]

---

[241] FHC film of St. Michael's Church Records, Mohawk Hill, New York
[242] Obituary Utica Newspaper April 15, 1923
[243] Genealogy from Herbert Schrader
[244] Genealogy from Herbert Schrader
[245] Obituary Utica Newspaper February 27, 1981
[246] Genealogy from Herbert Schrader
[247] FHC film of St. Michael's Church Records, Mohawk Hill, New York
[248] Family information from Tom Acquaviva
[249] 1900 Rochester, New York Census
[250] 1900 Rochester, New York Census

Generation Five

21. Anthony Urtz[5] (Ann Schroeder[4], Matthew Schroeder[3], Nicolas[2], Nicolas[1]) was born 3 November 1861 in Highmarket, New York.[251] Anthony was baptized in St. Michael's Church, Mohawk Hill, New York and his Godparents were his Uncle Anthony Urtz and

Maria Salome Schroeder.[252] He died 1 March 1893.[253] He married Clara VanDenbure. Anthony's funeral took place from the home of his sister, Mrs. Frank Hart, 26 Chestnut St., Utica, New York. The name on his tombstone is Anton Uertz and he is buried with his parents in St. Joseph's Cemetery, Utica, New York.

Photo of Anthony Urtz from the collection of Thomas Schafer used with permission.

Anthony Urtz and Clara VanDenbure had the following child:

　　　　i.　　Anthony Urtz died at age 8 months 7 days.

22. John E. Urtz[5] (Ann Schroeder[4], Matthew Schroeder[3], Nicolas[2], Nicolas[1]) was born 5 December 1863 in West Leyden, New York.[254] John was baptized in St. Michael's Church, Mohawk Hill, New York and his Godparents were John Uertz and Margaretha Schroeder.[255] He died 19 November 1945 at Clinton Road, New Hartford, New York.[256] He married Sarah C. Shepard 27 June 1889, the daughter of James and Ann Shepard. Sarah was born in 1867 in Chadwicks, New York and died 23 April 1941 in Utica, New York.[257] John was one of a family of 21 children. He came to Chadwicks with his family at the age of 14 and was employed by the Willowvale Bleachery Company for 51 years. For many years, he was a foreman, retiring January 1, 1933. He was a member of St. Anthony of Padau Church, Chadwicks, New York and its Holy Name Society. He was also a member of the Fourth Degree, Knights of Columbus and a life honorary member of Utica Council 189; a life member of the Order of the Alhambra; a life member of Santa Fe Caravan, No. 40, Utica, New York. Sarah was a charter member of the former Utica

[251] Genealogy from Herbert Schrader
[252] FHC film of St. Michael's Church Records, Mohawk Hill, New York
[253] Death Notice Utica, New York Newspaper March 2, 1893
[254] Obituary Utica Newspaper November 20, 1945
[255] FHC film of St. Michael's Church Records, Mohawk Hill, New York
[256] Obituary Utica Newspaper November 20, 1945
[257] Obituary Utica Newspaper April 24, 1941

Chapter, Daughters of Isabella, a member of St. Anthony of Padua Church and its Rosary Society, and a member of the Sauquoit Valley Home Bureau.

John E. Urtz and Sarah C. Shepard had the following child:

      i.   Margaret Urtz was born 11 May 1899 in Chadwicks, New York and died 17 June 1979 at the Eden Park Nursing Home, Utica, New York.[258] Margaret married Robert J. Thomas in 1920 in New Hartford, New York.[259] Robert was born 8 August 1897 in New Hartford, New York, and was the son of Owen E. Thomas and Elizabeth Williams. He died 12 March 1973 in Faxton Hospital, Utica, New York. Margaret was educated in New Hartford, New York Schools and was a graduate of Utica School of Commerce. She was a member of St. Thomas Church, New Hartford, New York.   She was a former member of the Faxton Council and the Yahnundasis Golf and Country Club. She had no children. Robert J. Thomas graduated from New Hartford High School, New Hartford, New York and the American Institute of Banking. He was Secretary and Director of the Sturges Manufacturing Company in Utica, New York and was associated with the company for 30 years. He was a member of the First United Methodist Church of New Hartford, a 50-year member of Amicable Lodge, F & AM, a 32nd degree mason, of the Mohawk Valley Consistory, Ziyara Temple of Utica, Greater Utica Chamber of Commerce, Utica Kiwanis, Yahnundasis Golf Club, Credit Bureau of Utica and the National Association of Accountants. For 16 years he was Supervisor of the Town of New Hartford and he had served on the first Airport Committee.

23. Matthew Uertz[5] (Ann Schroeder[4], Matthew Schroeder[3], Nicolas[2], Nicolas[1]) was born 27 March 1865 in Lewis County, New York and died 3 April 1937 in New Hartford, New York[260] He was baptized in St. Michael's Church, Mohawk Hill, New York 20 May

Photo of Matthew Uertz and his daughter Anna from the collection of Thomas Schafer and used with permission.

---

[258] Obituary Utica Newspaper June 18, 1979
[259] Obituary Utica Newspaper June 18, 1979
[260] New York State Vital Records

1865 and his Godparents were Mathias Schroeder and his Aunt Elizabeth Urtz Pelser. He married Cora Stratton 5 October 1887[261] in New Hartford, New York, the daughter of Isaac and Catherine Stratton. She was born 7 June 1870 in Chadwicks, New York and died 10 April 1934 in Oswego, New York.[262]Matthew died at the home of his brother, Jacob Uertz in Willowvale, New York after a four day illness. Matthew and his wife worked at the Utica-Willowvale Bleachery Company for 54 years. They were both members of St. Anthony of Padua Church, Chadwicks, New York.

Matthew Uertz and Cora Stratton had the following children:

51.   i.   Anna (Lulu) Uertz was born in August 1889 and died 14 January 1972.[263]

52.   ii.   Blanche Mary Uertz was born August 1896[264] and died June 24, 1967 at the Dowling Nursing Home, Utica, New York.[265]

53.   iii.   Roy J. Uertz was born 20 February 1898 in Chadwicks, New York and died 3 January 1974 in Faxton Hospital, Utica, New York[266] [267]

54.   iv.   Floyd Uertz was born 4 August 1899 in Chadwicks, New York and died 17 October 1972 in Brookside Mobile Court, Chadwicks, and New York.[268] [269]

24.   Margaret D. Urtz[5] (Ann Schroeder[4], Matthew Schroeder[3], Nicolas[2], Nicolas[1]) was born 27 October 1867 in Lewis County, New York.[270] Margaret was baptized in St. Michael's Church, Mohawk Hill, New York and her Godparents were her Uncle John Pelser and Aunt Margaret Urtz.[271] She died 23 November 1950 in Chadwicks, New York.[272] She married John Chadwick in December 1887 in Utica, New York, the son of John Melvin Chadwick and Lavina Lintney. He was born 7 April 1868 in Chadwicks, New York and died 17 January 1929 in Chadwicks, New York.[273] Margaret moved from West Leyden, New York to New York Mills when she was a child and later to Chadwicks, New York where she had lived for 69 years. She and her husband owned and operated the Chadwicks Hotel for over 20 years retiring from business in 1913. She

---

[261] Rome, New York Newspaper marriage announcement October 1887
[262] Obituary Utica Newspaper April 11, 1934
[263] Family information from Michael Terrell
[264] 1900 New Hartford, New York Census
[265] Obituary Utica Newspaper June 25, 1967
[266] Obituary Utica Newspaper January 4, 1974
[267] Social Security Death Index from Ancestry.com
[268]Obituary Utica Newspaper October 18, 1972
[269] Social Security Death Index from Ancestry.com
[270] Genealogy from Herbert Schrader
[271] FHC film of St. Michael's Church Records, Mohawk Hill, New York
[272] Obituary Utica Newspaper November 24, 1950
[273] Obituary Utica Newspaper January 18, 1929

was a member of St. George's Episcopal Church and its Women's Auxiliary, Chadwicks, New York.

Photo of Margaret Urtz, John Chadwick, Anna Urtz and Frank Hart from the collection of Thomas Schafer used with permission.

Margaret D. Urtz and John Chadwick had the following children:

    i.   Anna Chadwick was born 14 September 1888 in Chadwicks, New York and died 21 May 1969 in Faxton Hospital, Utica, New York.[274] She married Maurice J. Kelley in 1917 in Utica, New York. He was born 26 February 1882 and died 18 April 1968 in Chadwicks, New York.[275] Anna was a member of St. George's Episcopal Church and its Women's Auxiliary, Chadwicks, New York. She did not have children. Maurice J. Kelley attended Utica, New York schools. He moved to Chadwicks in 1911 where he was employed by the Standard Silk Company as a loom fixer. He was the former owner and operator of a drug and variety store in Chadwicks, New York.

55.   ii.   John M. Chadwick was born 19 March 1890 in Chadwicks, New York and died 12 August 1940 in Chadwicks, New York.[276]

    iii.   Lucy V. Chadwick was born 14 November 1893 in Chadwicks, New York and died 3 February 1979 in Utica, New York.[277] She married Leo M. Hahn 6 September 1948 in Utica, New York. Leo was born 9 May 1895 in Utica, New York and died 6 August 1988.[278] Lucy was educated in Chadwicks and New Hartford, New York schools. She was of the Episcopal faith. She lived at 34 Brookline Drive, Chadwicks, New York at the time of her death.

Photo of Lucy Chadwick taken about 1914 and in the author's collection.

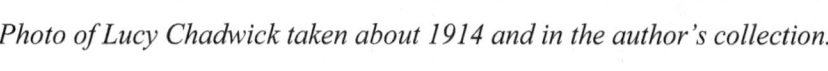

---

[274] Obituary Utica Newspaper May 22, 1969
[275] Social Security Death Index from Ancestry.com
[276] Obituary Utica Newspaper August 13, 1940
[277] Obituary Utica Newspaper February 4, 1979
[278] Social Security Death Index from Ancestry.com

25.   Anna Maria Urtz[5] (Ann Schroeder[4], Matthew Schroeder[3], Nicolas[2], Nicolas[1]) was born 16 May 1870 in Highmarket, New York.[279] Anna Maria was baptized in St. Michael's Church, Mohawk Hill, New York and her Godparents were Ana Maria Pelser and Carolus Schmidt.[280] She died 21 May 1947 in Ilion Hospital, Ilion, New York.[281] She married Frank (George) Hart in 1888 in Utica, New York. He was born 1864 and died 31 December 1932 in Ilion, New York.[282] Anna had lived for 41 years in Ilion, New York. She was a member of the Church of the Annunciation in Ilion, New York.

Anna Maria Urtz and Frank (George) Hart had the following children:
56.   i.   George H. Hart was born 15 January 1890 and died 7 June 1975 in North Miami, Florida.[283]

ii.   Mary K. Hart was born in 1895 and died 23 May 1913 in Ilion, New York.[284]

26.   Joseph S. Urtz[5] (Ann Schroeder[4], Matthew Schroeder[3], Nicolas[2], Nicolas[1]) was born 15 March 1874 in Lewis County, New York.[285] Joseph was baptized in St. Michael's Church, Mohawk Hill, New York and his Godparents were Joseph Moltz and Anna Pelser.[286] He died 5 January 1957 in Frankfort, New York.[287] He married Julia M. Sins 26 June 1901 in Chadwicks, New York, the daughter of John Sins and Margaret Link. She was born 29 April 1879 in Mohawk Hill, New York and died 26 March 1960 in Rogers and Lucy Nursing Home, Mohawk, New York.[288]

Photo of Joseph S. Urtz and Julia Sins from the collection of Thomas Schafer used with permission.

Joseph was a resident of Ilion, New York for about 45 years, moving to Ilion from Chadwicks, New York, and was a machine operator in Remington Rand for many years. He was a member of the Church of the Annunciation, the Holy Name Society and Ilion

---

[279] Genealogy from Herbert Schrader
[280] FHC film of St. Michael's Church Records, Mohawk Hill, New York
[281] Obituary Utica Newspaper January 1, 1933
[282] New York State Vital Records
[283] Obituary Utica Newspaper June 8, 1975
[284] Genealogy from Herbert Schrader
[285] Genealogy from Herbert Schrader
[286] FHC film of St. Michael's Church Records, Mohawk Hill, New York
[287] Obituary Utica Newspaper January 6, 1957
[288] Obituary Utica Newspaper March 27, 1960

Council 518, Knights of Columbus, Ilion, New York. His wife was also a member of the Church of the Annunciation in Ilion, New York.

Joseph S. Urtz and Julia M. Sins had the following children:

      i.   Margaret Rose Urtz was born 1904 and died 15 March 1905 at the age of 7 months.[289]

57.   ii.   Clarence Urtz was born 9 September 1905 in Chadwicks, New York and died 30 January 1998 in Faxton Hospital, Utica, New York.[290]

58.   iii.   Jerome Urtz was born 8 February 1907 and died 1 May 1993 in Ilion, New York.[291]

      iv.   Mary M. Urtz was born 26 May 1908 and died 9 February 1910.[292]

59.   v.   Robert J. Urtz was born 16 October 1910 in West Winfield, New York and died 31 October 1994 in East Hartford, Connecticut.[293]

      vi.   Thomas J. Urtz was born 22 October 1912 and died 5 July 1933 in Ilion, New York.[294]

60.   vii.   Rita Urtz was born 11 June 1914 in Ilion, New York and died 2 November 1991 in Ilion, New York.[295]

      viii.   Paul Urtz was born 12 May 1916 in Ilion, New York and died 30 July 1995 in DeBary, Florida.[296] He married Margaret Latt 14 February 1946 in Annunciation Church, Ilion, New York. Paul graduated from Ilion High School and was a veteran of World War II serving in the U.S. Navy. He was employed as a polisher at the Remington Arms, Ilion, New York for 33 years. He was a member of the Ilion Knight of Columbus, the Annunciation Church, Ilion, New York, St. Ann's Church in DeBary, Florida and the Holy Name of St. Ann's. He was an amateur Radio Operator. He did not have children.

61.   ix.   Living Urtz

62.   x.   Living Urtz

      xi.   Leonia J. Urtz was born in 1922 in Ilion, New York and died in 1922 in Ilion, New York.[297] Leonia only lived two days. She was a blue baby.

---

[289] Genealogy from Herbert Schrader
[290] Obituary Utica Newspaper January 31, 1998
[291] Social Security Death Index from Ancestry.com
[292] St. Mary's Cemetery tombstone, Clayville, New York
[293] Obituary Utica Newspaper November 1, 1994
[294] Genealogy from Herbert Schrader
[295] Obituary Utica Newspaper November 3, 1991
[296] Obituary Utica Newspaper July 31, 1995
[297] Genealogy from Herbert Schrader

27. Elizabeth Urtz[5] (Ann Schroeder[4], Matthew Schroeder[3], Nicolas[2], Nicolas[1]) was born 1 July 1875 in Mohawk Hill, New York. Elizabeth was baptized in St. Michael's Church, Mohawk Hill, New York and her Godparents were James Stal and Elisabeth Beha.[298]She died 21 August 1955 at 359 Oneida Street, Sauquoit, New York.[299] She married George J. Schafer 1 January 1893 in St. John the Evangelist Church, New Hartford, New York.[300] He was the son of Jacob Schafer and Margaret Moore. He was born 24 February 1870 in Utica, New York and died 4 February 1949 in Sauquoit, New York.[301] Elizabeth was a communicant of St. Anthony of Padua Church, Chadwicks, New York and a member of its Rosary and Alter Society. George had spent his life in the Sauquoit Valley. For 25 years he operated a farm in Sauquoit and prior to that he was employed for 25 years at the Willowvale Bleachery, Chadwicks, New York. He was a member of St. Anthony of Padua Church and its Holy Name Society.

Photo of Elizabeth Urtz from the collection of Thomas Schafer and used with permission.

Elizabeth Urtz and George J. Schafer had the following children:

63. i. Arthur C. Schafer was born 20 February 1895 in New York State.[302] He died 27 September 1971 in Faxton Hospital, Utica, New York.[303]

64. ii. George J. Schafer Jr. was born 28 April 1896 in New Hartford, New York and died 30 November 1978 in Harding Nursing Home, Waterville, New York.[304]

65. iii. Edward J. Schafer was born 2 August 1897 in New York State and died 20 March 1984 in Mount Vernon, Texas.[305]

iv. Elma Schafer was born 15 September 1910 in New Hartford, New York and died 19 January 2005 in Sauquoit, New York. She married Lawrence L. Smith 22 May 1929.[306]He was born in 4 May 1905 in Sauquoit, New York the son of John Smith and Ida Day. He died 29 April 1995 at the Harding Nursing Home, Waterville, New

[298] FHC film of St. Michael's Church Records, Mohawk Hill, New York
[299] Obituary Utica Newspaper August 22, 1955
[300] Obituary Utica Newspaper August 22, 1955
[301] Obituary Utica Newspaper February 5, 1949
[302] World War I Draft Registration from Anestery.com
[303] Social Security Death Index from Ancestry.com
[304] Obituary Utica Newspaper December 1, 1978
[305] Social Security Death Index from Ancestry.com
[306] Obituary Utica Newspaper January 20, 2005

York.[307] Elma was a homemaker who enjoyed her home and garden. She spent many happy hours in the garden and then canning and preserving the crop. She was a member of St. Anthony of Padua Church in Chadwicks, New York and its Alter Rosary Society, the Sauquoit Fire Ladies, the Community Club and the Village Elders of Sauquoit. Elma did not have children. Lawrence received his education in Sauquoit Schools. For many years, he was employed as a milk truck driver and later as a dairy farmer. Prior to his retirement he was a self-employed carpenter. He was also a member of St. Anthony of Padua Church, Chadwicks, New York and the Sauquoit Volunteer Fire Department where he served as treasurer for over 50 years. He was also active in the Oneida County Cooperative Extension and was an avid gardener.

28. Lawrence Uertz[5] (Ann Schroeder[4], Matthew Schroeder[3], Nicolas[2], Nicolas[1]) was born 25 June 1882 in Chadwicks, New York and died 26 June 1928 in Ilion, New York.[308] He married Mary L. Harter in 1910 in Chadwicks, New York who was the daughter of John Harter and Sarah Collins. She was born 26 March 1886 in Waterville, New York[309] and died 26 February 1979 in Ilion, New York.[310] Lawrence moved to Ilion, New York in 1912. He was widely known in bowling and baseball circles and was an active member of the Ilion Fish and Game Club. He was employed in the P.M. department of the Remington Typewriter Company. He and his wife were members of the Church of the Annunciation, Ilion, New York and of its Holy Name Society. Mary was a self employed hairdresser until her retirement in 1967.

Lawrence Uertz and Mary L. Harter had the following children:
66. i.   Stanley Uertz was born 21 November 1914 in Ilion, New York and died in 1963.[311]
  ii.   Living Uertz

29. Rose C. Urtz[5](Ann Schroeder[4], Matthew Schroeder[3], Nicolas[2], Nicolas[1]) was born 17 March 1887 in Chadwicks, New York[312] and died 27 November 1974 in St. Luke's Hospital, New Hartford, New York. [313]She married Anthony Nicknish 22 October 1912

[307] Social Security Death Index from Ancestry.com
[308] Obituary Utica Newspaper June 26, 1928
[309] Social Security Death Index from Ancestry.com
[310] Obituary Utica Newspaper February 27, 1979
[311] Family information from Vincent Urtz
[312] Social Security Death Index from Ancestry.com
[313] Obituary Utica Newspaper November 28, 1974

in St. Anthony of Padua Church, Chadwicks, New York.[314]He was born 27 February 1885 in West Leyden, New York and died 19 August 1970 in St. Luke's Memorial Hospital, New Hartford, New York.[315] Rose attended Chadwicks School in Chadwicks, New York and was member of St. Paul's Church, Whitesboro, New York.

Rose Urtz and Anthony Nicknish, October 22, 1912 Wedding Photo from the collection of Thomas Schafer and used with permission.

Anthony Nicknish was a resident of Whitesboro for 56 years. He was employed by the Kelsey-Hayes Corporation retiring in 1957. He was a member of St. Paul's Church and it's Holy Name Society. He lived at 14 Clyne Pl, Whitesboro, New York at the time of his death.

Rose C. Urtz and Anthony Nicknish had the following child:

67. i. Roger A. Nicknish was born 14 August 1914 in Whitesboro, New York and died 29 July 2002 in the Presbyterian Nursing Home, New Hartford, New York.[316]

30. Henry Nicholas Schrader[5] (Nicholas Schrater[4], Matthew Schroeder[3], Nicolas[2], Nicolas[1]) was born 30 November 1866 in New York State[317] and died 11 February 1920. He married Nellie F. Daley *about* 1897 in St. Patrick's Church, Rome, New York. She was the daughter of Keyron Daley and Mary Carney. She was born October 1883 in Osceola, New York and died 11 August 1955 in St. Elizabeth Hospital, Utica, New York.[318]In the 1910 Town of Lewis Census, New York, Henry was listed as working in a saw mill as a miller.

---

[314] Obituary Utica Newspaper November 28, 1974
[315] Obituary Utica Newspaper August 20, 1970
[316] Obituary Utica Newspaper July 30, 2002
[317] Genealogy from Herbert Schrader
[318] Genealogy from Herbert Schrader

Henry Nicholas Schrader and Nellie F. Daley had the following children:

68.   i.   Ward J. Schrader was born 2 May 1898 in Florence, New York and died 6 July 1995.[319]

   ii.   Mary F. Schrader was born 14 June 1899 in Parkers, New York and died 22 November 1991.[320]She married a man by the name of Blomness.

   iii.   Laura Schrader was born 21 July 1900 in Osceola, New York and died 13 March 1996.[321] She married a man by the name of Seelman.

   iv.   Grace R. Schrader was born 1905 in Florence, New York.[322] She married a man by the name of Seelman.

31.   Margareth J. Thomann[5] (Barbara Schroeder[4], Matthew Schroeder[3], Nicolas[2], Nicolas[1]) was born 26 March 1870 in Highmarket, New York.[323] Margareth was baptized in St. Michael's Church, Mohawk Hill, New York and her Godparents were Joseph Beha and Huldengarde Schmidt of Lee Center.[324]She married Frederick Scott in 1888. He was born in January 1868.[325] She married Charles Stopel before 1897. Margaret lived in Manlius in 1908 and in Deerfield in 1900. In 1945, she was married to Charles Staples and lived in DeWitt, New York.

Margareth J. Thomann and Frederick Scott had the following children:
   i.   Sophia A. Scott was born February 1891 in New York State.[326]
   ii.   Charles Scott was born April 1893.[327]
Margareth J. Thomann and Charles Stopel had the following children:
   i.   Halea A. Stopel was born 1898.[328]

32. George Henry Thomann JR[5] (Barbara Schroeder[4], Matthew Schroeder[3], Nicolas[2], Nicolas[1]) was born 23 January 1874 in Utica, New York and died 18 July 1957 in Utica, New York.[329] He married Gertrude Cole 6 June 1897 in Utica, New York, the daughter of John Cole and Katherine McCann. She was born in 9 June 1873 in Utica, New York and

---

[319] Social Security Death Index from Ancestry.com
[320] Family information from Robert Mathis
[321] Family information from Robert Mathis
[322] Family information from Robert Mathis
[323] Genealogy from Herbert Schrader
[324] FHC film of St. Michael's Church Records, Mohawk Hill, New York
[325] 1900 Deerfield, New York Census
[326] 1900 Deerfield, New York Census
[327] 1900 Deerfield, New York Census
[328] 1920 Dewitt, New York Census
[329] Obituary Utica Newspaper July 19, 1957

died 4 June 1943 in Memorial Hospital, Utica, New York.[330] George lived in Utica in 1908. He was found in 1910 Utica, New York Census living at 336 Whitesboro Street and working as a molder in the foundry. George was a member of the Wood, Wire, and Metal Lather International Union, Local 52. He and his wife were communicants of St. Joseph's Church, Utica, New York.

George H. Thomann Jr. and Gertrude Cole had the following children:

69. i. Ella Thomann was born 27 August 1901 in New York State and died 29 July 1996 in Downey, Los Angeles, California.[331]

70. ii. John Henry Thomann was born 22 June 1904 in Utica, New York and died 24 November 1980 in American International Hospital, Zion, Illinois.[332]

iii. George A. Thomann was born 4 April 1906 in Utica, New York and died 31 March 1972 in St. Elizabeth Hospital, Utica, New York.[333]George lived in Coldbrook, New York at time of his death. He was a member of St. Joseph's - St. Patrick's Church, Utica, New York and the Metal Lather's Union.

71. iv. Violet M. Thomann was born 21 April 1908 in Utica, New York and died 30 August 1988 in St. Elizabeth Hospital, Utica, New York.[334]

v. Gertrude Joan Thomann was born in 14 April 1912 in Utica, New York and she died 26 September 1968 in St. Luke's Memorial Hospital, New Hartford, New

York.[335] She married Felix A. Kubik 2 November 1945.[336]Felix was born 6 March 1907 in Ipswich, Massachusetts and died 28 November 1991 in St. Elizabeth Hospital, Utica, New York.[337]Gertrude had lived in Utica, New York until about nine months before her death when she moved to Whitesboro, New York. She was a member of St. Joseph's and St. Patrick's Church, Utica, New York.

Photo of Violet M., George A., Gertrude Joan, John H., and Ella Thomann in the collection of Jane Spence and used with permission.

---

[330] Obituary Utica Newspaper June 5, 1943
[331] Social Security Death Index from Ancestry.com
[332] Obituary Utica Newspaper November 25, 1980
[333] Obituary Utica Newspaper April 1, 1972
[334] Obituary Utica Newspaper August 31, 1988
[335] Obituary Utica Newspaper September 27, 1968
[336] Wedding Announcement Utica Newspaper
[337] Obituary Utica Newspaper

33. Peter R. Thomann[5] (Barbara Schroeder[4], Matthew Schroeder[3], Nicolas[2], Nicolas[1]) was born 31 July 1878 in Utica, New York and died 25 April 1943 in Utica, New York.[338] He married Maude Dela Warren 29 November 1899, the daughter of Thomas Warren and Anna Wilson. She was born 11 August 1880 and died 7 January 1934 at 706 Bristol Street, Utica, New York.[339] Peter had been a commercial photographer located for 38 years on Columbia Street, Utica, New York.

Peter R. Thomann and Maude Dela Warren had the following children:

   i.   Mabel Ada Thomann was born 18 November 1900 in Utica, New York[340] and died 28 September 1901 in Utica, New York.[341]

   ii.   Edna May Thomann was born in1904 in Utica, New York and died 28 December 1969 at 728 LaFayette Street, Utica, New York.[342] Edna never married. She attended Utica Schools and worked as a clerk in Berger's Department Store in Utica, New York.

72.   iii.   Ada P. Thomann was born in 1908 in Utica, New York and died 30 October 1968 at 7 Trinity Avenue, Yorkville, New York.[343]

   iv.   Walter P. Thomann was born 20 September 1905 in Utica, New York[344] and died 21 May 1906 in Utica, New York.[345]

34. Mary Johanna Schmidt[5] (Catherine Schroeder[4], Matthew Schroeder[3], Nicolas[2], Nicolas[1]) was born 8 November 1864 in West Leyden, New York. Mary was baptized in St. Michael's Church, Mohawk Hill, New York and her Godparents were Joannes Phillip Schmidt and Magdalena Finster.[346]She died 5 January 1958 in Utica, New York. She married George Sifer 7 June 1892 in St. Mary's Church, Prussian Settlement, West Leyden, New York,[347] the son of Augustus Isaac Seifert and Catharina Gasser Preis. The witnesses at their wedding were Richard Uerz and Christina Link. George was born 11 April 1861 in West Leyden, New York and died 23 January 1945 in Utica, New York. [348] More information on the family of Mary Johanna Schmidt can be found in Chapter Two

---

[338] Obituary Utica Newspaper April 26, 1943
[339] New Forest Cemetery, Utica, New York
[340] Genealogy from Herbert Schrader
[341] Obituary Utica Newspaper September 29, 1901
[342] Obituary Utica Newspaper December 29, 1969
[343] Obituary Utica Newspaper October 31, 1968
[344] Birth Announcement Utica Newspaper September 22, 1905
[345] Obituary Utica Newspaper May 22, 1906
[346] FHC film of St. Michael's Church Records, Mohawk Hill, New York
[347] FHC film of St. Michael's Church Records, Mohawk Hill, New York
[348] Obituary Utica Newspaper January 24, 1945

of this book and more information on the family of George Sifer is found in Chapter Three of this book.

Mary Johanna Schmidt and George Sifer had the following children:

73.   i.   **Susanna Etta Sifer** was born 17 July 1893 in Ava, New York and died 20 June 1966 in St. Luke's Memorial Hospital, Utica, New York[349]

        ii.   George John Sifer was born 18 April 1900 in Utica, New York and died 27 January 1958 in Utica, New York[350] George was employed as an orderly at the Masonic Hospital in Utica, New York and was a member of St. Joseph's Church, Utica, New York. He never married.

35.   Joseph Lee Schmidt[5] (Catherine Schroeder[4], Matthew Schroeder[3], Nicolas[2], Nicolas[1]) was born 6 July 1867 in West Leyden, New York. Joseph was baptized in St. Michael's Church, Mohawk Hill, New York. His Godparents were Joseph Schmidt and Maria Schroeder.[351] He died 25 July 1945 in Rome Hospital, Rome, New York.[352] His first marriage was to Bertha Comstock. After her death, he married Clesta Lescarbeau 15 August 1904 in Utica, New York.[353] She was the daughter of Mr. and Mrs. Joseph Lescarbeau. She was born in 1856 in Salle, Canada and died 15 August 1939 in Rome, New York.[354] Joseph was listed under Joseph Smith in the 1900 Utica Census and was married to Bertha at that time. Joseph was a landscape grader by trade. His first grading job was at the House of Good Shepherd in Utica, New York. He later engaged in farming in the Town of Rome, New York. He was a member of the Presbyterian Church.

Joseph Lee Schmidt and Bertha Comstock had the following children:

74.   i.   Rebecca (Reba) Schmidt was born 11 August 1893 and died 23 March 1979 in Rochester, New York.[355]

75.   ii.   Frederick U. Schmidt was born 26 November 1894 in Schuyler, New York and died 7 October 1977 in Rome Hospital, Rome, New York.[356]

76.   iii.   Olivia Schmidt was born 31 July 1896 in North Gage, New York and died 25 December 1976 in Sunset Nursing Home, Boonville, New York.[357]

---

[349] Obituary Utica Newspaper June 21, 1966
[350] Obituary Utica Newspaper January 28, 1958
[351] FHC film of St. Michael's Church Records, Mohawk Hill, New York
[352] Obituary Utica Newspaper July 26, 1945
[353] Obituary Utica Newspaper August 16, 1904
[354] Obituary Utica Newspaper August 16, 1969
[355] Social Security Death Index from Ancestry.com
[356] Obituary Utica Newspaper October 8, 1978
[357] Obituary Utica Newspaper December 26, 1976

77.   iv.   Frances Schmidt was born 24 May 1898 and died August 1987 in Rensselaer, New York.[358]

v.   Douglas L. Schmidt was born August 1899.[359]

36. Herbert John Schrader[5] (Hubert Schroeder[4], Matthew Schroeder[3], Nicolas[2], Nicolas[1]) was born 31 December 1875[360] and died 12 June 1941 in Faxton Hospital, Utica, New York.[361] He married Elisabeth Agnes Dourhamer 27 February 1900 in St. Mary's Church, Utica, New York.[362] She was born in 1878 and died 8 November 1956 in Utica, New York.[363] Herbert was educated in Utica, New York schools and was a plumber by trade. He operated a plumbing shop on Columbia Street, Utica, New York for many years. He was a member of St. Francis deSales Church, Utica, New York.

Herbert John Schrader and Elisabeth Agnes Dourhamer had the following children:
78.   i.   Charles H. Schrader was born 26 February 1901 in Utica, New York and died 6 July 1956 at 1412 Dudley Ave., Utica, New York.[364]
79.   ii.   Mary E. Schrader was born 1904 in New York State.[365]
iii.   Edward J. Schrader was born in 1906 Edward was an electrician by trade. He moved to Cahoes, New York.[366]
80.   iv.   Leo Michael Schrader was born in 1909 in New York State and died 21 December 1971.[367]
81.   v.   Gertrude Norma Schrader was born 5 April 1911 and died 10 April 1986 in Arnot-Ogden Hospital, Elmira, New York.[368].
82.   vi.   Jane Schrader was born 11 March 1913 and died 31 January 1995 in St. Luke's Hospital, Utica, New York.[369]

37.   Charles (Carl) Peter Schrader[6] (Peter Schrader[5], Matthew Schroeder[4], Nicolas[3], Nicolas[2], Nicolas[1]) was born 8 June 1890 in Utica, New York[370] and died 15 November 1950.[371] He married Mildred Guske 1 June 1914. She was born in 1892 and died 18 February 1992.[372]

---

[358] Social Security Death Index from Ancestry.com
[359] 1900 Utica, New York Census
[360] World War I draft registration from Ancestery.com
[361] Obituary Utica Newspaper June 13, 1941
[362] Wedding Announcement Utica Newspaper February 28, 1900
[363] Genealogy from Herbert Schrader
[364] Genealogy from Herbert Schrader
[365] 1910 Utica, New York Census Ward Three
[366] Genealogy from Herbert Schrader
[367] Genealogy from Herbert Schrader
[368] Obituary Utica Newspaper April 11, 1986
[369] Obituary Utica Newspaper February 1, 1995
[370] World War I draft registration from Ancestery.com
[371] Genealogy from Herbert Schrader
[372] Genealogy from Herbert Schrader

Charles (Carl) Peter Schrader and Mildred Guske had the following children:

83.   i.   Mary E. Schrader was born 15 November 1916 in Utica, New York and died 9 September 1997 in Faxton Hospital, Utica, New York.[373]

         ii.   Helen R. Schrader was born 30 September 1919 in Utica, New York and died 11 June 2007 in Faxton-St. Lukes Healthcare, Utica, New York.[374] Helen had attended Utica schools. She was employed for many years by Johanna's Children's Clothing Store in New Hartford. She was a member of St. Joseph's and St. Patrick's Catholic Church, Utica, New York.

84.   iii.   Living Schrader

38. Mary Frances Schrader[5] (Peter Schrader[4], Matthew Schroeder[3], Nicolas[2], Nicolas[1]) was born 12 July 1892 in New York State[375] and died 14 July 1964.[376] She married Morris F. Jones in1923. He was born 4 September 1887 in Dwllheli, Wales and died 7 September 1974 in Faxton Hospital, Utica, New York.[377]In the 1900 Utica 11th Ward Census, Mary was listed as a saleslady. She lived in Chadwicks, New York later in her life. Morris F. Jones had come to America at the age of 3. He had been a resident of Sauquoit, New York for 50 years. He was a toolmaker at Kelsey Hayes and Savage Arms retiring several years before his death.

Mary Frances Schrader and Morris F. Jones had the following child:

85.   i.   Living Jones

39. Ernest W. Schrader[5] (Francis Schrader[4], Matthew Schroeder[3], Nicolas[2], Nicolas[1]) was born August 1878 in New York State[378] and died 1 November 1904 at 112 Schuyler Street Utica, New York.[379]He married Myrtice E. Quincy in 1896.

Ernest W. Schrader and Myrtice E. Quincy had the following child:

         i.   Ira Josephine Schrader was born 1 November 1902 in Utica, New York.[380]

40. Luella G. Schrader[5](Francis Schrader[4], Matthew Schroeder[3], Nicolas[2], Nicolas[1]) was born 29 August 1882 in Lee, New York and died 13 February 1952 in St. Luke's Memorial Hospital, Utica, New York.[381] She married Frederick E. Bennett in 1906 in Rome, New York.[382]He was born in 1868 in New York State[383] and died before 1930.[384]

---

[373] Obituary Utica Newspaper September 10, 1997

[374] Obituary Utica Newspaper June 12, 2007

[375] Family information from Mary Jane Chynoweth

[376] Obituary Utica Newspaper July 15, 1964

[377] Obituary Utica Newspaper September 8, 1974

[378] 1900 Utica, New York Census Ward Nine

[379] Death Announcement Utica Newspaper November 2, 1904

[380] Birth Announcement Utica Newspaper November 11, 1902

[381] Obituary Utica Newspaper February 14, 1952

[382] Obituary Utica Newspaper February 14, 1952

[383] 1920 Rome, New York Census

Luella lived in Rome in 1925. The 1930 Census showed Luella and her son living with her brother, Leo and his family. Luella came to Utica as a young woman with her family. She was a member of St. Joseph's Church, Utica, New York.

Luella G. Schrader and Frederick E. Bennett had the following child:

86.   i.   Clarence E. Bennett was born in 1904 in Rome, New York and died 17 June 1971 in St. Luke's Memorial Hospital, Utica, New York.[385]

41. Leo P. Schrader[5] (Francis Schrader[4], Matthew Schroeder[3], Nicolas[2], Nicolas[1]) was born 1 July 1890 in Lee Center, New York and died 24 June 1967.[386] [387] He married Eva H. Lavoie 14 January 1910.[388] She was born in 1890 in Massachusetts and died 22 December 1961 at 1012 Steuben Street, Utica, New York.[389] Leo operated the East Utica Welding Company, having his shop in Frankfort, New York. He later worked as a stationary engineer at Griffiss Air Force Base in Rome, New York. He was a member of St. John's Church, Frankfort, New York.

Leo P. Schrader and Eva H. Lavoie had the following children:

87.   i.   Helen S. Schrader was born 13 December 1910 in Norwich, New York and died 25 January 1981 in Ft. Lauderdale, Florida.[390]

         ii.   Anne Belle (Sister Francis Eymard) Schrader was born in 1913 in Utica, New York and died 11 March 1978 in Convent St. Joseph's, East Syracuse, New York.[391] Anne joined the St. John the Baptist Convent in Syracuse, New York and went under the name of Sister Frances Eymaird. She was a sister of St. Joseph for 45 years.

88.   iii.   Bertha Schrader was born 8 March 1914 in Utica, New York and died 24 March 1961 in Sauquoit, New York.[392]

89.   iv.   Leo P. Schrader Jr. was born 3 November 1915 in Frankfort, New York and died 29 January 2001 in Utica, New York.[393]

90.   v.   Gilbert C. Schrader was born 1917 in Frankfort, New York and died 13 August 1966.[394]

91.   vi.   Karl E. Schrader was born 8 February 1919 and died 11 September 1972.[395]

---

[384] 1930 Rome, New York Census
[385] Obituary Utica Newspaper June 18, 1971
[386] Obituary Utica Newspaper June 25, 1967
[387] Social Security Death Index from Ancestry.com
[388] Wedding Announcement Utica Newspaper
[389] Obituary Utica Newspaper December 23, 1961
[390] Obituary Utica Newspaper January 26, 1981
[391] Obituary Utica Newspaper March 12, 1978
[392] Obituary Utica Newspaper March 25, 1961
[393] Obituary Utica Newspaper January 30, 2001
[394] Genealogy from Herbert Schrader
[395] Social Security Death Index from Ancestry.com

92.   vii.   Living Schrader

93.   viii.   Elizabeth Schrader was born 12 July 1922 in Frankfort, New York and died 13 April 2005 in the Presbyterian Home, New Hartford, New York.[396].

   ix.   Arthur W. Schrader was born 9 February 1924 in Frankfort, New York and died 5 September 1936 in 1012 Steuben Street, Utica, New York.[397] Arthur was a member of St. Agnes Church and had attended St. Agnes School. For the last year he had been a member of St. John's Church.

   x.   Living Schrader.

42.   Mary Catherine Mirkes[5] (Anna Maria Schroeder[4], Matthew Schroeder[3], Nicolas[2], Nicolas[1]) was born 21 July 1877[398] and died 30 November 1901 in Deerfield, New York.[399] She married William A. Clark in 1893 in Rome, New York.   According to Forest Hill Cemetery records, Mary's body was removed to St. Agnes Cemetery 6 May 1912. Mary was educated in St. John's School, Utica, New York. She had lived in Rome, New York for five years following her marriage she moved to Deerfield, New York where she lived until her death.

Mary Catherine Mirkes and William A. Clark had the following children:
   i.   Ruth Lillian Clark was born in 1895 in Deerfield, New York.[400]
   ii.   Mary Marguerita Clark was born in 1899 in Deerfield, New York.[401]
   iii.   Frederick M. Clark was born in 1900 in Deerfield, New York.[402]

43. Nicholas Matthew Schrader[5] (Richard Otto Schrader[4], Matthew Schroeder[3], Nicolas[2], Nicolas[1]) was born 16 August 1888 in Utica, New York[403] and died 16 February 1935 in Utica, New York.[404] He married Anna Christine Kler 28 May 1912 in St. Mary's Church, Utica, New York, daughter of John Kler and Barbara Kotary. She was born 13 March 1888 in Alsace, France and died 21 August 1980 in Stonebridge Nursing Home, Rome, New York.[405]Nicholas was educated in St. Mary's School. He worked for the New York Central Railroad and later was a building contractor. He was a member of Church of the Sacred Heart, its Men's Club and the Holy Name Society. He was also a member of the Utica Lodge 22 B.P.O. Elks.

---

[396] Obituary Utica Newspaper April 14, 2005
[397] Obituary Utica Newspaper September 5, 1936
[398] Forest Hill Cemetery Records, Utica, New York
[399] Obituary Utica Newspaper December 2, 1901
[400] Genealogy from Herbert Schrader
[401] Genealogy from Herbert Schrader
[402] Genealogy from Herbert Schrader
[403] World War I draft registration from Ancestery.com
[404] Obituary Utica Newspaper February 17, 1935
[405] Obituary Utica Newspaper August 22, 1980

Nicholas Matthew Schrader and Anna Christine Kler had the following children:

94.   i.   Eleanor Magdalena Schrader was born 2 May 1913 and died 23 July 1991 in West Palm Beach, Florida.[406]

95.   ii.   Mary Agnes Schrader was born 10 August 1916[3 and died 17 October 2002 in Strong Memorial Hospital, Rochester, New York.[407]

96.   iii.   Living Schrader

97.   iv.   Living Schrader

98.   v.   Living Schrader

44.   Howard M. Schrader[5](Richard Otto Schrader[4], Matthew Schroeder[3], Nicolas[2], Nicolas[1]) was born 29 May 1891 in West Leyden, New York and died 19 March 1964 in Faxton Hospital, Utica, New York.[408] He married Margaret Lorena Irving in 1914, the daughter of Thomas Irving and Harriet Golden. She was born 25 October 1897 in Utica, New York and died 27 December 1970 in St. Elizabeth Hospital, Utica, New York.[409] Howard was a self-employed building contractor. He came to Utica in 1903 and was a member of St. Francis de Sales Church, Utica, New York.

Howard M. Schrader and Margaret Lorena Irving had the following children:

99.   i.   Thelma Elizabeth Schrader was born 10 August 1916 in Utica, New York and died 13 February 2004 in Largo, Florida.[410]

            ii.   Rosemary Schrader was born 6 May 1918 in Utica, New York and died 24 November 1989 in St. Joseph's Nursing Home, Utica, New York.[411] She married Victor Levi Martin 4 May 1940 in St. Frances de Sales Church, Utica, New York. Victor was born 31 October 1912 in Crogan, New York and died 15 September 1980 in Utica, New York. He was the son of James Martin and Mary Burdick.[412] Rosemary did not have children.

100.   iii.   Richard Paul Schrader was born 27 September 1920 in Utica, New York and died 1 April 2002 in Utica, New York.[413]

101.   iv.   Charles Harold Schrader was born 25 August 1926 in Utica, New York and died 17 January 1973 in St. Elizabeth Hospital, Utica, New York.[414]

102.   v.   Edward Thomas Schrader was born 25 October 1927 in Utica, New York[415] and died 15 October 1976 in St. Luke's Memorial Hospital, New Hartford, New York.[416]

---

[406] Social Security Death Index from Ancestry.com
[407] Social Security Death Index from Ancestry.com
[408] Obituary Utica Newspaper March 20, 1964
[409] Obituary Utica Newspaper December 27, 1970
[410] Social Security Death Index from Ancestry.com
[411] Obituary Utica Newspaper November 25, 1989
[412] Obituary Utica Newspaper September 16, 1980
[413] Social Security Death Index from Ancestry.com
[414] Genealogy from Herbert Schrader
[415] Genealogy from Herbert Schrader
[416] Obituary Utica Newspaper October 16, 1976

103. vi. Robert Kenneth Schrader was born 1 May 1928 in Utica, New York[417] and died 31 October 1995 in Faxton Hospital, Utica, New York.[418]

104. vii. John Adam Schrader was born 11 August 1929 in Utica, New York and died 11 August 1967.[419]

viii. William M. Schrader was born 24 August 1930 in Utica, New York and died 15 October 1987 in St. Elizabeth Hospital, Utica, New York.[420]He was married 13 August 1966 in Sacred Heart Church, Utica, New York. William was a Maintenance Mechanic for the Board of Water Supply in Utica and later was employed by the Labor Union. William served in the U.S. National Guard for many years. He did not have any children.

ix. Gloria Ann Schrader was born 1931 in Utica, New York and died 22 March 1933 in Utica, New York.[421]

x. Living Schrader

105. xi. Living Schrader

106. xii. Patricia Mae Schrader was born 9 March 1935 in Utica, New York[422] and died 14 November 1981 in St. Elizabeth Hospital, Utica, New York.[423]

107. xiii. Margaret Schrader was born 11 November 1936 in Utica, New York[424] and died 19 August 2008 at Faxton St. Luke's Healthcare, Utica, New York.[425]

ivx. Nicholas Matthew Schrader was born 14 May 1938 in Utica, New York and died 13 May 1992 at 1218 Conkling Avenue, Utica, New York[426] He was married 6 May 1967 in St. Francis deSales Church, Utica, New York.[427]Nicholas worked for Univac and then for Calvary Cemetery. He also worked for the Indium Corporation of America in Utica, New York. He was a member of St. Mary's Church in Utica, New York. Nicholas did not have children.

108. xv. Sue Ann Schrader was born 19 May 1939 in Utica, New York[428]and died 10 November 2003 in Faxton Hospital, Utica, New York.[429]

45. Emory Sentiff[5] (Joseph Sentiff[4], Margaret Schroeder[3], Nicolas[2], Nicolas[1]) was born 10 August 1881 in Rochester, New York and died 8 March 1963 in Rochester, New

[417] Genealogy from Herbert Schrader
[418] Obituary Utica Newspaper November 1, 1995
[419] Genealogy from Herbert Schrader
[420] Obituary Utica Newspaper October 16, 1987
[421] Genealogy from Herbert Schrader
[422] Genealogy from Herbert Schrader
[423] Obituary Utica Newspaper November 15, 1981
[424] Genealogy from Herbert Schrader
[425] Obituary Utica Newspaper August 20, 2008
[426] Obituary Utica Newspaper May 14, 1992
[427] Wedding Announcement Utica Newspaper May 14, 1967
[428] Genealogy from Herbert Schrader
[429] Obituary Utica Newspaper November 11, 2003

York.[430] He married Sophia B. who was born in 1881 and died 30 July 1958 in Rochester, New York.[431]

Emory Sentiff and Sophia B. had the following children:
109.   i.   Robert Sentiff was born 28 October 1907 in Rochester, New York and died October 1986 in Rochester, New York.[432]

       ii.   Hazel Sentiff was born 1910.[433]

      iii.   Madeline Sentiff was born 1913.[434]

46.   Florence Sentiff[5] (Joseph Sentiff[4], Margaret Schroeder[3], Nicolas[2], Nicolas[1]) was born in August 1883 and died 26 November 1969 in Rochester, New York.[435] She married Franklin J. McGee, the son of John McGee and Mary Oberst. He was born in 1880 and died in 12 October 1955 in Rochester, New York.[436]

Florence Sentiff and Franklin J. McGee had the following children:
110.   i.   Joseph Warren McGee was born 25 June 1921 in Rochester, New York and died 19 December 2007 in Rochester, New York.[437]

      ii.   Franklin McGee was born Rochester, New York.[438]

47.   Joseph Anthony Sentiff[5] (Joseph Sentiff[4], Margaret Schroeder[3], Nicolas[2], Nicolas[1]) was born 31 July 1891 in Webster, New York[439] and died in Rochester, New York.[440] He married Martha Lederthil. She was born 27 November 1894 and died August 1987 in Rochester, New York.

Joseph Anthony Sentiff and Martha Lederthil had the following children:
      i.   Living Sentiff

      ii.   Living Sentiff

      iii.   Living Sentiff.

      iv.   William Sentiff was born in 1918 and died 20 December 1923.[441].

      v.   Harry J. Sentiff was born 23 August 1916 and died July 14, 2009.[442]

      vi.   Martha Sentiff was born 23 February 1929 and died 4 July 1987.[443].

---

[430] Family information from Tom Acquaviva
[431] Family information from Tom Acquaviva
[432] Family information from Tom Acquaviva
[433] Family information from Tom Acquaviva
[434] Family information from Tom Acquaviva
[435] Family information from Tom Acquaviva
[436] Family information from Tom Acquaviva
[437] Family information from Tom Acquaviva
[438] Family information from Tom Acquaviva
[439] Family information from Tom Acquaviva
[440] Family information from Tom Acquaviva
[441] Family information from Tom Acquaviva
[442] Family information from Tom Acquaviva

48. Harold Sentiff[5] (Joseph Sentiff[4], Margaret Schroeder[3], Nicolas[2], Nicolas[1]) was born 18 November 1897 in Rochester, New York and died 13 August 1968 in Rochester, New York[444]He married Loretta J. Lefrois. She was born in 1896 in Rochester, New York and died 6 March 1965 in Rochester, New York.[445]

Harold Sentiff and Loretta J. Lefrois had the following children:
114. i. Harold J. Sentiff was born 24 July 1926 in Rochester, New York. He died 8 October 1991 in Rochester, New York.
115. ii. Living Sentiff

49. Genevieve (Jeannette) Turck[5] (Margaret Sentiff[4], Margaret Schroeder[3], Nicolas[2], Nicolas[1]) was born in January 1885.[446] She married Leon John Lewis *about* 1906. Leon was born 30 March 1885 in Georgetown, New York and died 11 October 1907 in Utica, New York.[447] Leon John Lewis died young with diabetes. He had lived in Utica for 11 years. He graduated from the Advanced School and began working for the Globe Woolen Mill. He gave up that position and went to work for the American Express Company as a bill clerk. He was last a messenger of the M & M road and until his failing health he was a fireman on the M & M road. He was a member of St. Luke's Church, Utica, New York.

Genevieve later married John E. Moran 25 December 1912 in St. Peter's Church, Deerfield, New York.[448]He was born in 1891 in New York State.[449] Genevieve sued John E. Moran for inhuman treatment and other complaints in 1922 after John narrowly escaped death from suffocation. The 1920 Utica, New York census stated that John E Moran was a teamster and was in the industry of wholesale food.

Genevieve (Jeannette) Turck and Leon John Lewis had the following child:
i. Marian B Lewis was born 1907.[450] Marian was an infant when her father died in 1907.

50. Caroline (Carrie) E. Turck[5](Margaret Sentiff[4], Margaret Schroeder[3], Nicolas[2], Nicolas[1]) was born October 1889 in Deerfield, New York and died 26 February 1981 in Faxton Hospital, Utica, New York.[451] She married Ernest C. Burton 25 April 1916 in St.

[443] Family information from Tom Acquaviva
[444] Family information from Tom Acquaviva
[445] Family information from Tom Acquaviva
[446] Genealogy from Herbert Schrader
[447] Obituary Utica Newspaper October 12, 1907
[448] Wedding Announcement Utica Newspaper
[449] 1920 Utica, New York Census
[450] 1910 Utica, New York Census
[451] Obituary Utica Newspaper February 27, 1981

Peter's Church, Deerfield, New York.[452] She was born 8 July 1892 in Marcy, New York and died 6 June 1972 in Faxton Hospital, Utica, New York.[453]Carrie was educated in the Utica, New York Schools. Ernest was born in Marcy, New York and attended area schools. He was a World War I Army veteran and was a member of the VFW.

Caroline (Carrie) E. Turck and Ernest C. Burton had the following children:
i.   Living Burton
ii.   Elsie F. Burton was born 30 March 1922 in Deerfield, New York and died 15 October 2004 in St. Elizabeth Medical Center, Utica, New York.[454]Elsie was a member of St. Peter's Church, North Utica, New York.
iii.   Living Burton

Generation Six

51.   Anna (Lulu) Uertz[6] (Matthew Uertz[5], Ann Schroeder[4], Matthew Schroeder[3], Nicolas[2], Nicolas[1]) was born in August 1889 and died 14 January 1972.[455] She married John Clawson 23 December 1916 in South Street Methodist Church, Utica, New York.[456]

Anna (Lulu) Urtz and John Clawson had the following child:
i.   Ruth Clawson who married a man by the name of Gimmilaro.

52.   Blanche Mary Uertz[6] (Matthew Uertz[5], Ann Schroeder[4], Matthew Schroeder[3], Nicolas[2], Nicolas[1]) was born August 1896.[457]She married James E. McMahon Sr. 4 March 1918 in Chadwicks, New York, the son of James E. McMahon and Mary Wengert. He was born 15 February 1899 in Boonville, New York and died 1 July 1949 in Hawkinsville, New York.[458]After the death her first husband, Blanche married Frank Wright in 1962 and he died in 1966. Blanche had been a buyer for J.B.Wells Company and Berger Department Store retiring in 1962.

Blanche Mary Urtz and James E. McMahon Sr. had the following child:
i.   James E. McMahon Jr. was born 17 February 1919 in Utica, New York and died 3 October 1988 in St. Elizabeth Hospital, Utica, New York.[459]He was married 28 October 1942 in Utica, New York. James settled in Stittville after his marriage but

---

[452] Obituary Utica Newspaper April 26, 1916
[453] Obituary Utica Newspaper June 7, 1972
[454] Obituary Utica Newspaper October 16, 2004
[455] Family information from Michael Terrell
[456] Wedding Announcement Utica Newspaper
[457] 1900 New Hartford, New York Census
[458] Obituary Utica Newspaper July 2, 1949
[459] Obituary Utica Newspaper October 4, 1988

went back to Utica in 1971. He was employed by Bossert Manufacturing Company in Utica, New York for 41 years, and was a member of the International Association of Machinists and Aerospace Workers.

53. Roy J. Uertz[6] (Matthew Uertz[5], Ann Schroeder[4], Matthew Schroeder[3], Nicolas[2], Nicolas[1]) was born 20 February 1898 in Chadwicks, New York[460]and died 3 January 1974 in Faxton Hospital, Utica, New York.[461] He married Mirty L. Reese 16 May 1917 in the Willowvale United Methodist Church, Chadwicks, New York, the daughter of Evan Reese and Lizzie Williams. She was born 2 January 1897 in Washington Mills, New York and died 20 March 1978 in St. Luke's Hospital, Utica, New York.[462] The 1910 Census showed Roy and his brother Floyd living with Catherine Straton as a boarder on School Street in Chadwicks, New York. Roy was employed by Chicago Pneumatic for 15 years retiring in 1965. He also conducted a general insurance business for 40 years retiring in 1972. He was a member of Willowvale United Methodist Church. . He lived on Red Hill Road in the 1930 New Hartford, New York Census. Roy was ill a long time before his death.

Roy J. Uertz and Mirty L. Reese had the following children:

    i.   Esther Uertz was born 30 September 1918 in New Hartford, New York and died 6 February 2006 in the Presbyterian Home, New Hartford, New York.[463]She married William Boyd 26 May 1945 in the Willowvale Methodist Church, Chadwicks, and New York.[464]William was born 16 September 1920 and died 5 December 1969 in Mount Vernon Hospital, Mount Vernon, New York.[465] Esther graduated from Chadwicks High School and the Utica Conservatory of Music. She was employed with the Social Services Department for the State of New York and later with the Office of Vocational Rehabilitation in the Education Department. She retired in 1979. She also worked for NBC Music in New York City. She was a member of the Sauquoit Valley United Methodist Church and the B Sharp Music Club.

    ii.   Glenn R. Uertz was born in 1922 in Chadwicks, New York and died 26 August 1965 in Veteran's Hospital, East Orange, New Jersey.[466] He married Evelyn Hauver in 1948 in Utica, New York. She died 30 August 1978.[467]Glenn was a graduate of Chadwicks High School, Chadwicks, and New York. He was a self-employed television and radio technician. He enlisted in the US Army January 27, 1943.

    iii.   Living Uertz

[460] Social Security Death Index from Ancestry.com
[461] Obituary Utica Newspaper January 4, 1974
[462] Obituary Utica Newspaper March 21, 1978
[463] Obituary Utica Newspaper February 7, 2006
[464] Obituary Utica Newspaper February 7, 2006
[465] Sauquoit Valley Cemetery tombstone, Church Road, Sauquoit, New York
[466] Sauquoit Valley Cemetery tombstone, Church Road, Sauquoit, New York
[467] Family information from Michael Terrell

54.   Floyd Uertz[6](Matthew Uertz[5], Ann Schroeder[4], Matthew Schroeder[3], Nicolas[2], Nicolas[1]) was born 4 August 1899 in Chadwicks, New York and died 17 October 1972 of heart disease in Brookside Mobile Court, Chadwicks, New York.[468]He married Clara Shephard February 1920 in Utica, New York. She was born 31 October 1900 in Chadwicks, New York and died 9 February 1958 in Faxton Hospital, Utica, New York.[469] In the 1910 Census, he and his brother Roy were listed as living with Catherine Straton as a boarder on School Street in Chadwicks, New York. He lived in Utica in 1937. He attended Chadwicks School in Chadwicks, New York. He was a member of St. George's Episcopal Mission. Floyd worked for Savage Arms Corp for 30 years as a welder.

55.   John M. Chadwick[6] (Margaret D. Urtz[5], Ann Schroeder[4], Matthew Schroeder[3], Nicolas[2], Nicolas[1]) was born 19 March 1890 in Chadwicks, New York and died 12 August 1940 in Chadwicks, New York.[470]He married Bertha Thomas 22 December 1922 in Chadwicks, New York, the daughter of David Thomas and Gladys Mainwaring. Bertha was born 22 October 1900 in Plains, Pennsylvania and died 14 March 1953 in Sidney, New York.[471]John graduated from New Hartford High School and the Utica School of Commerce. For several years he was connected with the Adrain Knitting Company, both in Sauquoit and Adrian, Michigan. He later served as Superintendent of the Sauquoit Knitting Company. He was a World War I Veteran and a member of the St. George's Episcopal Church. Bertha died in an automobile accident near Sidney, New York. Bertha ran the Chadwicks Wholesale Candy Company for 13 years prior to her death.

John M. Chadwick and Bertha Thomas had the following children:
    i.   Living Chadwick
    ii.   Gordon T. Chadwick was born 2 February 1927 in New York State and died 25 February 1980 in Ventura, California.[472]

56.   George H. Hart[6] (Anna Maria Urtz[5], Ann Schroeder[4], Matthew Schroeder[3], Nicolas[2], Nicolas[1]) was born 15 January 1890 and died 7 June 1975 in North Miami, Florida.[473]He married Anna K. She was born 5 February1887 in New York State and died 3 December 1981 in Miami, Florida.[474]George was a past grand knight, fourth degree, and past district deputy of Ilion Council 518, Knights of Columbus and was a past president of the Remington Arms 25 year club. He had worked for Remington Arms for 36 years.

---

[468] Obituary Utica Newspaper October 18, 1972
[469] Obituary Utica Newspaper February 10, 1958
[470] Obituary Utica Newspaper August 13, 1940
[471] Obituary Utica Newspaper March 15, 1953
[472] California Death Index at Ancestry.com
[473] Florida Death Index 1877-1998 at Ancestry.com
[474] Florida Death Index 1877-1998 at Ancestry.com

George H. Hart and Anna K. had the following children:

      i.   Lucille A. Hart was born 1915.[475] Lucille married a man named Beck.

      ii.   Marie A. Hart was born 17 June 1914 and died 19 October 2002 in Los Alamos, New Mexico.[476]

      iii.   Frank B. Hart was born 1921.[477]

57.   Clarence Urtz[6] (Joseph S. Urtz[5], Ann Schroeder[4], Matthew Schroeder[3], Nicolas[2], Nicolas[1]) was born 9 September 1905 in Chadwicks, New York and died 30 January 1998 in Faxton Hospital, Utica, New York.[478] He married Bertha Shutts 25 May 1934 in Ilion, New York. She was born 18 February 1907[479] and died 8 March 1987.[480] Clarence was a finish gun quality auditor for 46 years at Remington Arms Company, retiring in 1970. He was a member of the Church of the Annunciation, National Rifle Association, and Ilion Fish and Game Club all in Ilion, New York. He was also a 70 year member of the Ilion Knights of Columbus and its Fourth Degree Assembly. For over 50 years, he enjoyed his camp and gardening at Canadarago Lake. Clarence Urtz and Bertha Shutts had three children all of whom may still be living.

58.   Jerome Urtz[6] (Joseph S. Urtz[5], Ann Schroeder[4], Matthew Schroeder[3], Nicolas[2], Nicolas[1]) was born 8 February 1907 and died 1 May 1993 in Ilion, New York.[481] He married Agnes Hayse. She was born 5 July 1907 and died 29 April 2002 in Mystic, Connecticut.[482] Jerome Urtz and Agnes Hayse had one child who may still be living.

59.   Robert J. Urtz[6] (Joseph S. Urtz[5], Ann Schroeder[4], Matthew Schroeder[3], Nicolas[2], Nicolas[1]) was born 16 October 1910 in West Winfield, New York and died 31 October 1994 in East Hartford, Connecticut.[483] He married Dorothy E. Farmer. She was born in 1910.[484] Robert was employed at the Remington Arms Company, of Ilion, New York for many years. He attended the Church of the Annunciation and was a member of the Ilion K of C 518 and its 4th Degree Assembly and the Ilion Elks Lodge all in Ilion, New York. Robert J. Urtz and Dorothy E. Farmer had two children both of whom may still be living.

60.   Rita Urtz[6] (Joseph S. Urtz[5], Ann Schroeder[4], Matthew Schroeder[3], Nicolas[2], Nicolas[1]) was born 11 June 1914 in Ilion, New York and died 2 November 1991 in Ilion, New York.[485] She married Howard Wheelock, who was born in 1918[486] and died 6 June

[475] 1930 Ilion, New York Census
[476] Social Security Death Index from Ancestry.com
[477] 1930 Ilion, New York Census
[478] Obituary Utica Newspaper January 31, 1998
[479] Social Security Death Index from Ancestry.com
[480] Obituary in the Herkimer Telegram, Herkimer, New York
[481] Social Security Death Index from Ancestry.com
[482] Social Security Death Index from Ancestry.com
[483] Obituary Utica Newspaper November 1, 1994
[484] Family information from Vincent Urtz
[485] Obituary Utica Newspaper November 2, 1991

1943.[487]Rita was a housekeeper at London Bridge Medial Group, Ilion for eight years retiring in 1972. She was a member of the Church of the Annunciation, Ilion, New York, former secretary of Litchfield Cemetery Association and former member of the Home Bureau and the Election Board. She had 18 grandchildren and 15 great-grandchildren at the time of her death as indicated in her obituary.

Rita Urtz and Howard Wheelock had the following child:

      i.   Marjorie Wheelock was born 2 April 1938 in Ilion, New York and died 21 September 2006 in Gloversville, New York.[488]She was married 16 February 1957.
Following High school graduation, Marjorie attended Central City Business Institute in Syracuse. For a short time she was employed by General Electric in Utica. She and her husband owned and operated Johnson Ave. Sales, Johnstown, New York. She was a secretary for 21 years at Auto World Sales and Service in Johnstown, New York. She was a member of St. Mary of Mount Carmel Church in Gloversville, New York. Marjorie and her husband had seven children all of whom may still be living.

63. Arthur C. Schafer[6](Elizabeth Urtz[5], Ann Schroeder[4], Matthew Schroeder[3], Nicolas[2], Nicolas[1]) was born 20 February 1895 in New York State and died 27 September 1971 in Faxton Hospital, Utica, New York.[489]He married Anna Gaffey 17 January 1915 in Mohawk, New York,[490] the daughter of John Gaffey and Julia Quinn. Anna was born 28 September 1889 in Osceola, New York and died 4 December 1983 at 3040 Mohawk St., Sauquoit, New York.[491]Arthur was born in Washington Mills, New York. He was a 42-year resident of Sauquoit and had previously lived in New Hartford and Whitesboro. He operated a grocery store in Chadwicks several years, and also operated his own paper hanging business. He was a member of St. Anthony of Padua Church, Chadwicks, New York, a trustee of the church and a member of its Holy Name Society. He also was a member of the Knights of Columbus; the Sauquoit Fire Department and a past fire commissioner.

Arthur C. Schafer and Anna Gaffey had the following children:

      i.   Living Schafer
      ii.   Russell A. Schafer was born 7 February 1916 in Whitesboro, New York and died 8 August 1983 in 3040 Mohawk St., Sauquoit, New York.[492]Russell lived in Sauquoit, New York for 59 years and was a graduate of Sauquoit Valley High School. Until his retirement in 1977, he operated his own dairy farm and a retail milk delivery business. He was a member of St. Anthony of Padua Church, Chadwicks, New York.

---

[486] Family information from Vincent Urtz
[487] Family information from Michael Terrell
[488] Obituary Utica Newspaper September 21, 2006
[489] Social Security Death Index from Ancestry.com
[490] Obituary Utica Newspaper September 28, 1971
[491] Obituary Utica Newspaper December 5, 1983
[492] Obituary Utica Newspaper August 9, 1983

He was also a member of the Sauquoit Volunteer Fire Department, serving as its Chief for 25 years from 1957 until 1982.

      iii.   Living Schafer.

      iv.   Living Schafer

      v.   Lawrence (Larry) Schafer was born 28 July 1928 in Sauquoit, New York and died 23 April 2003 in Macon, Georgia.[493]

64.   George J. Schafer Jr[6] (Elizabeth Urtz[5], Ann Schroeder[4], Matthew Schroeder[3], Nicolas[2], Nicolas[1]) was born 28 April 1896 in New Hartford, New York and died 30 November 1978 in Harding Nursing Home, Waterville, New York.[494] He married Elizabeth Delahunt 23 June 1921 in Chadwicks, New York, daughter of Thomas and Johanna Delahunt. Elizabeth was born in Brooklyn, New York and died on 21 May 1935 in Utica, New York.[495]He married Helen Paye in 1940 in New Hartford, New York, the daughter of Edgar S. Paye and Mary Jane Donahue. She was born 26 September 1911 in Utica, New York and died 5 December 1979 in St. Luke's Memorial Hospital, Utica, New York.[496] George had been employed as a manager for 37 years with the A & P Tea Company, and for 15 years was the manager of the New Hartford store, retiring in 1960. He was a member of St. Anthony of Padua Church, Chadwicks, New York and an honorary member of its Holy Name Society. George J. Schafer Jr. and Helen Paye had one child who is still living.

65. Edward J. Schafer[6] (Elizabeth Urtz[5], Ann Schroeder[4], Matthew Schroeder[3], Nicolas[2], Nicolas[1]) was born 2 August 1897 in New York State[497]and died 20 March 1984 in Mount Vernon, Texas.[498]He married Ella French Moyer and she died in 1969.[499] Edward lived in Sauquoit all of his life and in Texas since 1982. He has been employed by the Sauquoit Valley Central School, Sauquoit, New York, retiring in 1969. Edward J. Schafer and Ella French Moyer had one child who may still be living.

66. Stanley Uertz[6] (Lawrence Uertz[5], Ann Schroeder[4], Matthew Schroeder[3], Nicolas[2], Nicolas[1]) was born 21 November 1914 in Ilion, New York and died in 1963.[500] He married Jeanette Tymiak. Stanley Uertz and Jeanette Tymiak had one child who may still be living.

67. Roger A. Nicknish[6](Rose C. Urtz Nicknish[5], Ann 2002 in the Presbyterian Nursing Home, New Hartford, New York. He married Jane Sherman 6 June 1942 in St. Paul's

[493] Obituary Utica Newspaper April 24, 2003

[494] Obituary Utica Newspaper December 1, 1978

[495] Obituary Utica Newspaper May 22, 1935

[496] Obituary Utica Newspaper December 6, 1979

[497] Social Security Death Index from Ancestry.com

[498] Obituary Utica Newspaper March 21, 1984

[499] Obituary of husband Utica Newspaper March 21, 1984

[500] Obituary of mother Utica Newspaper February 27, 1979

Church, Whitesboro, New York.[501] Roger worked at Utica National Insurance Company for many years, retiring in 1976. Roger A. Nicknish and Jane Sherman had two children who may still be living.

68. Ward J. Schrader[6] (Henry Nicholas Schrader[5], Nicholas Schrater[4], Matthew Schroeder[3], Nicolas[2], Nicolas[1]) was born 2 May 1898 in Florence, New York and died 6 July 1995.[502]He married Anna Mary Mathis 14 October 1924 in St. Peter and Paul's Church, Fish Creek, West Turin, New York. She was born 24 April 1898 at Mathis Road, Town of Lewis, New York and died 17 January 1994.[503] Ward J. Schrader and Anna Mary Mathis had two children who may still be living.

69. Ella Thomann[6] (George H. Thomann Jr[5], Barbara Schroeder, [4] Matthew Schroeder[3], Nicolas[2], Nicolas[1]) was born 27 August 1901 in New York State and died 29 July 1996 in Downey, Los Angeles, California.[504]Ella married Louis Charles Haas who was born 24 September 1899 in New York State and died 12 June 1974 in California. After the death of her first husband, she married Louis Allen Brannies who was born 29 December 1907 in Texas.[505]He died 11 October 1988 in Los Angeles, California.[506]Ella lived in Long Beach, California in 1943 and in Los Angeles, California in 1972. Ella Thomann and Louis Charles Haas had two children who are still living.

70. John H. Thomann[6](George H. Thomann Jr.[5], Barbara Schroeder[4], Matthew Schroeder[3], Nicolas[2], Nicolas[1]) was born 22 June 1904 in Utica, New York and died 24 November 1980 in American International Hospital, Zion, Illinois.[507]He married Bertha Freson 22 July 1924 in St. Joseph's Church, Utica, New York,[508] the daughter of William Freson and Elizabeth Oenick.   Bertha was born 25 May 1909 in Utica, New York and died 21 February 1952 in Utica, New York.[509]John married Mary Strilka in 1968. John worked as a lather for various construction companies retiring in 1972. He attended St. Joseph's - St. Patrick's Church, Utica, New York. He was a member of the Wood, Wire, Metal Lather International Union and Lodge #450 Loyal Order of Moose.
Schroeder[4], Matthew Schroeder[3], Nicolas[2], Nicolas[1]) was born 14 August 1914 in Whitesboro, New York and died 29 July

John H. Thomann and Bertha Freson had the following children:
   i. Living Thomann

---

[501] Obituary Utica Newspaper July 30, 2002
[502] Social Security Death Index from Ancestry.com
[503] Family information from Robert Mathis
[504] Social Security Death Index from Ancestry.com
[505] Social Security Death Index from Ancestry.com
[506] Social Security Death Index from Ancestry.com
[507] Obituary Utica Newspaper November 25, 1980
[508] Obituary Utica Newspaper July 23, 1924
[509] Obituary Utica Newspaper February 22, 1952

> ii.   Living Thomann
> iii.   Living Thomann
> iv.   Living Thomann
>   v.   Evelyn Marie Thomann was born 21 July 1925 in Utica, New York and died 21 January 1952 in Utica, New York.[510]Evelyn was educated in St. Joseph School, Kernan School and Utica Free Academy all in Utica, New York. She was employed by the Kirk Guild, Whitesboro, New York. She died as a result of an auto accident.
>   vi.   John G. Thomann was born 30 June 1926 in Utica, New York and died 24 October 2002 in Faxton Hospital, Utica, New York.[511]John was a Navy veteran and served in both World War II and the Korean War. For many years, John was employed with Thomann Construction and also for many years he owned and operated the Tollgate Inn in Remsen, New York. He was a member of St. Joseph's-St.Patrick's Church in Utica, New York. He was a member and past officer of the Boonville V.F.W. Post #5538, Boonville American Legion Post #406, the Carpenters Union and the Wood, Wire & Metal Lathe Union.

71.   Violet M. Thomann[7](George H. Thomann Jr.[6], Barbara Schroeder[5], Matthew Schroeder[4], Nicolas[3], Nicolas[2], Nicolas[1]) was born 21 April 1908 in Utica, New York and died 30 August 1988 in St. Elizabeth Hospital, Utica, New York. She married Fred C. Feisthamel in 1928. He was born in 1907 and died in 1976[512]

Violet M. Thomann and Fred C. Feisthamel had the following child:
>   i.   Frederick M. Feisthamel was born 16 July 1929 and died 9 January 2009 in Remsen, New York. Frederick was married 19 November 1955 in West Winfield, New York.[513]Frederick served in the Army during the Korean War.   In 1954, he was appointed to the New York State Police. In 1955, he transferred to the New York State Department of Environmental Conservation and served there for 27 years until his retirement. He attended St. Joseph's-St.Patrick's Church in Utica, New York. He was an avid hunter, fisherman, gun collector and a member of the NRA.

72.   Ada P. Thomann[6](Peter R. Thomann[5], Barbara Schroeder[4], Matthew Schroeder[3], Nicolas[2], Nicolas[1]) was born 1908 in Utica, New York[514]and died 30 October 1968 at 7 Trinity Avenue, Yorkville, New York.[515]She married George A. McCorduck in 1925. He was born 20 August 1905 in Utica, New York and died 22 April 1981 in St. Elizabeth Hospital, Utica, New York.[516]Ada attended Utica Schools.   She was a resident of

---

[510] Obituary Utica Newspaper January 22, 1952
[511] Obituary Utica Newspaper October 25, 2002
[512] St. Joseph's Cemetery tombstone, Utica, New York
[513] Obituary Utica Newspaper January 9, 2009
[514] 1930 Utica, New York Census
[515] Obituary Utica Newspaper October 31, 1968
[516] Obituary Utica Newspaper April 23, 1981

Yorkville for 32 years and was a member of Grace Episcopal Church in Utica, New York.

Ada P. Thomann and George A. McCorduck had the following children:

     i.   George E. McCorduck was born 25 June 1927 in Utica, New York and died 20 March 1997 in the Oneida Healthcare Center, Oneida, New York.[517] He was married 21 February 1948 in Utica, New York. George graduated from Whitesboro High school and served in the U.S. Navy during World War II. He was a retired employee of Agway of Syracuse and for 30 years served as a part time building inspector for the Oneida Savings Bank. He attended Christ Church United Methodist of Sherrill and was a member of the Ziyara Temple Shrine Oriental Lodge of Utica and the Western Shrine Club. He was a former member of the Sherrill Rotary Club. George had eight grandchildren at the time of his death as indicated in his obituary.

     ii.   Donald R. McCorduck was born 29 May 1929 and died 13 June 2007 in Oriskany, New York.[518]

     iii.   Robert McCorduck was born 28 February 1935 in Utica, New York and died 25 January 2009 in Heritage Healthcare Center, Utica, New York. Robert was married 14 March 1959.[519] Robert was raised and educated in Yorkville, New York. He graduated from Whitesboro High School in 1953 and attended Utica College. He was a veteran of the United States Army and served as a cryptographer during the Korean Conflict. For many years Bob was employed by the Jones and Stack Chemical Companies as a chemical salesman. He was a lifetime member of the Veterans of Foreign Wars Post #7393 in New York Mills and a 27 year member of the American Legion Post #1113 of Whitesboro, New York, serving as Color Guard at both Posts.

73. Susanna Etta Sifer[6] (Mary Johanna Schmidt Sifer[5], Catherine Schroeder,[4] Matthew Schroeder[3], Nicolas[2], Nicolas[1]) was born 17 July 1893 in Ava, New York[520] and died 20 June 1966 in Utica, New York.[521] She married George Francis Bowman 8 September 1916 in St. Joseph's Church, the son of George Bowman and Rose Hahn. He was born 18 December 1891 in Jersey City, New Jersey[522] and

Photo of George Bowman and Susanna Etta Sifer taken in 1914. Photo is in the author's collection.

---

[517] Obituary Utica Newspaper March 21, 1997
[518] Social Security Death Index from Ancestry.com
[519] Obituary Utica Newspaper March 15, 1959
[520] Social Security Death Index from Ancestry.com
[521] Obituary Utica Newspaper June 21, 1966
[522] FHC film 1403369, St. Patrick's Church, Jersey City, New Jersey

died 8 January 1957 in Utica, New York.[523]For more information on Susanna Etta Sifer see Chapter Three, Generation Three. For more information on George Francis Bowman see Chapter Four.

74. Rebecca (Reba) Schmidt[6] (Joseph Lee Schmidt[5], Catherine Schroeder, [4] Matthew Schroeder[3], Nicolas[2], Nicolas[1]) was born 11 August 1893[524] and died 23 March 1979 in Rochester, New York.[525]She married George Haggerty. Reba lived in Rochester, New York in 1945 and in Yuma, Arizona in 1977. She was a member of the Melba Rebecca Lodge and the Germania Chapter of the Eastern Star.

Rebecca (Reba) Schmidt and George Haggerty had the following children:
      i.   Franklin James Haggerty was born between 1909-1910 in New York State.[526]Franklin was living with his grandparents in 1920 and 1930 according to the Utica, New York census.
      ii.   John W. Haggerty was born 1912 in New York State.[527]John was living with his grandparents in 1920 and 1930 according to the Utica, New York census.

75. Frederick U. Schmidt[7](Joseph Lee Schmidt[6], Catherine Schroeder[5], Matthew Schroeder[4], Nicolas[3], Nicolas[2], Nicolas[1]) was born 26 November 1894 in Schuyler, New York and died 7 October 1977 in Rome Hospital, Rome, New York.[528] He married Gertrude J. Batchelor 9 September 1920,[529]the daughter of William Batchelor and Frances Thomas. She was born 1 March 1900 in Utica, New York and died 14 June 1967 in Oriskany, New York.[530] Frederick registered for the draft June 5, 1917 in Utica and was single at the time. Frederick came to Oriskany, New York in 1936 and was employed by the Rome Air Depot during World War II. He was a member of St. Mark's Church, Clark Mills, New York. As indicated in his obituary, Fred had 26 grandchildren and 12 great grandchildren at the time of his death.

Frederick U. Schmidt and Gertrude J. Batchelor had the following children:
      i.   Living Schmidt
      ii.   Edmond D. Schmidt was born 20 December 1922 in Utica, New York and died 7 May 2004 in Rome, New York.[531]He married 26 July 1942 in Stuttgart, Arkansas.[532] Edmond entered the Army Air Corps in 1941. He retired from the Air

---

[523] Obituary Utica Newspaper January 9, 1957
[524] Social Security Death Index from Ancestry.com
[525] Obituary Utica Newspaper March 23, 1979
[526] 1930 Utica, New York Census
[527] 1930 Utica, New York Census
[528] Obituary Utica Newspaper October 8, 1977
[529] Wedding Announcement Utica Newspaper
[530] Obituary Utica Newspaper June 15, 1967
[531] Social Security Death Index from Ancestry.com
[532] Obituary Utica Newspaper May 7, 2004

Force as a Chief Master Sgt. and Aircraft Maintenance Supervisor at Griffiss Air Force Base in 1963. He had been awarded the Good Conduct Medal with four bronze Oak Leaf Clusters, American Defense Service Medal, American Campaign Medal, Asiatic-Pacific Campaign Medal, World War II Victor medal, Army of Occupation Medal, Air Force Longevity Service Award Ribbon, United Nations Service Medal and Distinguished Unit Award. He was then employed as Supervisor of the Maintenance and Reliability Programs at Mohawk Airlines and by the Rite Aid Distribution Center. Ed was a devoted father, an avid hunter, and fisherman and outdoors man. He was a member and past president of the Rome Photo Club, Rome, New York.

      iii.   Frances (Jane) Schmidt was born 18 February 1925 in Utica, New York and died 19 July 2001 in Rome, New York.[533]She married 18 April 1944 in Utica, New York.

      iv.   Helen Schmidt was born 18 December 1927 in Utica, New York and died 31 December 1990 in Crouse Irving Memorial Hospital, Syracuse, New York.[534]She married 24 August 1954 in Westmoreland, New York.

      v.   Walter J. Schmidt Sr was born 16 June 1937 in Utica, New York and died 31 December 1989 in Vernon Center, New York.[535]He was married in January 1962 in St. Mark's Church, Clark Mills, New York. Walter attended Oriskany Schools in Oriskany, New York and was a graduate of Mohawk Valley Community College receiving his certificate in Police Science. He was employed as a machinist for the Oneida Molded Plastics Company, Oneida, New York and was the former chief of Police of the Village of Clinton, New York. He was of the Episcopal faith.

      vi.   Frederick U. Schmidt was born in 1921 and died 30 June 1929 in Utica, New York.[536]

76. Olivia Schmidt[6](Joseph Lee Schmidt[5], Catherine Schroeder[4], Matthew Schroeder[3], Nicolas[2], Nicolas[1]) was born 31 July 1896 in North Gage, New York and died 25 December 1976 in Sunset Nursing Home, Boonville, New York.[537]She married Charles Smith who died in 1939.[538]Olivia attended North Gage schools in North Gage, New York. During World War II she was employed at Griffiss Air Force Base. She was a member of the Tabernacle Baptist Church. To find children for Olivia Schmidt and Charles Smith, see Chapter Two.

77. Frances Schmidt[6] (Joseph Lee Schmidt[5], Catherine Schroeder,[4] Matthew Schroeder[3], Nicolas[2], Nicolas[1]) was born 24 May 1898 and died August 1987 in Rensselaer, New

[533] Obituary Utica Newspaper July 20, 2001
[534] Obituary Utica Newspaper January 1, 1991
[535] Obituary Utica Newspaper January 1, 1990
[536] . Death Notice Utica, New York Newspaper June 30, 1929
[537] Obituary Utica Newspaper December 26, 1976
[538] Obituary Utica Newspaper December 26, 1976

York.[539]She married Thomas Lazot. He was born 3 July 1896. He died July 1971 in Troy, New York.[540]Frances Schmidt and Thomas Lazot had one child who may still be living.

78. Charles H. Schrader[6] (Herbert John Schrader[5], Hubert Schroeder[4], Matthew Schroeder[3], Nicolas[2], Nicolas[1]) was born 26 February 1901 in Utica, New York and died 6 July 1956 in 1412 Dudley Ave., Utica, New York.[541]He married Louise Searle 20 July 1931,[542] the daughter of Joseph Searle and Anna Blake. She was born 27 September 1900 in Clinton, New York and died 3 February 1984 in St. Elizabeth Hospital, Utica, New York.[543]Charles went to elementary school in Utica, New York and then attended Utica Vocational School. He had been employed by Langdon and Hughes Electric Company and prior to that he was self-employed in Clinton, New York conducting a radio and television repair shop. He was a communicant of St. Mary's Church in Clinton, New York and the Utica Amateur Radio Club. Charles H. Schrader and Louise Searle had one child who may still be living.

79. Mary E. Schrader[6] (Herbert John Schrader[5], Hubert Schroeder[4], Matthew Schroeder[3], Nicolas[2], Nicolas[1]) was born in 1904 in New York State.[544]

80. Leo Michael Schrader[6] (Herbert John Schrader[5], Hubert Schroeder[4], Matthew Schroeder[3], Nicolas[2], Nicolas[1]) was born in 1909 in New York State and died 21 December 1971.[545]He married Lois E. Cook in 1936 in Utica, New York, the daughter of Steward Cook and Ethel McGuley. She was born in 1915 in Utica, New York and died 27 July 1980 in St. Elizabeth Hospital, Utica, New York.[546]Leo Michael Schrader and Lois E. Cook had five children who may still be living.

81. Gertrude Norma Schrader[6](Herbert John Schrader[5], Hubert Schroeder[4], Matthew Schroeder[3], Nicolas[2], Nicolas[1]) was born 5 April 1911 and died 10 April 1986 in Arnot-Ogden Hospital, Elmira, New York.[547]She married Joseph F. Ferriter 20 September 1941 in St. Francis deSales Church, Utica, New York, the son of James Ferriter and Elizabeth Sweeney.[548]He was born 23 November 1910 in Utica, New York and died 17 August 1991 in VA Hospital, Canandiagua, New York.[549]Gertrude and her husband were members of St. Patrick's Church, Forestport, New York and are buried in St. Patrick's

---

[539] Social Security Death Index from Ancestry.com
[540] Social Security Death Index from Ancestry.com
[541] Genealogy from Herbert Schrader
[542] Obituary Utica Newspaper July 7, 1956
[543] Obituary Utica Newspaper February 4, 1984
[544] 1910 Utica, New York Census, Ward Three
[545] Genealogy from Herbert Schrader
[546] Obituary Utica Newspaper July 28, 1980
[547] Obituary Utica Newspaper April 11, 1986
[548] Obituary Utica Newspaper April 11, 1986
[549] Obituary Utica Newspaper August 18, 1991

Cemetery in Forestport. Gertrude Norma and Joseph F. Ferriter had four children who may still be living.

82.   Jane Schrader[6](Herbert John Schrader[5], Hubert Schroeder[4], Matthew Schroeder[3], Nicolas[2], Nicolas[1]) was born 11 March 1913 and died 31 January 1995 in St. Luke's Hospital, Utica, New York.[550]She married John F. Clair 8 February 1941 in St. Francis deSales Church, Utica, New York. He was born 9 June 1911 and died October 1978.[551] Jane Schrader and John F. Clair had four children who may still be living.

83.   Mary E. Schrader[6](Charles (Carl) Peter Schrader[5], Peter Schrader[4], Matthew Schroeder[3], Nicolas[2], Nicolas[1]) was born 15 November 1916 in Utica, New York and died 9 September 1997 in Faxton Hospital, Utica, New York.[552]She married Charles Christensen 14 July 1940 in Utica, New York. He was born 15 November 1904 and died 13 August 1974.[553]Mary received her education in Utica schools. She was a chef at the Adirondack League Club, Old Forge, New York and at Keyes Manor Inn, Forestport, New York. She also owned and operated the Christmas Corner Gift Shop in Forestport. She was a member of St. Patrick's Church, Forestport, New York and the American Federation of Chefs, Mid-York Chapter for 25 years.

Mary E. Schrader and Charles Christensen had the following children:
i.	William Patrick Christensen died between 1997-2007
ii.	Living Christensen
iii.	Living Christensen.
iv.	Carl Peter Christensen died in 1941.[554]

86.   Clarence E. Bennett[6](Luella G. Schrader[5], Francis Schrader[4], Matthew Schroeder[3], Nicolas[2], Nicolas[1]) was born in 1904 in Rome, New York and died 17 June 1971 in St. Luke's Memorial Hospital, Utica, New York.[555]He married Bernice J. Zajac in1942 in Utica, New York, the daughter of Albert and Josephine Zajac. She was born 22 October 1904 in Utica, New York and died 9 September 1986 in St. Luke's Hospital Memorial Hospital, New Hartford, New York.[556]Clarence was a self employed accountant. He was a former member of Maynard Volunteer Fire Department and of the Moose Club. Clarence E. Bennett and Bernice J. Zajac had one child who may still be living.

87.   Helen S. Schrader[6] (Leo P. Schrader[5], Francis Schrader[4], Matthew Schroeder[3], Nicolas[2], Nicolas[1]) was born 13 December 1910 in Norwich, New York and died 25

---

[550] Obituary Utica Newspaper February 1, 1995
[551] Social Security Death Index from Ancestry.com
[552] Obituary Utica Newspaper September 10, 1997
[553] Social Security Death Index from Ancestry.com
[554] Obituary of his mother in the Utica Newspaper September 10, 1997
[555] Obituary Utica Newspaper June 18, 1971
[556] Obituary Utica Newspaper September 10, 1986

January 1981 in Ft. Lauderdale, Florida.[557]She married William O. Every 8 June 1935 in Our Lady of Lourdes Church, Utica, New York, the son of Frank Every and Laura Canfield. He was born 26 March 1913 in Ilion, New York and died 10 March 1988 at 25 Prospect Street, Utica, New York.[558]

Helen S. Schrader and William O. Every had the following child:
    i.   Donald W. Every died 2 September 1980.[559]

88.   Bertha Schrader[6] (Leo P. Schrader[5], Francis Schrader[4], Matthew Schroeder[3], Nicolas[2], Nicolas[1]) was born 8 March 1914 in Utica, New York and died 24 March 1961 in Sauquoit, New York.[560]She married Joseph G. Dwyer 23 April 1937 in St. John's Church, Utica, New York, the son of John David Dwyer and Esther C. Loftus. He was born 1 November 1915 in Utica, New York and died 24 October 1962 in Utica, New York.[561]Bertha was a member of St. John's Catholic Church in New Hartford, New York. Joseph was the superintendent of service at Hotel Hamilton in 1937 and died of a heart attack while operating an elevator at the Hotel. He lived at 15 Evalon Road, New Hartford, New York at the time of his death. He was a member of St. John's Roman Catholic Church in New Hartford. Bertha Schrader and Joseph G. Dwyer had two children who may still be living.

89.   Leo P. Schrader Jr[6] (Leo P. Schrader[5], Francis Schrader[4], Matthew Schroeder[3], Nicolas[2], Nicolas[1]) was born 3 November 1915 in Frankfort, New York and died 29 January 2001 in Utica, New York.[562]He married Marion Fay 1939 in St. John's Church, Utica, New York, the daughter of Edward Fay and Estelle Cleary. She was born 10 September 1910 in Clinton, New York and died 2 December 1983 in St. Elizabeth Hospital, Utica, New York.[563]Leo served in the Navy during World War II. For 25 years until his retirement Leo was employed by Bramley's in Utica. He was a parishioner of Historic Old St. John's Church, Utica. Leo was a former Boy Scout Leader in the Utica, New York area and in his earlier years served in the Civilian Conservation Corps. Leo is survived by 11 grandchildren and three great grandchildren as indicated by his obituary.

Leo P. Schrader Jr. and Marion Fay had the following children:
    i.   Living Schrader
    ii.   Living Schrader
    iii.   Living Schrader

---

[557] Genealogy from Herbert Schrader
[558] Obituary Utica Newspaper March 11, 1988
[559] Obituary Utica Newspaper September 3, 1980
[560] Obituary Utica Newspaper March 25, 1961
[561] Obituary Utica Newspaper October 24, 1962
[562] Obituary Utica Newspaper January 30, 2001
[563] Obituary Utica Newspaper December 3, 1983

iv.   Leo P. III Schrader was born 31 January 1940 in Utica, New York and died 18 February 1997 in St. Elizabeth Medical Center, Utica, New York.[564]He was married 12 July 1969.[565]Leo was a member and former captain with the Clinton Fire Department in Clinton, New York. He was a co-founder and former lieutenant with the Central Oneida County Volunteer Ambulance Corps., having designed their logo. He was also an active member of the Adirondack Motorcycle Club.

90.   Gilbert C. Schrader[6] (Leo P. Schrader[5], Francis Schrader[4], Matthew Schroeder[3], Nicolas[2], Nicolas[1]) was born in 1917 in Frankfort, New York and died 13 August 1966.[566]He married Rose E. Dale in 1940 in Utica, New York. She was born June 20, 1918 in Utica, New York and died in 19 March 1979 in Lakeworth, Florida.[567]Gilbert was killed in a truck accident in Forestport, New York. Gilbert C. Schrader and Rose E. Dale had two children who may still be living.

91.   Karl E. Schrader[6] (Leo P. Schrader[5], Francis Schrader[4], Matthew Schroeder[3], Nicolas[2], Nicolas[1]) was born 8 February 1919 and died 11 September 1972. He was married 23 October 1943 in St. Peter's Church, Utica, New York.[568]Karl had worked as an inspector at Kelsey Hayes in Whitesboro, New York for 20 years. He was awarded a Bronze Star in World War II while with the artillery. Karl E. Schrader and his wife had one child who may still be living.

93.   Elizabeth Schrader[6] (Leo P. Schrader[5], Francis Schrader[4], Matthew Schroeder[3], Nicolas[2], Nicolas[1]) was born 12 July 1922 in Frankfort, New York and died 13 April 2005 in the Presbyterian Home, New Hartford, New York[569]She married Walter A. Hughes 14 April 1945 in Delaware, Maryland. Walter was born 18 September 1918 in Utica, New York, the son of Arthur Hughes and Lillian Henzler. He died 15 August 1986.[570]After the death of her first husband, Elizabeth married Francis G. Bahr July 1989, the son of Frank H. Bahr and Ursula Casey. He was born 11 June 1908 in Utica, New York and died 7 December 1999 in New Hartford, New York.[571]Elizabeth was a veteran of the United States Navy and served during World War II. For many years until her retirement, she worked for the General Electric Company.   She was a parishioner of Historic Old St. John Church in Utica, New York and a member of the Yorkville Highlanders.   Elizabeth Schrader and Walter A. Hughes had two sons who may still be living.

---

[564] Obituary Utica Newspaper February 19, 1997
[565] Engagement Announcement Utica Newspaper
[566] Genealogy from Herbert Schrader
[567] Obituary Utica Newspaper March 20, 1979
[568] Genealogy from Herbert Schrader
[569] Obituary Utica Newspaper April 14, 2005
[570] Obituary Utica Newspaper August 15, 1986
[571] Obituary Utica Newspaper December 8. 1999

94. Eleanor Magdalena Schrader[6] (Nicholas Matthew Schrader[5], Richard Otto Schrader[4], Matthew Schroeder[3], Nicolas[2], Nicolas[1]) was born 2 May 1913 and died 23 July 1991 in West Palm Beach, Florida.[572]She married John Elmer Wheeler 16 June 1943 in Sacred Heart Church, Utica, New York, [573] the son of Katherine Wheeler. He was born 1 July 1907 and died 17 February 1987 in West Palm Beach, Florida.[574]Eleanor Magdalena Schrader and John Elmer Wheeler had two children who may still be living.

95.   Mary Agnes Schrader[6] (Nicholas Matthew Schrader[5], Richard Otto Schrader[4], Matthew Schroeder[3], Nicolas[2], Nicolas[1]) was born 10 August 1916 and died 17 October 2002 in Strong Memorial Hospital, Rochester, New York.[575]She married Joseph Dee Vosburgh 1 May 1937 in Sacred Heart Church, Utica, New York.[576]He was born 1 April 1915 and died 25 October 2000. She married again 31 December 1957. Mary was educated in Utica Catholic Schools. She was a buyer for Berger Department Store in Utica, New York. She was the secretary for many years in Rochester, New York at Bausch and Lomb. Mary Agnes Schrader and Joseph Dee Vosburgh had two children who may still be living.

99.   Thelma Elizabeth Schrader[6] (Howard M. Schrader[5], Richard Otto Schrader[4], Matthew Schroeder[3], Nicolas[2], Nicolas[1]) was born 10 August 1916 in Utica, New York and died 13 February 2004 in Largo, Florida.[577]She married Herman John Colacicco 6 September 1937 in St. Frances de Sales Church, Utica, New York,[578] the son of Vincenzo Colacicco and Maria Massa. He was born 11 January 1914 and died 4 October 1996 in Largo, Florida.[579]Thelma Elizabeth Schrader and Herman John Colacicco had one child who may still be living.

100.   Richard Paul Schrader[6] (Howard M. Schrader[5], Richard Otto Schrader[4],   Matthew Schroeder[3], Nicolas[2], Nicolas[1]) was born 27 September 1920 in Utica, New York and died 1 April 2002 in Utica, New York.[580]He married Amy Lorena Bebee 6 June 1944 in St. Francis deSales Church, Utica, New York, daughter of Rev William Lorne and Amy Sheets Bebee. She was born 29 July 1921 in Flackville, New York and died 31 July 2007 in the Heritage Home, Utica, New York.[581]Richard was employed with the Utica Board of Water Supply until his retirement in 1985 was been president of the union. He was a disabled American veteran serving in World War II in the European Theater with the 9th

---

[572] Social Security Death Index from Ancestry.com
[573] Wedding Announcement Utica Newspaper July 14, 1943
[574] Social Security Death Index from Ancestry.com
[575] Obituary Utica Newspaper October 18, 2002
[576] Wedding Announcement Utica Newspaper May 4, 1937
[577] Social Security Death Index from Ancestry.com
[578] 50th Wedding Anniversary Announcement Utica Newspaper, Utica, New York
[579] Obituary Utica Newspaper October 5, 1996
[580] Social Security Death Index from Ancestry.com
[581] Obituary Utica Newspaper August 1, 2002

Air Force. Dick served in the C.C.'s at Blue Mountain Lake and Boonville. He was a steadfast and dedicated husband and father.   Richard Paul Schrader and Amy Lorena Bebee had four daughters who may still be living.

101. Charles Harold Schrader[6](Howard M. Schrader[5], Richard Otto Schrader[4], Matthew Schroeder[3], Nicolas[2], Nicolas[1]) was born 25 August 1926 in Utica, New York and died 17 January 1973 in St. Elizabeth Hospital, Utica, New York.[582]He married Dolores McCracken 8 November 1947, the daughter of Frederick McCracken and Marie Peterson. She died 4 November 1975.[583]Charles was a chef in various local restaurants. He died as a result of a two car accident on 4 January 1973.   Charles Schrader and Dolores McCracken had two daughters who may still be living.

102.   Edward Thomas Schrader[6](Howard M. Schrader[5], Richard Otto Schrader[4], Matthew Schroeder[3], Nicolas[2], Nicolas[1]) was born 25 October 1927 in Utica, New York[584]and died 15 October 1976 in St. Luke's Memorial Hospital, New Hartford, New York.[585] He married Gloria Angeline Papa in 1945, the daughter of Luigi Papa and Angela Palladino. She was born in 1927 in Utica, New York[586] and died 15 December 1973 in St. Luke's Memorial Hospital, New Hartford, New York.[587]Edward worked as a taper machine operator at Mohawk Containers for 12 years prior to his death. He and his wife were members of Sacred Heart Church, Utica, New York.   Edward Thomas Schrader and Gloria Angeline Papa had four children who may still be living.

103.   Robert Kenneth Schrader[6](Howard M. Schrader[5], Richard Otto Schrader[4], Matthew Schroeder[3], Nicolas[2], Nicolas[1]) was born 1 May 1928 in Utica, New York and died 31 October 1995 in Faxton Hospital, Utica, New York.[588]He was married 31 July 1957.[589] He married again 1 July 1988.[590]Robert was educated in Utica, New York Schools. He served his country in the United States Army during the Korean War. He was employed by Continental Baking Company for many years, retiring in 1984. Robert Kenneth Schrader and his wife had two sons who may still be living.

104. John Adam Schrader[6] (Howard M. Schrader[5], Richard Otto Schrader[4], Matthew Schroeder[3], Nicolas[2], Nicolas[1]) was born 11 August 1929 in Utica, New York and died 11 August 1967.[591]

---

[582] Obituary Utica Newspaper January 18, 1973
[583] Genealogy from Herbert Schrader
[584] Genealogy from Herbert Schrader
[585] Obituary Utica Newspaper January October 16, 1976
[586] Genealogy from Herbert Schrader
[587] Obituary Utica Newspaper December 16, 1973
[588] Social Security Death Index from Ancestry.com
[589] Genealogy from Herbert Schrader
[590] Genealogy from Herbert Schrader
[591] Genealogy from Herbert Schrader

John Adam Schrader and his wife had the following children:

     i.   Barbara R. Schrader was born 1 April 1954 in Utica, New York and died 22 January 2009 in St. Elizabeth Medical Center, Utica, New York[592] She was married 17 September 2006.[593]Barbara was a graduate of Utica Free Academy, Utica, New York. She was a member of Historic Old St. John's Church, Utica, New York. Barbara and her first husband had five children who may still be living.

     ii.   Living Schrader.

     iii.   Living Schrader.

106. Patricia Mae Schrader[6](Howard M. Schrader[5], Richard Otto Schrader[4], Matthew Schroeder[3], Nicolas[2], Nicolas[1]) was born 9 March 1935 in Utica, New York[594]and died 14 November 1981 in St. Elizabeth Hospital, Utica, New York.[595] She was married 1 January 1954 in St. Agnes Church, Utica, New York.[596]Patricia was educated in Utica, New York schools. She attended St. Francis de Sales Church, Utica, New York.

Patricia Mae Schrader and her husband had the following children:

     i.   Living Murphy

     ii.   Patricia J Murphy was born 12 July 1957 in Utica, New York and died 5 October 1958 in Utica, New York[597]

107. Margaret Schrader[6] (Howard M. Schrader[5], Richard Otto Schrader[4], Matthew Schroeder[3], Nicolas[2], Nicolas[1]) was born 11 November 1936 in Utica, New York.[598] She died 19 August 2008 in Faxton St. Luke's Healthcare, Utica, New York.[599]She married Hubert Chapman 23 December 1966, [600]son of James and Helen Chapman. He was born 25 August 1931 in Pulaski, New York and died 27 June 1990 in 711 Rutger Street, Utica, New York.[601]Margaret loved Alfred Hitchcock movies, various TV shows and chocolate, coffee in the morning, ice cream, and games with her grandchildren. Margaret Schrader and Hubert Chapman had seven children all of whom are still living.

108. Sue Ann Schrader[6](Howard M. Schrader[5], Richard Otto Schrader[4], Matthew Schroeder[3], Nicolas[2], Nicolas[1]) was born 19 May 1939 in Utica, New York[602]and died 10 November 2003 in Faxton Hospital, Utica, New York.[603]She married 15 June 1961 in

---

[592] Obituary Utica Newspaper January 23, 2009
[593] Obituary Utica Newspaper September 18, 2006
[594] Genealogy from Herbert Schrader
[595] Obituary Utica Newspaper November 15, 1981
[596] Obituary Utica Newspaper January 2, 1954
[597] Obituary Utica Newspaper October 6, 1958
[598] Genealogy from Herbert Schrader
[599] Obituary Utica Newspaper August 20, 2008
[600] Obituary Utica Newspaper December 24, 1966
[601] Obituary Utica Newspaper June 28, 1990
[602] Genealogy from Herbert Schrader
[603] Obituary Utica Newspaper November 11, 2003

Holy Trinity Church, Utica, New York.[604]Sue Ann attended Utica, New York Schools and graduated from Utica Free Academy.   Sue Ann and her husband had the following children:

    i.   Living Weise

    ii.   Kirk Eric Weise was born 10 February 1963 in New Hartford, New York, and died 21 September 1983[605] in a motorcycle accident. He was educated in local schools and was as a machine operator at the Lally Manufacturing Company, Utica, New York.

    iii.   Living Weise

    iv.   Living Weise

109. Robert Sentiff[6] (Emory Sentiff[5], Joseph Sentiff[4], Margaret Schroeder[3], Nicolas[2], Nicolas[1]) was born 28 October 1907 in Rochester, New York and died October 1986 in Rochester, New York.[606] He married a woman named Frances who was born 28 November 1916 and died 23 August 1986 in Rochester, New York.[607]Robert and Frances Sentiff had three children who may still be living.

110. Joseph Warren McGee[6] (Florence Sentiff[5], Joseph Sentiff[4], Margaret Schroeder[3], Nicolas[2], Nicolas[1])) was born 25 June 1921 in Rochester, New York and died 19 December 2007 in Rochester, New York.[608]He married Eileen E. Corcoran, daughter of Thomas Corcoran and Virginia Weiss. Eileen was born 3 April 1924 and died in May 1996.[609]

Joseph Warren McGee and Eileen E. Corcoran had the following children:

    i.   Living McGee

    ii.   Living McGee

    iii.   Vincent Edward McGee was born 06 July 1955 in Rochester, New York, and died 6 July 1955 in Rochester, New York.[610]

114. Harold J. Sentiff[6] (Harold Sentiff[5], Joseph Sentiff[4], Margaret Schroeder[3], Nicolas[2], Nicolas[1]) was born 24 July 1926 in Rochester, New York. He died 8 October 1991 in Rochester, New York.[611]

---

[604] Obituary Utica Newspaper November 11, 2003
[605] Genealogy from Herbert Schrader
[606] Family information from Tom Acquaviva
[607] Family information from Tom Acquaviva
[608] Family information from Tom Acquaviva
[609] Social Security Death Index from Ancestry.com
[610] Family information from Tom Acquaviva
[611] Family information from Tom Acquaviva

Harold J. Sentiff and his wife had the following children:

    i.   John Sentiff was born 11 October 1953 in Rochester, New York and died 13 October 1953 in Rochester, New York.[612]

    ii.   Living Sentiff

    iii.   Living Sentiff

    iv.   Living Sentiff

    v.   Living Sentiff

---

[612] Family information from Tom Acquaviva

Chapter Two

Descendants of John Philip Schmidt

Generation One

1. John Philip Schmidt[1] was born *about* 1815 in Württemberg, Germany York[1] He died 17 February 1873 in Utica, New York.[2] He married Walburga (Mary) Fischer Schmidt prior to 1839 in Würtemberg, Germany York. She was born *about* 1810 in Würtemberg, Germany[3] and died 16 June 1882 in Utica, New York.[4]

John and his family came to America in June of 1852 with four children. Their son, Joseph, was 16 months old at the time of the crossing.[5]   They were first mentioned in the 1855 Utica, New York Census taken June 28, 1855. This census indicated he was not a naturalized citizen, and he had been living in Utica for six months. His occupation was listed as a shoemaker. His naturalization papers indicated that the witnesses to his naturalization were John Wolf of Rome, New York and Francis I. Dorn of Lee Center, New York. The Naturalization papers dated October 23, 1860 indicated he came from Württemberg and was living in Lee Center at that time.   John and his family were not listed in the 1860 Census in either Oneida or Lewis County.   However, they were listed in 1865 and 1870 in the Town of Lewis Census, Lewis County, New York. The 1870 Town of Lewis, Lewis County Census indicated that John was unable to read or write and listed his occupation as a Day Laborer.

The 1870 Census indicated Mary had given birth to nine children. It has not been determined if they left children behind in Germany. As the family story goes they had a

---

[1] 1870 Town of Lewis Census, Lewis County, New York
[2] St. Joseph's Church records, Utica, New York
[3] 1855 Town of Deerfield, Utica, New York Census
[4] St. Joseph's Church records, Utica, New York
[5] Family story from Hazel Wooding

three year old son who died during the crossing and was buried at sea. More of the family story says there was a member of the family who had a stained glass factory in Germany. My great grandmother corresponded with this family in Germany. She was told there was money for her if she could get to Germany to get it. But, of course, she did not have the means to do that. Then more of the story says the factory was destroyed during World War II. I have not been able to prove this story. John and his wife Mary must have left Lewis County, New York between 1870 and 1873 as John died in 1873 and was buried from St. Joseph's Church in Utica, New York.

The following was found in the Sunday Tribune - Utica, New York - June 18, 1882 - Death Notices:

> SCHMIDT: In Whitesboro, June 16, 1882, Mrs. Mary Schmidt, mother
> of Joseph and John J. Schmidt of this city aged 75 years.

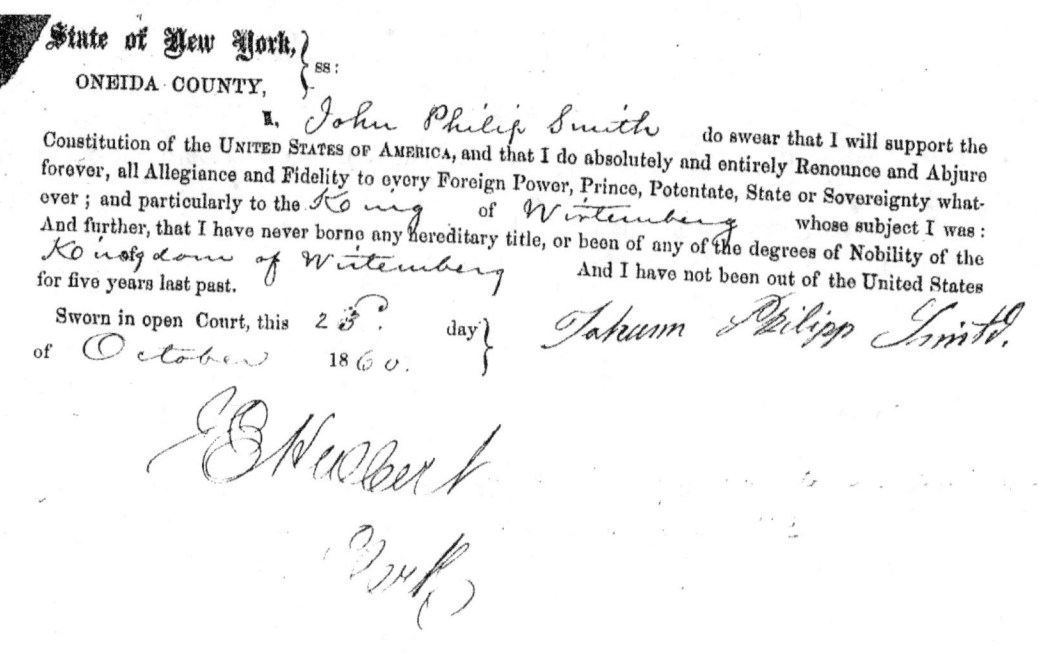

Copy of Naturalization papers for John Philipp Smith.

The 1870 Lewis County Census listed Mary as a housekeeper, unable to read or write and she had nine children. In 1875 she was living with her son, John, in the Town of Lewis, with no mention of her husband. In the 1880 Utica Census she was living with her son, John, in Utica, New York.

John Philip Schmidt and Walburga (Mary) Fischer Schmidt had the following children:

2.   i.   **John Jacob Schmidt**[6] was born 18 September 1841 in Württemberg, Germany and died 6 August 1891 at 12 Wiley Street, Utica, New York.[7]

3.   ii.   Christina Schmidt was born in 1847 in Württemberg, Germany[8] and died *before* 1892.

iii.   Boy Schmidt was born *about* 1849 in Württemberg, Germany and died *about* 1852. This child died at age 3 during the crossing of the Atlantic and was buried at sea.[9]

4.   iv.   Joseph Smith was born 11 February 1851 in Württemberg, Germany,[10] and died 8 June 1927 in Detroit, Michigan.[11]

5.   v.   Cornelia Schmidt was born in July 1854 in Oneida County, New York[12] and died 14 June 1896 at 37 Stark Street, Utica, New York.[13]

Generation Two

2. John Jacob Schmidt[2](John Philip Schmidt[1]) was born 18 September 1841 in Würtemberg, Germany and died 6 August 1891 at 12 Wiley Street, Utica, New York.[14] He married Catherine Schroeder about 1864[15], the daughter of Matthew Schroeder and Maria Salome Sasgas. She was born 30 August 1847 in Ava, New York[16] and died in February 1871 in West Leyden, Lewis County, New York.[17] Catherine Schroeder was baptized in St. Michael's Church, Mohawk Hill, New York and her Godparents were Francis Sentiff and Anna Caterina Hoffmann.[18] Catherine died at a very young age, only 24 years old as indicated in her husband's Civil War pension records. Her death has been a mystery to me. I have searched for her grave, and suspect that she was buried in West Leyden, New York without a marker. I have been unable to find her exact date of death or what caused her death at such a young age.

After Catherine's death, John married Philomena Ritter 1 February 1872 in St. Joseph's Church, Utica, New York, the daughter of Mathias (Martin) Ritter and Catherine Krailer.

---

[6] The bold print indicates that John Jacob Schmidt is a direct descendant of the authors.
[7] Obituary Utica Newspaper August 7, 1891
[8] 1855 Town of Deerfield, Utica, New York Census
[9] Family information from Jean Langford
[10] Family information from Jean Langford
[11] Obituary Utica Newspaper June 9, 1927
[12] 1855 Town of Deerfield, Utica, New York Census
[13] Obituary Utica Newspaper June 15, 1896
[14] Obituary Utica Newspaper August 7, 1891
[15] John J. Schmidt's Civil War papers
[16] Oneida County Gen Web page list of births from 1847 to 1851
[17] John J. Schmidt's Civil War papers
[18] FHC film of St. Michael's Church Records, Mohawk Hill, New York

Witnesses to this marriage were George Spran and Catharine Ritter. Philomena was born 25 March 1849 in Baden, Germany.[19]She died 30 September 1918 in Utica, New York.[20]

Philomena was forced to file for civil war pension benefits through her deceased husband, John Schmidt. Following the funeral of John, the surviving Company C Soldiers took up a collection for Philomena and her family as she had no means of support and was considered destitute.   Philomena was born in Baden, Germany as were her parents. Philomena emigrated with her parents in 1851 from Germany. According to John J. Schmidt's Civil War Pension records, Philomena lived in Kansas City, Kansas in 1904. Philomena married John Muthig after John Schmidt's death. She was taken ill while walking on the street with her daughter-in-law and taken into Donaldson's Drug Store at the corner of Columbia and Varick Street. She died within a half hour.   Philomena lived at 924 Whitesboro Street, Utica, New York at time of her death.

Photo of Philomena Ritter Schmidt from the collection of Jean Langford and used with permission.

The following obituary was taken from the Utica Morning Herald on August 7, 1891:

John J. Schmidt

Yesterday at his residence No. 12 Wiley Street occurred the death of John J. Schmidt, aged 49 years. The deceased was born in Germany, but came to this country when 9 years of age with his parents, locating in Utica. After living here a short time he moved to Point Rock, where he resided for several years, before returning to Utica. When the Civil War broke out the deceased enlisted in Company C, Fourteenth regiment New York Volunteers. When mustered out of service, Mr. Schmidt returned to Utica and took a great interest in the City's welfare. He was at one time a member of Hutchinson Guards of the Old 26th Battalions. He was a member of Post Mcquade, G.A.R., Order of United Friends, German Rifle Corps and the Carpenters and Jointers Union. Mr. Schmidt was twice married. His first wife, Catherine Schrader, died March 1870. The following January he married Minnie(Philomena) Ritter, who survives him with nine children.

[19] St. Joseph's Cemetery tombstone, Utica, New York
[20] Obituary Utica Newspaper October 1, 1918

Civil War Journey of
John Jacob Schmidt

The Civil War records on John J. Schmidt indicated that at the of age 21 years he enlisted in Company C 14th New York Infantry of the Civil War July 8, 1862 at Utica, New York. He mustered in as a private to serve 3 years. The 14th Regiment NY Infantry itself mustered in May 17, 1861 and mustered out May 24, 1863. On July 19, 1862 he arrived at Harrison Landing Recruit from Depot. From September to November 1862 and January 1863 John was on daily duty. From February to April 1863 he was on duty with the ambulance Corp. May 12, 1863 John along with about 70 other soldiers was left at Stonemans Switch near Fredericksburg, VA without arms or equipment of supplies and that their said regiment went home and was mustered out of service. A that time, John was troubled with Rheumatism and was sent to the field Hospital. According to the Surgeon General's Office - John J. Schmidt was admitted April 27th and discharged June 16, 1863 from Harewood General Hospital, at Potomac Crux, Virginia with a diagnosis of Typhoid Fever. On June 17, 1863 he was sent to Camp Convalescence near Alexandria, VA. He was then sent to Camp Distribution where he remained to Aug 7th, 1863 when he was sent to his home.[21]

His company was transferred June 24, 1863 to Co. F 44th infantry – There is no record of John joining this company to which he was transferred. The record transfer of John to Co F 44 NY Volunteers is cancelled and he is discharged July 15, 1863 by order of the Secretary of War to complete his military record as John F. Schmidt having fought July 2, 1863 at Gettysburg, Little Round Top facing Devil's Run. The personal description from the Adjutant General's Office stated he was born in Germany York, age 21, occupation, farmer; eyes, dark; hair, dark; complexion, dark; height 5 ft 7 in. He was also listed on the rolls as John J. Smith.[22]

Photo of John Jacob Schmidt in his Civil War uniform in the author's collection.

---

[21] John J. Schmidt's Civil War papers
[22] John J. Schmidt's Civil War papers

John was found in the 1865, 1870, and 1875 in the Town of Lewis Census, Lewis County, New York. By 1875 John was married to Philomena, had two more children, and his mother was living with him. His occupation in 1875 was growing potatoes. In 1880 Utica, New York Census, John and his family were living in Utica at 252 Whitesboro St, Ward Six. The census said he was a naturalized citizen and his occupation was a carpenter. He was a member of the German Rifles and served as the shooting master.

John Jacob Schmidt and Catherine Schroeder had the following children:
6.   i.   **Mary Johanna Schmidt** was born 8 November 1864 in West Leyden, New York and died 5 January 1958 in Utica, New York.

         ii.   Maria Magdalena Schmidt was born 6 April 1866 in West Leyden, New York[23] and died between 1870 and 1875. Maria was baptized at St. Michael's Church, Mohawk Hill, New York and her Godparents were Hubertus Schroeder and Marie Magdalena Finster.[24] The 1870 Town of Lewis Census, Lewis County, New York listed her as Lena. She was not in the 1875 Town of Lewis Census or 1880 Utica Census. A death record on her on her has never been found.

7.   iii.   Joseph Lee Schmidt was born 6 July 1867 in West Leyden, New York[25] and died 25 July 1945 in Rome Hospital, Rome, New York.[26]

John Jacob Schmidt and Philomena Ritter had the following children:
8.   i.   John Philippey Schmidt was born 15 November 1872 in Utica, New York[27] and died 20 March 1948 in Soldiers and Sailors Memorial Hospital, Masonic Home, Utica, New York. [28]

9.   ii.   George E. Schmidt (Smith) Sr was born 11 June 1874 in Utica, New York and died 18 December 1929 in Utica, New York. [29]

10.   iii.   Margaret (Maggie) Schmidt was born 1 March 1876 in Utica, New York and died 2 January 1942 in 1018 Court St., Utica, New York.[30]

11.   iv.   Anna M. Schmidt was born 19 March 1878 in Utica, New York and died 17 January 1962 in Utica, New York.[31]

12.   v.   Philomena (Minnie) M. Schmidt was born 17 March 1880 in Utica, New York[32] and died 23 September 1958 in Beverly, New Jersey.[33]

---

[23] FHC film of St. Michael's Church Records, Mohawk Hill, New York
[24] FHC film of St. Michael's Church Records, Mohawk Hill, New York
[25] FHC film of St. Michael's Church Records, Mohawk Hill, New York
[26] Obituary Utica Newspaper July 26, 1945
[27] St. Joseph's Church records, Utica, New York
[28] Obituary Utica Newspaper March 21, 1948
[29] Death announcement Utica Newspaper December 19, 1929
[30] Obituary Utica Newspaper January 3, 1942
[31] Obituary Utica Newspaper January 18, 1962
[32] Family information from Arlene Turner
[33] Ancestry.com US Veterans Cemeteries

13.   vi.   Frank Xavier Schmidt was born 7 June 1883 in Utica, New York[34]and died 23 September 1957 in New Hartford, New York.[35]

vii.   Matthew (Mathias) Peter Schmidt was born 18 November 1887 in Utica, New York[36]and died 30 May 1922 in Utica, New York.[37] Matthew was baptized in St. Joseph's Church, Utica, New York and his Godparents were Joanes Schmidt and Philomena Schafer.[38]Matthew lived in Utica at time of his mother's death but in March of 1920 he lived in Hammond, Indiana. He was said to be a "helpless child" by the Civil War Pension Board and received benefits throughout his life. He suffered from Spinal Meningitis. He lived with his sister, Margaret Uerz, for the last three and a half years of his life. He was a member of St. Joseph's church and its Holy Name Society. He was also affiliated with the Sons of Veterans.

Photo of Matthew Schmidt from the author's collection.

3. Christina Schmidt[2] (John Philip Schmidt[1]) was born in 1847 in Württemberg, Germany York.[39]She died *before* 1891. She married Jacob Roser *about* 1866, the son of Andrew and Catherine Elizabeth Roser. He was born in 1839 in New York State.[40] Christina was living next door to her parents in the 1870 Town of Lewis Census, Lewis County, New York.   The 1880 Town of Lewis Census, Lewis County, New York indicated she was born in Württemberg and her parents were born in Baden.   She lived two houses away from her sister, Cornelia, in the 1880 Town of Lewis Census. She was not mentioned in the obituaries of her brother, John, in 1891 or in her sister, Cornelia's in 1896.   Jacob was found living with his brother, Andrew in the 1892 Census. Jacob lived alone in the 1905 Town of Lewis Census, Lewis County, New York.

---

[34] World War I draft registration from Ancestery.com
[35] Obituary Utica Newspaper September 23, 1957
[36] St. Joseph's Church records, Utica, New York
[37] Obituary Utica Newspaper May 31, 1922
[38] St. Joseph's Church records, Utica, New York
[39] 1855 Town of Deerfield, Utica, New York Census
[40] 1880 Town of Lewis, New York Census

Christina Schmidt and Jacob Roser had the following children:

    i.   Jacob Roser Jr was born 21 July 1867 in Town of Lewis, Lewis County, New York. He was baptized 15 August 1867 at St. Michael's Church, Mohawk Hill, New York and his Godparents were Jacobus Baulig and Maria Salomia Schroeder.[41]
He was listed in the 1870 Census, Town of Lewis, as being 3 years old. He did not appear in the 1875 or 1880 Census. He may have died.

    ii.   Caroline Roser was born in 1869 in Lewis County, Town of Lewis, New York.[42] She was 11 years old when found in the 1880 Town of Lewis Census. I have searched and searched and have not been able to find out what happened to Caroline.

4. Joseph Smith[2] (John Philip Schmidt[1]) was born 11 February 1851 in Württemberg, Germany[43] and died 8 June 1927 in Detroit, Michigan.[44] He married Elizabeth Schrader *about* 1872. After her death, he married Louisa Yob *about* 1876 in Utica, New York, the daughter of Frederick G. Yob. She was born 17 September 1859 in Stittville, New York and died 12 July 1936 in Detroit, Michigan.[45]

Photo of Joseph Smith and his wife, Louisa Yob from the collection of Jean Langford and used with permission.

The following obituary for Joseph Smith was taken from the Utica Daily Press June 13, 1927:

Word has been received here of the death of Joseph Smith, formerly of Utica, at the home of his son, George, 15781 Joslyn Avenue, Detroit, Wednesday. Mr. Smith was born in Germany York, in 1851, and came to this country with his parents and settled in West Leyden, Lewis County, when a boy. Mr. Smith was well known in this city. He was one of the best known wood workers in this section, having been employed by the Sylvester Deering, C.C. Kellogg & Sons and Denton and Waterbury Company. He was a member of the Dering Guards. Besides his wife he leaves 11 children, John, Utica; Mrs. Edward Weber, Bellflower, Cal.; William J., Los Angeles; Mrs. John Venn, Utica; Frederick J., Oriskany, Frank J., Plymouth, Michigan; Mrs. Albert Smith, Detroit; Mrs. William Humphrey, Oriskany;

[41] FHC film of St. Michael's Church Records, Mohawk Hill, New York
[42] 1880 Town of Lewis, New York Census
[43] Family information from Jean Langford
[44] Obituary Utica Newspaper June 9, 1927
[45] Family information from Jean Langford

Mrs. William Beil, Utica; George and Mrs. Joseph McSweeney, Detroit. He leaves also 41 grandchildren and 14 great-grandchildren. Funeral services were held in Detroit Friday.

Joseph came to America when he was 16 months old. He lived at 5 Wiley St. Utica in 1878 and at 12 Wiley St. in 1894. The 1900 Utica Census said he lived at 6 Orchard Street Ward 9.

Joseph Smith and Elizabeth Schrader had the following children:

14.   i.   John Ignacious Schmidt was born 30 August 1873 in Utica, New York and died 6 October 1966 in Utica, New York.[46]

15.   ii.   Amelia Agnes Smith was born 26 October 1874 in New York State and died 09 December 1949 in Ventura, California.[47]

            iii.   William J. Smith was born 11 February 1876.[48] A very handsome man, he worked in a cigar factory and had a lot of money in a fairly poor family. He had one of the first cars and airplane. He married Flora Dower who eventually kicked him out and he moved to California.

Joseph Smith and Louisa Yob had the following children:

16.   i.   Wilhelmina Smith was born 15 July 1880 in Stittville, New York and died 9 November   1941 in 920 Kellogg St., Utica, New York.[49]

17.   ii.   Mary J. Smith was born 12 October 1879 in Stittville, New York and died 2 February 1912 in Utica, New York.[50]

18.   iii.   Frederick John Smith was born 12 July 1881 in Stittville, New York and died 5 January 1957 in Oriskany, New York.[51]

19.   iv.   Francis Jacob Smith was born 21 March 1884 in Utica, New York[52]and died 23 January 1959 in Garden City, Wayne, Michigan.[53]

20.   v.   Eva Smith was born 26 February 1886 in Utica, New York and died 30 December 1957 in Whitesboro, New York.[54]

21.   vi.   Louisa Smith was born 20 March 1888[55]and died 11 February in Hollywood, Florida.

22.   vii.   Margaret Smith was born 31 December 1888 in Utica, New York and died 4 December 1971 in New Hartford, New York.[56]

---

[46] Obituary Utica Newspaper October 7, 1966
[47] California Death Index at Ancestry.com
[48] Family information from Jean Langford
[49] Obituary Utica Newspaper November 10, 1941
[50] Obituary Utica Newspaper February 3, 1912
[51] Obituary Utica Newspaper January 6, 1957
[52] Family information from Jean Langford
[53] Family information from Karen Murdock
[54] Obituary Utica Newspaper December 31, 1957
[55] Family information from Jean Langford

viii.   Henry Smith was born 25 March 1893[57]and died in 1897 in New York State.[58]

23.   ix.   George Smith was born 26 February 1897 in Utica, New York and died May 1970 in Milan, Monroe, Michigan.[59]

24.   x.   Anna Smith was born 4 January 1900 in New York State.[60]

5. Cornelia Schmidt [2](John Philip Schmidt[1]) was born in July 1854 in Oneida County, New York[61]and she died 14 June 1896 in 37 Stark Street, Utica, New York.[62]She married John Shuemaker *about* 1872 shortly after the death of his first wife, Elizabeth. John was born 4 July 1840 in Michigan and died 28 May 1925 in Utica, New York.[63]

The following obituary for Cornelia Shuemaker was taken from the Utica Newspaper June 15, 1896:

> *Cornelia, wife of John Shuemaker, died at her late home, No. 37 Stark*
> *Street, at 1 a.m. yesterday, after a week's illness. The deceased was*
> *born in Lewis County 41 years ago and had lived in Utica for the past*
> *ten years. Twenty-four years ago she married John Shuemaker,*
> *who with the following children and step-children survives: Louis,*
> *George, Joseph and Edward Shuemaker, all of this city, and Misses*
> *Anna, Emma, Elizabeth and Susan Shuemaker, and Henry, Frank*
> *and Mary Shuemaker, also of Utica. One brother, Joseph Smith of*
> *this city also survives. The deceased attended St. Joseph's Church*
> *and her funeral will be held from there Thursday morning at 10 o'clock.*

 In the 1870 Town of Lewis Census, John Shuemaker and his wife Elizabeth lived two doors away from Cornelia and her family. Cornelia's sister, Christine Roser, lived next door. John was born in Michigan and came to New York State at the age of two. He lived with his parents in West Turin at the age of 8. He was a carpenter by occupation and helped erect many homes in Utica, New York. He retired from that trade several years before his death. He was a member of St. Joseph's Church, Utica, New York. He had eleven grandchildren at the time of his death as indicated in his obituary.

Cornelia Schmidt and John Shuemaker had the following children:

    i.   Louis Shuemaker was not alive in 1925 at the time of his father's death.
    ii.   Charles Shuemaker was born in 1870 and died 2 May 1892.

---

[56] Obituary Utica Newspaper December 5, 1971
[57] Family information from Jean Langford
[58] Family information from Karen Murdock
[59] Social Security Death Index from Ancestry.com
52 Family information from Karen Murdock
[61] 1855 Town of Deerfield, Utica, New York Census
[62] Obituary Utica Newspaper June 15, 1896
[63] Obituary Utica Newspaper May 29, 1925

iii.   Joseph Shuemaker was born 6 March 1873 in Town of Lewis, New York.[64]Joseph was baptized in St. Michael's Church, Mohawk Hill, New York and his Godparents were Valentinas Hoffman & Christina Roser. He lived in Utica in 1934.

iv.   George Ignatius Shuemaker was born 9 January 1875 in Town of Lewis, New York[65]and died 10 July 1950 in Syracuse, New York.[66]George was baptized in St. Michael's Church, Mohawk Hill, New York and his Godparents were Joannes Ignatius Schmitt and Catharine Heilig.[67]He married in 1900. George was a pattern maker, retiring in 1947. He lived in Syracuse, New York for 20 years and the last three years he lived in Clay, New York.

v.   Anna Christina Shuemaker was born 5 May 1876 in Town of Lewis, New York. Anna was baptized in St. Michael's Church, Mohawk Hill, New York and her Godparents were Franciscus Anton Mattles & Christina Schmitt.[68]

25.   vi.   Emma Shuemaker was born 5 March 1878 in Town of Lewis, New York[69] and died 14 January 1970 in 1606 Dudley Ave., Utica, New York.[70]

vii.   Lillie Shuemaker was born 4 March 1880 and died 7 August 1880.[71]

26.   viii.   Elisabeth Shuemaker was born 2 May 1880 in Town of Lewis, New York[72] and died 19 June 1976 in Hobokus, New Jersey.[73]

ix.   Susanna Shuemaker was born 22 February 1882 in Town of Lewis, New York[74]and died 6 March 1967 in Benn Nursing Home, Marcy, New York.[75]Susanna was baptized in St. Michael's Church, Mohawk Hill, New York and her Godparents were Jacob Seelman and Sara Kanover *nata* Groneiser.   She married Arthur Francis Foxenberger in 1904 in Utica, New York, the son of Frank X Foxenberger and Margaret Ribolin. He was born 4 August 1882 in Utica, New York and died in 6 November 1934 in Utica, New York.[76]Susan was born in Mohawk Hill and moved to Utica when she was a child. She was a member of St. Joseph and St. Patrick's Church, Utica, New York. She did not have children.

x.   Joseph Shuemaker was born 5 September 1883 in Utica, New York[77] and died 24 February 1953 at 1204 Schuyler Street, Utica, New York.[78]He was baptized in St. Michael's Church, Mohawk Hill, New York and his Godparents were George Kiefer & Cathrina Kiefer *nata* Seelmann. Joseph was a carpenter and paperhanger and operated

---

[64] FHC film of St. Michael's Church Records, Mohawk Hill, New York
[65] FHC film of St. Michael's Church Records, Mohawk Hill, New York
[66] Obituary Utica Newspaper July 11, 1950
[67] FHC film of St. Michael's Church Records, Mohawk Hill, New York
[68] FHC film of St. Michael's Church Records, Mohawk Hill, New York
[69] FHC film of St. Michael's Church Records, Mohawk Hill, New York
[70] Obituary Utica Newspaper January 15, 1970
[71] St. Joseph's Cemetery tombstone, Utica, New York
[72] FHC film of St. Michael's Church Records, Mohawk Hill, New York
[73] Obituary Utica Newspaper June 20, 1976
[74] FHC film of St. Michael's Church Records, Mohawk Hill, New York
[75] Obituary Utica Newspaper March 7, 1967
[76] Obituary Utica Newspaper November 7, 1934
[77] FHC film of St. Michael's Church Records, Mohawk Hill, New York
[78] Obituary Utica Newspaper February 25, 1953

his own business for many years. He did not marry. He was a member of St. Joseph's Church, Utica, New York.

      xi.   Linda Shuemaker was born 2 February 1886 and died 20 April 1887.[79]

      xii.   Edward Shuemaker was born 26 December 1888 in Utica, New York and died 1 January 1968 in St. Luke's Memorial Hospital, Utica, New York.[80]Edward was educated in the Utica public schools. He lived at 1204 Schuyler Street, Utica, New York at the time of his death. He had been employed on dairy farms in the Marcy area for many years before he retired in 1953. He was a member of St. Joseph's and St. Patrick Church, Utica, New York and was a United States Army veteran of World War I.

Generation Three

6. Mary Johanna Schmidt[3] (John Jacob Schmidt[2], John Philip Schmidt[1]) was born 8 November 1864 in West Leyden, New York. She died 5 January 1958 in Utica, New York. Mary was baptized in St. Michael's Church, Mohawk Hill, New York and her Godparents were Joannes Phill Schmidt and Magdalena Finster. She married George Sifer 7 June 1892 in St. Mary's Church, Prussian Settlement, West Leyden, New York[81] the son of Augustus Isaac Seifert and Catharina Gasser Preis. Witnesses to their wedding were Richard Uerz and Christina Link. He was born 11 April 1861 in West Leyden, New York. He died 23 January 1945 in Utica, New York.[82]For more information on George Sifer see Chapter Three, Descendants of Augustus Isaac Seifert.

For many years Mary J. Sifer was known to many Utica women as an exceptionally fine dressmaker. She was born in West Leyden, and lived on a farm there and attended West Leyden School until her family came to Utica to live. Here she attended St. Joseph's Parochial school. As a young woman she was employed as a children's nurse in the Park Avenue home of George L. Roberts, a nephew of Ellis H. Roberts, then U.S. Treasurer. She traveled considerably with the Roberts family, spending summers in the Catskills. Later on, she went to Kansas City, MO where she worked as a dressmaker for three years, returning to marry young George Sifer, who had a farm on Mohawk Hill, near West Leyden. They came to Utica around the turn of the century and lived on City Street, Sunset Avenue and also in Maynard, before taking up their residence on North Genesee Street.

---

[79] St. Joseph's Cemetery tombstone, Utica, New York
[80] Obituary Utica Newspaper January 2, 1968
[81] FHC film of St. Michael's Church Records, Mohawk Hill, New York
[82] Obituary Utica Newspaper January 24, 1945

Mary loved to trim the Christmas tree. She and her son-in-law, George Bowman, spent two weeks before Christmas trimming the tree and setting up a village under the tree. They would move all the furniture out of the living room to make room for this tree. They made village under the tree consisting of a train station, a church, a fire station, a school house, an airport, a ski slope and several little houses. George set up the train and Mary made clothes for the small people accordingly and made curtains for the windows. This tree took up their entire living room. Then a white fence would be set up around the

village. The public was invited to come in and look at this. Mary had a guest book for visitors to sign and the Utica Observer Dispatch newspaper came and took pictures of the tree and wrote an article about it. They would keep the tree up for two weeks after Christmas just for friends and neighbors to enjoy. Before Christmas, sheets were hung at the doorways to the living room so the children in the house could not see the tree until Christmas morning.

The children in the photo are Gertrude and Marvin Bowman. Photo in the author's collection

The following article was taken from Boonville Herald - June 9, 1892
> *Mohawk Hill - June 8 - On the 7th day of June, in St. Michael's Church, occurred the marriage of Miss Mary Smith of Utica to George Leifert[83] of Prussian Settlement. The bride looked very prettily attired in full bridal costume. Her dress was steel gray over which was draped a long white veil falling from a wreath on her head. The bridesmaid was dressed in*
> *the same colors. A bountiful wedding breakfast was served at John Sins.*

Mary Johanna Schmidt and George Sifer had the following children:
27.   i.   **Susanna Etta Sifer** was born 17 July 1893 in Ava, New York[84] and died 20 June 1966 in Utica, New York.[85]
        ii.   George John Sifer was born 18 April 1900 in Utica, New York and died 27 January 1958 in Utica, New York.[86]George was employed as an orderly at the Masonic Hospital, Utica, New York. He was a member of St. Joseph's Church, Utica, New York.

---

[83] In this newspaper article, Seifert was spelled Leifert
[84] Social Security Death Index from Ancestry.com
[85] Obituary Utica Newspaper June 21, 1966
[86] Obituary Utica Newspaper January 28, 1958

7.   Joseph Lee Schmidt[3] (John Jacob Schmidt[2], John Philip Schmidt[1]) was born 6 July 1867 in West Leyden, New York[87] and died 25 July 1945 in Rome Hospital, Rome, New York.[88] Joseph was baptized in St. Michael's Church, Mohawk Hill, New York and his Godparents were Joseph Schmidt and Maria Schroeder. He married Bertha Comstock and later married Clesta Lescarbeau 15 August 1904 in Utica, New York,[89] the daughter of Mr. and Mrs. Joseph Lescarbeau. She was born in 1856 in Salle, Canada and died 15 August 1939 in Rome, New York.[90] Joseph was a landscape grader by trade. His first grading job was at the House of Good Shephard in Utica, New York. He later engaged in farming in the Town of Rome. He was a member of the Presbyterian Church.

Photo Joseph Lee Schmidt and his wife in the author's collection.

Joseph Lee Schmidt and Bertha Comstock had the following children:

28.   i.   Rebecca (Reba) Schmidt was born 11 August 1893 and died 23 March 1979 in Rochester, New York.[91]

29.   ii.   Frederick U. Schmidt was born 26 November 1894 in Schuyler, New York and died 7 October 1977 in Rome Hospital, Rome, New York.[92]

 30.   iii.   Olivia Schmidt was born 31 July 1896 in North Gage, New York and died 25 December 1976 in Sunset Nursing Home, Boonville, New York.[93]

31.   iv.   Frances Schmidt was born 24 May 1898 and died August 1987 in Rensselaer, New York.[94]

           v.   Douglas L. Schmidt was born in August 1899. Douglas was listed with his parents in the 1910 Utica Census (Schuyler).

---

[87] FHC film of St. Michael's Church Records, Mohawk Hill, New York
[88] Obituary Utica Newspaper July 26, 1945
[89] Obituary Utica Newspaper August 15, 1939
[90] Obituary Utica Newspaper August 15, 1939
[91] Social Security Death Index from Ancestry.com
[92] Obituary Utica Newspaper October 8, 1977
[93] Obituary Utica Newspaper December 26, 1976
[94] Social Security Death Index from Ancestry.com

8. John Philippey Schmidt[3](John Jacob Schmidt[2], John Philip Schmidt[1]) was born 15 November 1872 in Utica, New York[95] and died 20 March 1948 in Soldiers and Sailors Memorial Hospital, Masonic Home, Utica.[96] John was baptized in St. Michael's Church, Mohawk Hill, New York and his Godparents were Joannes Phillippey Schmidt and Catharina Ritter.[97]He married Sophia Marie Dies Schmidt 12 December 1893 in St. Luke's Rectory, Utica, New York, the daughter of Nicholas Dies and Christina Roser Dies. Sophia was born 9 February 1872 in Fish Creek, New York and died 30 January 1957 in Soldiers and Sailors Memorial Hospital, Utica, New York.[98]John attended the local schools in Utica, New York and later worked as a barber. John was a life member of the Oriental Lodge 224, F&AM; past Thrice Potent Master of the Lodge of Perfection; a member of the Yahnundahsis Bodies of Scottish Rite Masons and a member of Ziyara Temple, Nobles of the Mystic Shrine. The family story says that John went to St. Joseph, Missouri to learn to be a barber. Sophie was from Mohawk Hill, New York. She was a member of Zion Lutheran Church and its Ladies Aid Society.

John Philippey Schmidt and his wife, Sophia Marie Dies. Photo in the author's collection.

John Philippey Schmidt and Sophia Marie Dies had the following children:

32.　i.　Florence Schmidt was born 19 July 1894 in Utica, New York and died 19 January 1980 in Riverhead, Long Island, New York[99]

33.　ii.　Lillian M. Schmidt was born 10 February 1896 in Utica, New York and died 20 September 1966 in Faxton Hospital, Utica, New York.[100]

34.　iii.　Alice May Schmidt was born 29 October 1899 in Utica, New York and died 26 May 1968 in Chicago, Illinois.[101]

35.　iv.　Edna Bertha Schmidt was born 11 May 1902 in Utica, New York and died 26 March 1974 in New Jersey.[102]

---

[95] St. Joseph's Church records, Utica, New York

[96]Obituary Utica Newspaper March 21, 1948

[97] FHC film of St. Michael's Church Records, Mohawk Hill, New York

[98] Obituary Utica Newspaper January 31, 1957

[99] Family information from Donald Moon

[100] Family information from Donald Moon

[101] Family information from Donald Moon

[102] Family information from Donald Moon

36.   v.   John Peter Schmidt was born December 1907 in Utica, New York[103] and died 29 December 1970 in Woodgate, New York.[104]

vi.   Arthur Lee Schmidt was born 14 October 1910 in Utica, New York[105]and died 10 February 1976 in Oneida, New York.[106]Arthur was educated in Utica, New York schools. He had been employed in the shipping department of Oneida Ltd., Sherrill, New York for 40 years retiring in 1973. He was a World War II veteran and a member of the American Legion, Sherrill; Oriental Lodge F&AM, Utica; Utica Commandery; Ziyara Temple; Utica Maennerchor and Zion Lutheran Church. Arthur was married briefly and had no children.

Photo of Arthur Lee Schmidt in the author's collection.

9. George E. Schmidt (Smith) Sr[3](John Jacob Schmidt[2], John Philip Schmidt[1]) was born 11 June 1874 in Utica, New York and died 18 December 1929 in Utica, New York.[107]He married Jessie Whalen 17 October 1894 in St. Joseph's Church, Utica, New York, the daughter of James Whalen and Fidelia Geer. She was born 14 August 1876 in Norwich, New York and died in 31 July 1960 in Gable's Nursing Home.[108] George E. Schmidt changed his name to Smith. He was hit by a car driven by Michael Hanna coming out of a bar on Lafayette Street, Utica, New York and died of a fractured skull.   He worked for 30 years at the International Heater Company, Utica, New York. He was a veteran of the United States Army.

Photo of George E Schmidt and his wife, Jessie Whalen, and their children, James Howard, George E .Jr and William J. Schmidt in the author's collection.

---

[103] Family information from Katherine Schmidt
[104] Obituary Utica Newspaper December 30, 1970
[105] Family information from Donald Moon
[106] Obituary Utica Newspaper February 11, 1976
[107] Death Notice in Utica Newspaper December 19, 1929
[108] Obituary Utica Newspaper August 1, 1960

George E. Schmidt (Smith) Sr. and Jessie Whalen had the following children:

37.   i.   James Howard Schmidt, B: 27 August 1898 in Utica, New York and died 28 April 1984 in St. Elizabeth Hospital, Utica, New York.[109]

38.   ii.   George E. Schmidt Jr was born 17 February 1900 in New York State and died 2 March 1964 in New Hartford, New York.[110]

39.   iii.   William J. Schmidt was born 18 June 1902 in Utica, New York[111] and died 29 September 1959 in Rome, New York.[112]

40.   iv.   Mary Irene Schmidt was born 28 October 1907 in Utica, New York and died 22 February 1975 in Syracuse, New York.[113]

10. Margaret (Maggie) Schmidt^3(John Jacob Schmidt^2, John Philip Schmidt^1) was born 1 March 1876 in Utica, New York and died 2 January 1942 at 1018 Court Street, Utica, New York.[114]She married John Francis Uerz 8 September 1896 in Utica, New York, the son of John Uerz and Elizabeth Deusch. He was born 22 May 1875 in Utica, New York and died 20 January 1933 in Utica, New York.[115]

Margaret Schmidt with her husband, John Uerz, and Their children John Jr, Margaret P. and Gertrude. Photo in the author's collection.

Margaret (Maggie) Schmidt and John Francis Uerz had the following children:

41.   i.   Margaret P. Uerz was born 9 January 1898 in Utica, New York and died 8 August 1969 in St. Elizabeth Hospital, Utica, New York.[116]

42.   ii.   John Francis Urtz Jr was born 22 November 1899 in Utica, New York[117] and died 19 August 1941 in Hammond, Indiana.[118]

iii.   Gertrude Uerz was born in 1901 in Utica, New York and died 18 February 1966 in St. Lukes-Memorial Hospital, Utica, New York.[119]Gertrude worked for 19 years as a housekeeper at Utica State Hospital. She was a member of St. Joseph's Church, Utica, New York and the New York State Civil Service Employees Association. She did

---

[109] Obituary Utica Newspaper April 29, 1984

[110] Family Information from Nancy Schmidt Salecki

[111] New York State Vital Records

[112] Obituary Utica Newspaper September 30, 1959

[113] Obituary Syracuse Newspaper February 23, 1975

[114] Obituary Utica Newspaper January 3, 1942

[115] Obituary Utica Newspaper January 21, 1933

[116] Obituary Utica Newspaper August 9, 1969

[117] World War I draft registration from Ancestery.com

[118] Obituary Utica Newspaper August 20, 1941

[119] Obituary Utica Newspaper February 19, 1966

not have children. She lived at 704 Saratoga Street, Utica, New York at the time of her death.

11. Anna M. Schmidt[3](John Jacob Schmidt[2], John Philip Schmidt[1]) was born 19 March 1878 in Utica, New York and died 17 January 1962 in Utica, New York.[120]She married

Fred H. Ulrich 24 February 1897 in Utica, New York, the son of Ludwig Ulrich and Katherine Brown. Fred was born 22 February 1877 in Wellsboro, New York and died 5 April 1970 in Utica, New York.[121]Anna had attended Utica, New York schools and was of the Lutheran faith.

Photo of Anna M. Schmidt and Mary Muthig
in the author's collection.

Anna M. Schmidt and Fred H. Ulrich had the following children:
43.   i.   Charles H. Ulrich, was born 25 October 1897 in Utica, New York and died 3 June 1969 in Utica, New York.[122]
44.   ii.   Loretta M. Ulrich was born 9 May 1899 in Utica, New York[123]and died 26 November 1960 in Auburn Memorial Hospital, Auburn, New York.[124]
45.   iii.   Catherine M. Ulrich was born 8 November 1900 in Utica, New York and died 13 June 1990 in Faxton-Sunset-St. Luke's Health Related Facility, Utica, New York.[125]
46.   iv.   Walter W. Ulrich was born 3 June 1904 in Utica, New York and died 11 December 1956 at 1118 Orchard Street, Utica, New York.[126]
47.   v.   Kenneth J. Ulrich was born 19 September 1912 in Utica, New York and died 24 January 1971 in St. Luke's Memorial Hospital, New Hartford, New York.[127]
48.   vi.   Raymond A. Ulrich was born 25 June 1915 in Utica, New York and died 10 November 1953 in St. Luke's Hospital, New Hartford, New York.[128]

---

[120] Obituary Utica Newspaper January 18, 1962
[121] Obituary Utica Newspaper April 6, 1970
[122] Obituary Utica Newspaper June 4, 1969
[123] New York State Vital Records
[124] Obituary Utica Newspaper November 27, 1960
[125] Obituary Utica Newspaper June 14, 1990
[126] Obituary Utica Newspaper December 12, 1956
[127] Social Security Death Index from Ancestry.com
[128] Obituary Utica Newspaper November 11, 1953

12. Philomena (Minnie) M. Schmidt[3] (John Jacob Schmidt[2], John Philip Schmidt[1]) was born 17 March 1880 in Utica, New York. She died on 23 September 1958 in Beverly, New Jersey.[129] She married Adam Wendelin Muthig 4 October 1899 in St. Patrick's Church, Utica New York, [130] the son of John Adam Muthig and Margaretha Beltz Muthig. He was born 27 February 1877 in Germany York and died 20 June 1963 in Beverly, New Jersey.[131] Philomena and Wendelin Muthig moved to Philadelphia, Pennsylvania and spent the rest of their lives there.

Photo of Philomena Schmidt and her husband, Adam Muthig circa 1900 from the collection of Debbie Leach and used with permission.

Philomena (Minnie) M. Schmidt and Adam Wendelin Muthig had the following children:

49.   i.   Maurice John Muthig Sr was born 15 March 1900, [132] and died in 1983 in New Jersey.

50.   ii.   Rosalie Muthig was born 5 September 1901 in Utica, New York[133] and died in 1934 as a result of a fire.[134]

13. Frank Xavier Schmidt[3] (John Jacob Schmidt[2], John Philip Schmidt[1]) was born 7 June

1883 in Utica, New York and died 23 September 1957 in New Hartford, New York.[135] He married Carrie Barnes 22 November 1903 in Utica, New York, the daughter of William Barnes and Carrie Phifster. She was born 14 July 1886 in Boonville, New York and died 22 November 1953 in 1008 Cleveland Ave., Utica, New York.[136] Frank attended St. Joseph's Church and school in Utica, New York. He had been employed as a welder by the International Heater County, for 45 years, until his retirement in 1952. Frank lived at 1008 Cleveland Avenue, Utica at the time of his death.

Photo of Frank X. Schmidt from the collection of Debbie Leach and used with permission.

---

[129] Ancestry.com US Veterans Cemeteries
[130] Wedding Announcement Utica Newspaper October 5, 1899
[131] Family information from Debbie Leach
[132] Family information from Debbie Leach
[133] Birth announcement Utica Newspaper September 13, 1901
[134] Family information from Rosalie Barili
[135] Obituary Utica Newspaper September 24, 1957
[136] Obituary Utica Newspaper November 23, 1953

Frank Xavier Schmidt and Carrie Barnes had the following children:

51.   i.   William G. Schmidt was born 4 December 1904 in Boonville, New York and died 1 August 1937 in Rome, New York.[137]

52.   ii.   Blanche L. Schmidt was born 19 November 1906 in Boonville, New York and died 25 November 2001 in Eden Park Nursing Home, Utica, New York.[138]

53.   iii.   Florence Schmidt was born 1 November 1908 in Boonville, New York and died 27 September 2002 in Martin Luther Nursing Home, Clinton, New York.[139]

54.   iv.   Ruth Schmidt was born 26 April 1910 in Utica, New York and died 23 September 1993 in Faxton Hospital, Utica, New York.[140]

55.   v.   Mildred Schmidt was born 23 September 1912 and died 5 September 2001 in St. Elizabeth Hospital, Utica, New York.[141]

56.   vi.   Ethel Schmidt was born 1 May 1914 in Utica, New York and died 30 September 2002 in Crossville, Tennessee.[142]

57.   vii.   Frank X. Schmidt Jr., B: 09 May 1915 in Utica, New York and died 5 May 1991 in St. Elizabeth Hospital, Utica, New York.[143]

58.   viii.   Carrie Schmidt was born 16 April 1917 in Utica, New York and died 1 July 1990 in Utica, New York.[144]

14. John I. Schmidt[3] (Joseph Smith[2], John Philip Schmidt[1]) was born 30 August 1873 in Utica, New York and died 6 October 1966 in Utica, New York.[145] He married Charlotte M. Ezzard 20 May 1896 in St. Joseph's Church, Utica, New York[146] the daughter of William Ezzard and Elizabeth Bolton. Charlotte was born in 1871 in England[147] and died 8 June 1961 in Utica, New York.[148] The 1925 Utica Census 16th Ward indicated he was living at 463 Coventry Avenue, Utica, New York and he worked in a knitting mill. John attended St. Joseph's School and Utica Public Schools in Utica, New York. He had been employed a number of years

Photo of John I. Schmidt from the collection of Jean Langford and used with permission.

[137] Death announcement Utica Newspaper August 2, 1937

[138] Obituary Utica Newspaper November 26, 2001

[139] Obituary Utica Newspaper September 28, 2002

[140] Obituary Utica Newspaper September 24, 1993

[141] Obituary Utica Newspaper September 6, 2001

[142] Obituary Utica Newspaper October 1, 2002

[143] Obituary Utica Newspaper May 6, 1991

[144] Obituary Utica Newspaper July 2, 1990

[145] Obituary Utica Newspaper October 7, 1966

[146] 50th Wedding anniversary announcement Utica newspaper May 21, 1946

[147] 1920 Utica, New York Census

[148] Obituary Utica Newspaper June 9, 1961

by Charles C. Kellogg Lumber Company, and retired from the Philip Thomas Lumber County in 1941. He was a member of St. Joseph's - St. Patrick's Church in Utica.

John I. Schmidt and Charlotte M. Ezzard had the following children:

59.   i.   Gertrude Schmidt was born 8 May 1897 in Utica, New York and died 13 February 1993 in Mohawk Valley Nursing Home, Ilion, New York.[149]

Photo of John I. Schmidt and his wife in the collection of Karen Schmidt and used with permission.

       ii.   Grace Schmidt was born 24 September 1899 in New York State and died 17 November 2000 in Troy, New York[150]She married a man by the name of Snyder.

60.   iii.   Herbert J. Schmidt was born in 1902 in Utica, New York and died 12 April 1982 in Faxton Hospital, Utica, New York.[151]

61.   iv.   Elizabeth P. Schmidt was born 20 August 1903 in Utica, New York and died 18 December 2001 in St. Joseph's Nursing Home, Utica, New York.[152]

Photo of the three sisters, Gertrude, Grace and Elizabeth Schmidt from the collection of Dorothy Wallace and used with permission.

       v.   John I. Schmidt Jr was born in July 22, 1910.[153] John married Dorothy Helen Loomis 31 January 1934. John was recently honorably discharged from the U.S. Army Panama Air Corps where he served three years and received a rating of toolmaker and first class machinist. They had three children who are still living.

Photo of John I. Schmidt Jr. from the collection of Dorothy Wallace and used with permission.

15. Amelia Agnes Smith[3](Joseph Smith[2], John Philip Schmidt[1]) was born 26 October 1874 in New York State and died 9 December 1949 in Ventura, California.[154]She married Edward Weber who was born 2 June 1869 in New York State and died 3 May 1954 in Ventura, California.[155]

---

[149] Obituary Utica Newspaper February 14, 1993
[150] Social Security Death Index from Ancestry.com
[151] Obituary Utica Newspaper April 13, 1982
[152] Obituary Utica Newspaper December 19, 2001
[153] Family information from Karen Schmidt
[154] California Death Index at Ancestry.com

Amelia Agnes Smith and Edward Weber had the following children:

　　　　i.　　　　William Weber was born 22 December 1892 in Texas and died 21 November 1953 in Monterey, California.[156]

　　　　ii.　　　　Edward Francis Weber was born 1 February 1898 in New York State and died 18 August 1955 in Ventura, California.[157]

16. Wilhelmina Smith[3](Joseph Smith[2], John Philip Schmidt[1]) was born 15 July 1880 in Stittville, New York and died 9 November 1941 at 920 Kellogg St., Utica, New York.[158] She married John Venn 24 May 1897, the son of John Venn and Alice Cameron. He was born 16 February 1873 in London, Lambeth, Surrey, England[159]and died 6 March 1942 at 920 Kellogg St., Utica, New York.[160] He was born in England at 8 Clarence Place,

Vauxhall St., London, Lambeth, and Surrey. John came to Utica as a young man. He came about 1890 with his maternal aunts, Mary and Rose Cameron. He traveled in steerage while they booked passage in a better class. They were supposed to help him get an education and a good job in the US; however, they reneged on their promise and John went to work in the mills. This caused an estrangement between John and his aunts. He retired after being employed for 30 years as a spinner by the Utica Knitting Company. He was a member of the Dryer Memorial Church. He had two brothers and a sister in England.

Photo of Wilhelmina Smith Venn from the collection of Dianne Britting-Hayden and used with permission.

Wilhelmina Smith and John Venn had the following children:

62.　i.　　　　Alfred Frederick Venn was born 11 March 1898 in Oneida County, New York[161]and died 4 April 1973 in Homestead, Florida.[162]

　　　　ii.　　　　Alice R. Venn was born 18 March 1900 in Utica, New York and died 28 July 1980 in Faxton Hospital, Utica, New York.[163]For many years Alice worked at the Utica Knitting Company and later was employed by the J.B. Wells Department Store in Utica, New York. Alice was married to Lester Davis. They had a baby that died.

---

[155] California Death Index at Ancestry.com
[156] California Death Index at Ancestry.com
[157] California Death Index at Ancestry.com
[158] Obituary Utica Newspaper November 10, 1941
[159] Family information from Diane Britting-Hayden
[160] Obituary Utica Newspaper March 7, 1942
[161] World War I draft registration from Ancestery.com
[162] Obituary Utica Newspaper April 4, 1973
[163] Obituary Utica Newspaper July 29, 1980

17. Mary J. Smith[3](Joseph Smith[2], John Philip Schmidt[1]) was born 12 October 1879 in Stittville, New York and died 2 February 1912 in Utica, New York.[164]She married John H. Schreppel in January 1900 in Utica, New York, the son of Mr. and Mrs. John Schreppel. He was born 16 March 1879 in Utica, New York and died 24 February 1956 in Utica, New York.[165]

Mary J. Smith and John H. Schreppel had the following children:
63.   i.   Olive Mae Schreppel was born 14 September 1900 in Utica, New York and died 19 March 1990 in St. Elizabeth Hospital, Utica, New York.[166]
64.   ii.   William J. Schreppel was born 2 July 1902 in Utica, New York and died 9 February 1977 at 9 West St., Whitesboro, New York.[167]
65.   iii.   Mary Schreppel was born 24 May 1904 in Utica, New York[168]and died 19 December 1971 in St. Elizabeth Hospital, Utica, New York.[169]
66.   iv.   John H. Schreppel was born 21 August 1906[170]and died 8 January 1992 in Ormond Beach, Florida.[171]
         v.   Howard G. Schreppel was born 15 August 1908 in Utica, New York and died 30 September 1984 in Faxton Hospital, Utica, New York.[172]Howard was raised in Utica, New York and attended Utica schools. He was the owner and operator of the Schreppel 's Meat Market on Oneida Street from 1946 until he retired in 1980. He was a member of the Utica Lodge No. 33 B.P.O.E. Elks.

18. Frederick John Smith[3](Joseph Smith[2], John Philip Schmidt[1]) was born 12 July 1881 in Stittville, New York and died 5 January 1957 in Oriskany, New York.[173]He married Emily Bromwell 12 June 1907 in Utica, New York. She was born 12 July 1880 in Wales[174]and died 28 March 1941 in Oriskany, New York.[175]Fred lived in Oriskany in 1927 and in Rome 1941. He was a cabinet maker and had been employed by Denton & Waterbury in Whitesboro, New York and Kellogg Lumber Company in Utica, New York. He lived in Frankfort for a number of years. For the last six years he lived in Westdale, New York. He had 14 grandchildren and six great grandchildren at the time of his death as indicated by his obituary.

---

[164] Obituary Utica Newspaper February 3, 1912
[165] Obituary Utica Newspaper February 25, 1956
[166] Obituary Utica Newspaper March 20, 1990
[167] Obituary Utica Newspaper February 10, 1977
[168] Family information from Charles Paul
[169] Obituary Utica Newspaper December 20, 1971
[170] Social Security Death Index from Ancestry.com
[171] Obituary Utica Newspaper January 9, 1992
[172] Obituary Utica Newspaper October 1, 1984
[173] Obituary Utica Newspaper January 6, 1957
[174] Family information from Jean Langford
[175] Obituary Utica Newspaper March 29, 1941

Frederick John Smith and Emily Bromwell had the following children:

    i.   Boy Smith was born 10 August 1910and died as an infant. [176]

67.   ii.   Janet Louise Smith was born 20 October 1911 in East Schuyler, New York and died 30 May 2000 in Rome Memorial Hospital, Rome, New York.[177]

68.   iii.   Joseph Arthur Smith was born 24 March 1913 and died 23 November 1983 in Jamul, California.[178]

69.   iv.   Elsie Joyce Smith was born 13 January 1917 in Oriskany, New York and died 1 June 1974 in Rome Hospital, Rome, New York.[179]

19. Francis Jacob Smith[3](Joseph Smith[2], John Philip Schmidt[1]) was born 21 March 1884 in Utica, New York[180]and died 23 January 1959 in Garden City, Wayne, Michigan.[181]He married Fannie Alma Kilts 24 February 1909 in Forestport, New York,[182] the daughter of John Kilts and Alma Amana Russell. She was born 25 January 1888 in Stillwater, New York and died 15 March 1960 in Ann Arbor, Oakland, Michigan.[183]

Francis Jacob Smith and Fannie Alma Kilts had the following children:

    i.   Lynn Joseph Smith was born 10 March 1910 in Buffalo, New York and died 29 June 1960 in Michigan.[184]

70.   ii.   Glennwood John Smith was born 10 March 1910 in Buffalo, New York and died 30 November 2003 in Levering, Emmet Michigan.[185]

    iii.   Beatrice Jenny Smith was born 20 November 1912 in Canada and died 25 May 1991 in Roseville, Placer County, California.[186]She was married 28 June 1935 in Redford, Wayne, Michigan.

    iv.   Lester Yop Smith was born 17 April 1915 in Forestport, New York and died 28 August 1922 in Highland Park, Wayne, Michigan.[187]

    v.   Marjorie Eileen Smith was born4 February 1925 in Highland Park, Wayne County, Michigan and died 14 May 1989 in Killeen, Texas.[188]She married a man by the name of Cook.

    vi.   Betty Ruth Smith was born July 1927 in Plymouth, Wayne County, Michigan.[189]She was married 28 June 1946 in Plymouth, Wayne, Michigan to a man by the name of Yelle.[190]

---

[176] Family information from Jean Langford
[177] Obituary Rome, New York Newspaper May 31, 2000
[178] Family information from Jean Langford
[179] Obituary Utica Newspaper June 2, 1974
[180] Family information from Jean Langford
[181] Family information from Karen Murdock
[182] Family information from Karen Murdock
[183] Family information from Karen Murdock
[184] Family information from Karen Murdock
[185] Social Security Death Index from Ancestry.com
[186] Family information from Karen Murdock
[187] Family information from Karen Murdock
[188] Family information from Karen Murdock

20. Eva Smith[3](Joseph Smith[2], John Philip Schmidt[1]) was born 26 February 1886 in Utica, New York and died 30 December 1957 in Whitesboro, New York.[191]She married William Arthur Humphrey 12 January 1910 in Utica, New York. He was born 3 December 1887 in Whitesboro, New York and died 10 September 1969 in Oriskany, New York.[192]Eva attended Utica, New York schools.   She lived in Utica for ten years after her marriage and then moved to Oriskany.   She was a member of Waterbury Memorial Presbyterian Church in Oriskany, New York. William Humphrey retired from Federal Aeronautics Authority.   He was also a cabinet maker and a member of Waterbury Memorial Presbyterian Church.

Photo of Eva Smith Humphrey from the collection of Jean Langford and used with permission.

Eva Smith and William Arthur Humphrey had the following children:

71.   i.   Helen Rachel Humphrey was born 7 January 1911 in Whitesboro, New York[193]and died 1 April 2004 in Eastern Star Home, Oriskany, New York.[194]

72.   ii.   Hazel Eva Humphrey was born 6 August 1912.[195]

73.   iii.   Henry William Humphrey was born 27 March 1914 in Whitesboro, New York[196]and died 5 December 1993 in St. Luke's Memorial Hospital, Utica, New York.[197]

74.   iv.   Mary Jessie Humphrey was born 17 May 1918 in Yorkville, New York and died 9 September 1997 in Hamilton, New York.[198]

21. Louisa Smith[3] (Joseph Smith[2], John Philip Schmidt[1]1) was born 20 March 1888[199]and died 11 February in Hollywood, Florida. She married Albert Smith *about* 1908. Louisa was cremated and her ashes were scattered in Michigan.

---

[189] Family information from Karen Murdock
[190] Family information from Karen Murdock
[191] Obituary Utica Newspaper December 31, 1957
[192] Obituary Utica Newspaper September 11, 1969
[193] Family information from Jean Langford
[194] Obituary Utica Newspaper April 2, 2004
[195] Family information from Jean Langford
[196] Family information from Jean Langford
[197] Obituary Utica Newspaper December 6, 1993
[198] Family information from Jean Langford
[199] Family information from Jean Langford

Louisa Smith and Albert Smith had the following children:

    i.   Albert Smith Jr was married in Detroit, Michigan.

    ii.   Dr. Howard Smith was married in Detroit, Michigan. Howard was a dentist.

22. Margaret Smith[3](Joseph Smith[2], John Philip Schmidt[1]) was born 31 December 1888 in Utica, New York and died 4 December 1971 in New Hartford, New York.[200]She married William Joseph Beil 9 June 1909 in St. Joseph's Church, Utica, New York, the son of John Beil and Margaret Goppert. He was born in 1886 and died 26 March 1967 in New Hartford, New York.[201]Margaret worked for Joseph & Feiss in Utica, New York and was a member of St. John the Evangelist Church in New Hartford, New York.

Margaret Smith and her husband, William Beil wedding anniversary circa 1959.   Photo in Judy Agedal's collection and used with permission.

Margaret Smith and William Joseph Beil had the following children:

    i.   Regina Mary Beil was born 16 April 1910 in Utica, New York and died 10 September 1988 in California.[202]Regina never had children. She worked for Joseph & Feiss in Utica, New York.

76.   ii.   Raymond Smith Beil was born 7 February 1913 in Utica, New York and died 22 February 1988 in Presbyterian Home, New Hartford, New York.[203]

77.   iii.   Alma Louise Beil was born 3 August 1914 in Utica, New York and died 20 June 1976 in New Hartford, New York.[204]

    iv.   Ruth Amelia Beil was born 12 July 1918 in Utica, New York.[205]She was married 20 May 1972 in Las Vegas, Nevada to a man named Robert Thirion. Ruth served as an Army nurse in World War II and later worked as a nurse in the Panama Canal Zone. She never had children. She lived in Seal Beach, California in 1988.

23. George Smith[3](Joseph Smith[2], John Philip Schmidt[1]) was born 26 February 1897 in Utica, New York and died May 1970 in Milan, Monroe, Michigan.[206]He married Loretta M. Quinn *about* 1917 in Utica, New York, the daughter of Robert Quinn and Loretta

---

[200] Obituary Utica Newspaper December 5, 1971

[201] Family information from Jean Langford

[202] Family information from Jean Langford

[203] Social Security Death Index from Ancestry.com

[204] Family information from Jean Langford

[205] Family information from Judy Agedal

[206] Social Security Death Index from Ancestry.com

Christian. She was born in May 1900 in New York State.[207]George Smith and Loretta M. Quinn had five children who may still be living.

24. Anna Smith[3] (Joseph Smith[2], John Philip Schmidt[1]) was born 4 January 1900 in New York State.[208]She married John Francis McSweeney in 1924 in Detroit, Michigan.[209]He was born 25 December 1895 in Ohio and died on October 1968 in Detroit, Michigan.[210]

Anna Smith and John Francis McSweeney had the following children:
    i.   Lois Jean McSweeney was born 12 August 1925 in Michigan and died 12 June 2002 in Zephyrhills, Florida.[211]She married Jack Daly in Detroit, Michigan.
78.   ii.   Eugene F. McSweeney was born 7 October 1926 in Detroit, Michigan and died 10 July 1998 in Webster, Florida.[212]

25. Emma Shuemaker[3] (Cornelia Schmidt[2], John Philip Schmidt[1]) was born 5 March 1878 in Town of Lewis, New York[213]and died 14 January 1970 at 1606 Dudley Avenue, Utica, New York.[214]Emma was baptized in St. Michael's Church, Mohawk Hill, New York and her Godparents were Joseph and Emma Sellman. She married Jacob Heneka in 1900 in Utica, New York. He was born in 1869[215]and died in 1920.[216]She later married Edward Gallagher in 1923 in Utica, New York. He died in 1923.[217]Emma was a member of Blessed Sacrament Church. The 1910 Utica, New York Census indicated she had give birth to five children and three were living.

Emma Shuemaker and Jacob Heneka had the following children:
    i.   Helen Heneka was born 26 December 1916.[218]She married G. William Cooley.
    ii.   Marion Heneka was born 12 October 1902 in Utica, New York and died 29 April 1975 in Faxton Hospital, Utica, New York.[219]She married Harold C. Weeks in 1929 in Utica, New York. Marion attended Utica, New York schools and was a member of the Church of the Blessed Sacrament, Utica, New York. She did not have children.

---

[207] Family information from Diane Britting-Hayden
[208] Family information from Jean Langford
[209] 1930 Detroit, Michigan Census
[210] Social Security Death Index from Ancestry.com
[211] Social Security Death Index from Ancestry.com
[212] Obituary Daily Chronicle, Detroit, Michigan July 11, 1998
[213] FHC film of St. Michael's Church Records, Mohawk Hill, New York
[214] Obituary Utica Newspaper January 15, 1970
[215] 1910 Utica, New York Census
[216] Obituary Utica Newspaper January 15, 1970
[217] Obituary Utica Newspaper January 15, 1970
[218] Birthdatabase.com
[219] Obituary Utica Newspaper April 30, 1975

79.   iii.   Mildred Heneka was born in 1907 in New York State[220] and died 28 July 1977 in St. Elizabeth Hospital, Utica, New York.[221] Mildred married Otto Weber in 1926 and later married Roy MacArthur in 1950 in Utica, New York.

   iv.   Frederick Jacob Heneka was born 3 January 1909 and died 15 January 1993 in San Diego, California.[222]

Emma Shuemaker and Edward Gallagher had the following child:

   i.   Wallace B. Gallagher was born 21 March 1922 in New York State and died 11 July 2000 in Imperial Beach, California.[223]

26. Elisabeth Shuemaker[3] (Cornelia Schmidt[2], John Philip Schmidt[1]) was born 2 May 1880 in Town of Lewis, New York[224] and died 19 June 1976 in Hohokus, New Jersey.[225] Elisabeth was baptized in St. Michael's Church, Mohawk Hill, New York and her Godparents were Ansonius Dish and Elisabeth Greins.[226] She married Henry J. Ritzel who was born in November 1875 in New York State[227] and died in 1939.[228] Elizabeth was educated in Utica, New York schools. She moved to Hohokus, New Jersey in 1940 and was a member of St. Luke's Church and the Senior Citizens of Ridgewood and Glen Rock.

Elisabeth Shuemaker and Henry J. Ritzel had the following child:

   i.   Richard S. Ritzel was born 10 June 1911 and died in September 1977 in Hohokus, New Jersey.[229]

Generation Four

27. Susanna Etta Sifer[4] (Mary Johanna Schmidt[3], John Jacob Schmidt[2], John Philip Schmidt[1]) was born 17 July 1893 in Ava, New York[230] and died 20 June 1966 in Utica, New York.[231] Susanna was baptized in St. Michael's Church, Mohawk Hill, New York and her Godparents were Michael Isenecker and Susanna Brady.[232] She married George

---

[220] 1910 Utica, New York Census

[221] Obituary Utica Newspaper July 29, 1977

[222] California Death Index at Ancestry.com

[223] Social Security Death Index from Ancestry.com

[224] FHC film of St. Michael's Church Records, Mohawk Hill, New York

[225] Obituary Utica Newspaper June 20, 1976

[226] FHC film of St. Michael's Church Records, Mohawk Hill, New York

[227] 1900 Utica, New York Census

[228] Obituary Utica Newspaper June 20, 1976

[229] Social Security Death Index from Ancestry.com

[230] Social Security Death Index from Ancestry.com

[231] Obituary Utica Newspaper June 21, 1966

[232] FHC film of St. Michael's Church Records, Mohawk Hill, New York

Francis Bowman 8 September 1916 in St. Joseph's Church, the son of George Bowman and Rose Hahn. George was born 18 December 1891 in Jersey City, New Jersey[233]and died 8 January 1957 in Utica, New York.[234]A baptismal record was found in St. Patrick's Church Records, Jersey City, New Jersey saying the sponsor for George was Annie Clark and the priest was Rev. J.A. Sheehan. For more information on George Bowman, see Chapter Four.

Photo of Susanna Sifer and her husband, George Bowman circa 1945 in the author's collection.

Children of Susanna Etta Sifer Bowman and George Francis Bowman are:

80. i. George Marvin Bowman was 30 June 1917 in Utica, New York and died 19 March 1987 in Utica, New York.[235] He married Katherine McLaughlin 17 February 1940 in St. John's Church, New Hartford, New York.

81. ii. **Living Bowman (Gertrude Marie Bowman**)

28. Rebecca (Reba) Schmidt[4] (Joseph Lee Schmidt[3], John Jacob Schmidt[2], John Philip Schmidt[1]) was born 11 August 1893 and died 23 March 1979 in Rochester, New York.[236] She married George Haggerty. Reba lived in Rochester in 1945 and in Yuma, Arizona in 1977. She was a member of the Melba Rebecca Lodge and the Germania Chapter of the Eastern Star.

Rebecca (Reba) Schmidt and George Haggerty had the following children:

    i.   Franklin James Haggerty was born 1909-1910 in New York State.[237]

    ii.   John W. Haggerty was born in 1912 in New York State.[238]

29. Frederick U. Schmidt[4](Joseph Lee Schmidt[3], John Jacob Schmidt[2], John Philip Schmidt[1]) was born 26 November 1894 in Schuyler, New York and died 7 October 1977 in Rome Hospital, Rome, New York.[239]He married Gertrude J. Batchelor 9 September 1920, [240]the daughter of William Batchelor and Frances Thomas. She was born 1 March

---

[233] FHC Film 1403369 of St. Patrick's Church Records, Jersey City, New Jersey

[234] Obituary Utica Newspaper January 9, 1957

[235] Obituary Utica Newspaper March 20, 1987

[236] Social Security Death Index from Ancestry.com

[237] 1930 Utica, New York Census

[238] 1930 Utica, New York Census

[239] Obituary Utica Newspaper October 8, 1977

[240] Wedding Announcement Utica Newspaper

1900 in Utica, New York and died 14 June 1967 in Oriskany, New York.[241] Frederick registered for the draft June 5, 1917 in Utica and was single at the time. He went to Oriskany, New York in 1936 and was employed by the Rome Air Depot during World War II. He was a member of St. Mark's Church, Clark Mills, New York. He had 26 grandchildren and 12 great grandchildren at the time of his death as indicated in his obituary.

Frederick U. Schmidt and Gertrude J. Batchelor had the following children:

82.   i.   Living Schmidt

83.   ii.   Edmond D. Schmidt was born 20 December 1922 in Utica, New York and died 7 May 2004 in Rome, Oneida, New York, United States of America.[242]He was married 26 July 1942 in Stuttgart, Arkansas.[243]

84.   iii.   Frances (Jane) Schmidt was born 18 February 1925 in Utica, New York and died 19 July 2001 in Rome, New York.[244]She was married 18 April 1944 in Utica, New York.

Wedding photo of Frederick U. Schmidt and his wife, Gertrude Batchelor in the author's collection.

85.   iv.   Helen Schmidt was born 18 December 1927 in Utica, New York and died 31 December 1990 in Crouse Irving Memorial Hospital, Syracuse, New York.[245]She was married 24 August 1954 in Westmoreland, New York.

86.   v.   Walter J. Schmidt Sr was born 16 June 1937 in Utica, New York and died 31 December 1989 in Vernon Center, New York.[246]He was married in January 1962 in St. Mark's Church, Clark Mills, New York.

vi.   Frederick U. Schmidt Jr. was in 1921 and died 27 June 1929 in Utica, New York.[247]

30. Olivia Schmidt[4] (Joseph Lee Schmidt[3], John Jacob Schmidt[2], John Philip Schmidt[1]) was born 31 July 1896 in North Gage, New York and died 25 December 1976 in Sunset

[241] Obituary Utica Newspaper June 15, 1967
[242] Social Security Death Index from Ancestry.com
[243] Obituary Utica Newspaper July 27, 1942
[244] Obituary Rome, New York Newspaper July 20, 2001
[245] Obituary Utica Newspaper January 1, 1991
[246] Obituary Utica Newspaper January 1, 1990
[247] Death notice Utica Newspaper June 30, 1929

Nursing Home, Boonville, New York.[248]She married Charles Smith who died in 1939.[249]Olivia attended North Gage, New York schools. During World War II she was employed at Griffiss Air Force Base. She was a member of the Tabernacle Baptist Church, Utica, New York.

Olivia Schmidt and Charles Smith had the following children:

    i.   Dorothy Smith was born 12 March 1919.[250]She married Andrew Seelman who was born 28 Sep 1902 and died April 1976 in Boonville, New York.[251]

    ii.   Kenneth L. Smith.

31. Frances Schmidt[4] (Joseph Lee Schmidt[3], John Jacob Schmidt[2], John Philip Schmidt1) was born 24 May 1898 and died August 1987 in Rensselaer, New York.[252]She married Thomas Lazot. He was born 3 July 1896 and died July 1971 in Troy, New York.[253]Frances Schmidt and Thomas Lazot had one child who may be still living.

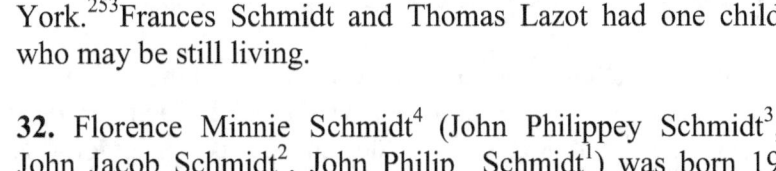

32. Florence Minnie Schmidt[4] (John Philippey Schmidt[3], John Jacob Schmidt[2], John Philip Schmidt[1]) was born 19 July 1894 in Utica, New York and died 19 January 1980 in Riverhead, Long Island, New York.[254]She married Louis Silva who was born 8 October 1888 in Puerto Rico and died 27 January 1972.[255]Florence Minnie Schmidt and Louis Silva had one child who may still be living.

Photo of Florence Schmidt taken in Philadelphia, September 11, 1919   Photo in the author's collection.

33. Lillian M. Schmidt[4] (John Philippey Schmidt[3], John Jacob Schmidt[2], John Philip Schmidt[1]) was born 10 February 1896 in Utica, New York and She died 20 September 1966 in Faxton Hospital, Utica, New York.[256]She married Floyd Dever Moon 23 June 1923 at Fay Street, Utica, New York. He was born 18 July 1894 in Norwich, New York and died 9 October 1975 in St. Luke's Hospital, New Hartford, New York.[257] Lillian attended Utica, New York schools. She was a former employee of the Utica Knitting

[248] Obituary Utica Newspaper December 26, 1976
[249] Obituary if wife Utica Newspaper December 26, 1976
[250] Birthdatabase.com
[251] Social Security Death Index from Ancestry.com
[252] Social Security Death Index from Ancestry.com
[253] Social Security Death Index from Ancestry.com
[254] Family information from Donald Moon
[255] Family information from Donald Moon
[256] Family information from Donald Moon
[257] Family information from Donald Moon

Mill and a member of Zion Evangelical Lutheran Church, New Hartford, New York. Floyd was a letter carrier for the Utica Post Office for more than 33 years retiring in 1959. On the day he was to retire he collapsed on the final block of his route. He was taken to St. Luke's Hospital where it was discovered he was suffering from exhaustion. He was a World War I Army veteran and a member of the National Association of Letter Carriers, Veterans of World War I of the U.S.A. and Zion Evangelical Lutheran Church in New Hartford, New York.

Wedding photo of Lillian Schmidt and Floyd Moon in the author's collection.

Lillian M. Schmidt and Floyd Dever Moon had the following children:

     i.   Floyd John Moon was born 26 October 1929 in Faxton Hospital, Utica, New York[258] and died 26 July 2001 in St. Luke's Memorial Hospital, New Hartford, New York.[259] Floyd (Jack) was a graduate of Utica Free Academy, Utica, New York. He was an Air Force Veteran, having served in the Korean Conflict. For a number of years until his retirement, he was employed by Chicago Pneumatic Tool Company, Utica, New York as a machinist. He was of the Lutheran faith and never married. Floyd was a member of the American Legion Post Charles H. Adrean Post #625 and the I.A.M. Forest Lodge.

     ii.   Donald George Moon was born 17 November 1937 in Faxton Hospital, Utica, New York[260] and died 30 June 2005 in Faxton-St. Lukes Healthcare Center, New Hartford, New York.[261] He was raised and educated in Utica graduating from Utica Free Academy, Utica, New York. He served four years with the United States Air Force from 1956 to 1960. He then went to work at Griffiss Air Force Base in Rome, New York. He was a Civil War buff and belonged to the Sons of the Union Veterans of the Civil War. Donald was an outdoorsman who enjoyed fishing and hunting. He was of the Lutheran faith and never married.

34. Alice May Schmidt[4] (John Philippey Schmidt[3], John Jacob Schmidt[2], John Philip Schmidt[1]) was born 29 October 1899 in Utica, New York and died 26 May 1968 in Chicago, Illinois.[262] She married Charles Hoelzle June 1918 in 912 Schuyler Street, Utica, New York.[263] He was born 15 May 1896 in Buffalo, New York.[264]

---

[258] Family information from Donald Moon
[259] Obituary Utica Newspaper July 27, 2001
[260] Family information from Donald Moon
[261] Obituary Utica Newspaper July 1, 2005
[262] Family information from Donald Moon
[263] Wedding Announcement Utica Newspaper
[264] World War I draft registration from Ancestery.com

Alice May Schmidt and Charles Hoelzle had the following children:

    i.   Twins Hoelzle died young.

    ii.   Living Hoelzle

Wedding photo of Alice Schmidt and Charles Hoelzle in the author's collection.

35. Edna Bertha Schmidt[4] (John Philippey Schmidt[3], John Jacob Schmidt[2], John Philip Schmidt[1]) was born 11 May 1902 in Utica, New York and died 26 March 1974 in New Jersey.[265] She married Francis Bailey 30 September 1923 in Constableville, New York. He was born on 1900 in New York State.[266] Edna Bertha Schmidt and Francis Bailey had one child who is still living.

Wedding photo of Edna Schmidt and Francis Bailey in the author's collection.

The following wedding announcement appeared in the Utica newspaper:

> ### Bailey - Schmidt
> *Miss Edna Schmidt, a daughter of Mr. and Mrs. J.P. Schmidt, 620 Schuyler Street, was married to Francis J. Bailey, a son of Mr. and Mrs. J. F. Bailey, 1006 Broad Street, at 3:30 Sunday afternoon at the home of the bride, the Rev. W.C. Nolte performing the ceremony. A sister and brother of the bride and bridegroom respectively Miss Jessie V. Bailey and John P. Schmidt, were the attending couple. The Bride wore a gown of blue satin and carried white roses. The bridesmaid wore a similar costume and her bouquet was of pink roses. After a western trip, the newly wedded couple will live in this city where they have a wide circle of well-wishing friends.*

---

[265] Family information from Donald Moon
[266] 1930 Utica, New York Census

6. John Peter Schmidt[4] (John Philippey Schmidt[3], John Jacob Schmidt[2], John Philip Schmidt[1]) was born 27 December 1907 in Utica, New York.[267]He died 29 December 1970 in Woodgate, New York.[268]He married Katherine Brucker 26 May 1932 at Coventry Avenue, Utica, New York, the daughter of Walter Brucker and Catherine Harris. She was born 1 February 1913 in Utica, New York and died 22 June 2002 in St. Elizabeth Medical Center, Utica, New York.[269]John had been a Meter Shop Foreman for the Utica Water Board for 44 years. He retired in 1969 and moved to Woodgate, New York. He attended the Zion Lutheran Church, New Hartford, New York and was a member of the Forestport Volunteer Fire Department, the White Otter Fish and Game Club and Oriental Lodge F&AM. He was past noble grand of the IOOF. Katherine worked as a switchboard operator at the former Boston Store in Utica. She had lived in

Woodgate since 1969. She was of Lutheran faith and was a member of the White Lake Cemetery Association and the White Otter Fish and Game Club. She greatly enjoyed cooking and embroidery and she loved flowers, plants and bird watching.

Photo of John P. Schmidt in the author's collection.

John Peter Schmidt and Katherine Brucker had the following children:

87. i. Living Schmidt
88. ii. Norman L. Schmidt was born 25 February 1937 in Utica, New York and died 28 June 1998 in Oriskany, New York.[270]He was married9 September 1961 in St. Mary's Church, Utica, New York.

89. iii. Living Schmidt

37. James Howard Schmidt[4] (George E. Schmidt (Smith) Sr[3], John Jacob Schmidt[2], John Philip Schmidt[1]) was born 27 August 1898 in Utica, New York and died 28 April 1984 in St. Elizabeth Hospital, Utica, New York.[271]He married Eleanor Clark 9 October 1918 in St. Anthony of Padua Church, Chadwicks, New York, the daughter of Michael Clark and Nora Kelleher. She was born 12 September 1900 in Carbondale, Pennsylvania and died 10 January 1989 in the Presbyterian Home, New Hartford, New York.[272]James lived at 33 Scott St., Utica, New York. He worked for the New York Central Railroad retiring in 1961. He and his wife were members of St. Frances deSales Church, Utica, New York.

---

[267] Family information from Katherine Schmidt
[268] Obituary Utica Newspaper December 30, 1970
[269] Obituary Utica Newspaper June 23, 2002
[270] Obituary Utica Newspaper June 29, 1998
[271] Obituary Utica Newspaper April 29, 1984
[272] Obituary Utica Newspaper January 11, 1989

James Howard Schmidt and Eleanor Clark had the following children:

90.   i.   James H. Schmidt Jr was born 4 October 1919 in Utica, New York and died 18 December 1996 in Utica, New York.[273] He was married 30 April 1949 in St. Patrick's Church, Utica, New York.

    ii.   Living Schmidt

    iii.   Living Schmidt

38. George E. Schmidt Jr[4] (George E. Schmidt (Smith) Sr[3], John Jacob Schmidt[2], John Philip Schmidt[1]) was born 17 February 1900 in New York State and died 2 March 1964 in New Hartford, New York. [274] He married Frieda Curtis 1928 in Alamo, Texas, daughter of Walter and Anna Curtis. She was born 7 August 1905 in Wichita, Kansas and died 3 March 1997 in Clinton, New York.[275] George E. Schmidt Jr. and Frieda Curtis had three children who may still be living.

Photo of George E. Schmidt and his wife, Frieda in 1942 in the author's collection.

39. William J. Schmidt[4] (George E. Schmidt (Smith) Sr[3], John Jacob Schmidt[2], John Philip Schmidt[1]) was born 18 June 1902 in Utica, New York[276] and died 29 September 1959 at New London Road, Rome, New York.[277] He married Elizabeth Alsheimer 10 February 1926,[278] the daughter of Andrew Alsheimer and Mary Blair. She was born 26 June 1906 in Utica, New York and died 20 February 1944 in Memorial Hospital, Utica, New York.[279] After the death of his first wife, Elizabeth, he married Hattie Fobare 4 August 1945.

William J. Schmidt and Elizabeth Alsheimer had the following children:

    i.   Living Schmidt

    ii.   Living Schmidt

    iii.   Living Schmidt

    iv.   Richard A. Schmidt, Sr was born 14 February 1931 in Utica, New York and died 12 May 2009 at Faxton-St. Lukes Healthcare. He was married 3 June 1950 at St. Patrick's Church, Utica, New York. He had been employed by Niagara Mohawk Power Company and retired after 33 years of service as Supervisor of Gas Operations.

---

[273] Obituary Utica Newspaper December 19, 1996
[274] Family Information from Nancy Schmidt Salecki
[275] Family Information from Nancy Schmidt Salecki
[276] New York State Vital Records
[277] Obituary Utica Newspaper September 30, 1959
[278] Obituary Utica Newspaper September 30, 1959
[279] Obituary Utica Newspaper February 21, 1944

He was an honorary member of the New York Mills Fire Department and past board member of the Eastern Snowmobile Racing Association.

      v.   Andrew H. Schmidt was born 17 October 1929 in Utica, New York and died 27 June 1944 in Memorial Hospital, Utica, New York.[280]Andrew died after an illness of one week.

William J. Schmidt and Hattie Fobare had one child who may still be living.

40. Mary Irene Schmidt[4] (George E. Schmidt (Smith) Sr[3], John Jacob Schmidt[2], John Philip Schmidt[1]) was born 28 October 1907 in Utica, New York and died 4 July 1989 in Syracuse, New York.[281]She married Floyd Allison Bristol in 1929. He was born 15 January 1899 and died 22 February 1975 in Syracuse, New York.[282]Mary lived in Syracuse, New York since 1961. She had been employed by Griffiss Air Force Base, Rome, New York as a parachute packer. She was a member of Immaculate Heart of Mary Church, Syracuse, New York.

Mary Irene Schmidt and Floyd Allison Bristol had the following children:

      i.   Robert A. Bristol

94.   ii.   Shirley Bristol was born 19 February 1932 in Utica, New York and died 29 July 1997 in Vero Beach, Florida.[283]She married Patsy Oriend who was born 6 February 1925 and died 8 November 2007 in Waterloo, New York.[284]Shirley Bristol and Patsy Oriend had three children who may still be living.

41. Margaret P. Uerz[4](Margaret (Maggie) Schmidt[3], John Jacob Schmidt[2], John Philip Schmidt[1]) was born 9 January 1898 in Utica, New York and died 8 August 1969 in St. Elizabeth Hospital, Utica, New York.[285]She married Joseph Anthony Schmitt in 1917 in Utica, New York. He was born 16 September 1888 in Utica, New York and died 7 December 1983 in St. Mary's Hospital, Rochester, New York.[286]Margaret was a member of St. Joseph's - St. Patrick's Church, Utica, New York and its Alter Rosary Society and the Third Order of St. Francis.

Margaret P. Uerz and Joseph Anthony Schmitt had the following children:

      i.   Living Schmitt

---

[280] Obituary Utica Newspaper June 28, 1944
[281] Obituary Syracuse, New York Newspaper July 5, 1989
[282] Obituary Syracuse, New York Newspaper February 23, 1975
[283] Obituary Vero Beach Press, Vero Beach, Florida August 13, 1977
[284] Obituary Syracuse, New York Newspaper November 9, 2007
[285] Obituary Utica Newspaper August 9, 1969
[286] Obituary Utica Newspaper December 8, 1983

95.   ii.   John E. Schmitt was born in November 1921 and died 15 June 1977 in Utica, New York.[287]He was married in 1946 in Rochester, New York and divorces in 1968.

96.   iii.   Living Schmitt

iv.   Helen Margaret Schmitt was born 5 April 1924 in Utica, New York and died 29 July 1933 in St. Luke's Hospital, Utica, New York.[288]Margaret died following an operation for appendicitis. She attended St. Josephs Church and School in Utica, New York.

42. John Francis Urtz Jr[4] (Margaret (Maggie) Schmidt[3], John Jacob Schmidt[2], John Philip Schmidt[1]) was born 22 November 1899 in Utica, New York[289]and died 19 August 1941 in Hammond, Indiana.[290]He married a Christine J. who was born 25 June 1912 in Indiana and died 5 May 2007 in Crown Point, Lake, Indiana.[291] John had lived in Hammond, Indiana for the last 15 years of his live and had been ill for two years. John Francis and Christine had seven children all of whom may still be living.

43. Charles H. Ulrich[4] (Anna M. Schmidt[3], John Jacob Schmidt[2], John Philip Schmidt[1]) was born on 25 October 1897 in Utica, New York and died 3 June 1969 in Utica, New York.[292]He married Beulah Griffith Stoddard in 1926 in Utica, New York, the daughter of William Griffith and Anna Charles. She was born 21 September 1894 in Remsen, New York and died 2 August 1972 in St. Elizabeth Hospital, Utica, New York.[293]He married Ethel Beeman in1916, the daughter of Myron and Katherine Beeman. She was born 4 May 1895 in New London, New York and died 9 December 1920 in Utica, New York.[294]Charles moved to Barneveld in 1940 and worked for Barneveld Motor Sales.

Charles H. Ulrich and Beulah Griffith Stoddard had the following children:

97.   i.   Fred C. Ulrich was born 27 February 1928 in Utica, New York and died 11 July 2003 in Rome Memorial Hospital, Rome, New York.[295]He was married in 1946.

ii.   Living Ulrich.

Charles H. Ulrich and Ethel Beeman had the following child:

98.   i.   Elmer C. Ulrich was born 22 August 1920 in Utica, New York and died 12 April 1984 in St. Luke's Hospital, New Hartford, New York.[296]He was married 20 July 1940 in Whitesboro, New York.

---

[287] Obituary Utica Newspaper June 16, 1977
[288] Obituary Utica Newspaper July 30, 1933
[289] World War I draft registration from Ancestery.com
[290] Obituary Utica Newspaper August 19, 1941
[291] Social Security Death Index from Ancestry.com
[292] Obituary Utica Newspaper June 4, 1969
[293] Obituary Utica Newspaper August 3, 1972
[294] Obituary Utica Newspaper December 10, 1920
[295] Obituary Utica Newspaper July 12, 2003

44. Loretta M. Ulrich[4](Anna M. Schmidt[3], John Jacob Schmidt[2], John Philip Schmidt[1]) was born 9 May 1899 in Utica, New York[297]and died 26 November 1960 in Auburn Memorial Hospital, Auburn, New York.[298]She married Henry C. Young 14 August 1910 in St. Matthew's Lutheran Church, Utica, New York.[299]He was born in 1891 in New York State[300]and died before 1960.[301]Loretta moved from Utica New York in 1933 to Aurora and then to Port Byron and finally to Auburn, New York where she resided for the last 15 years of her life. She was a member of the First Baptist Church, Auburn, New York. Loretta M. Ulrich and Henry C. Young had the following children:

    i.   Living Young
    ii.   Living Young.
    iii.   Living Young
    iv.   Living Young
    v.   Living Young
    vi.   Loretta M. Young was born 14 April 1922 and died 11 September 1989.[302]She was married 5 September 1942 in Church of the Redeemer, Utica, New York.[303]
    vii.   Living Young
    viii.   Living Young
    ix.   Living Young
    x.   Robert G. Young was born in 1929 in Utica, New York and died 25 November 1986 at Mullen Drive, Auburn, New York.[304]

45. Catherine M. Ulrich[4](Anna M. Schmidt[3], John Jacob Schmidt[2], John Philip Schmidt[1]) was born 8 November 1900 in Utica, New York and died 13 June 1990 in Faxton-Sunset-St. Luke's Health Related Facility, Utica, New York.[305]She married Albert Lincoln (Red) Losch 7 February 1921 in Buffalo, New York[306]the son of Albert Losch and Bertha Miller. He was born 2 February 1895 in Pekin, Illinois[307]and died 10 October 1946 in Utica, New York.[308]She married Dewey W. Losch in 1952 in California. He was born 25 October 1897 and died 10 July 1983 in Sun City, Arizona.[309]Catherine was educated in Utica, New York schools. She moved to California and later to Sun City,

[296] Social Security Death Index from Ancestry.com April 13, 1984
[297] New York State Vital Records
[298] Obituary Utica Newspaper November 27, 1960
[299] Wedding Announcement Utica Newspaper
[300] 1930 Utica, New York Census
[301] Obituary of wife Utica Newspaper November 27, 1960
[302] Social Security Death Index from Ancestry.com
[303] Wedding Announcement Utica Newspaper
[304] Obituary Utica Newspaper November 26, 1986
[305] Obituary Utica Newspaper June 14, 1990
[306] Obituary Utica Newspaper February 8, 1921
[307] World War I draft registration from Ancestery.com
[308] Obituary Utica Newspaper October 11, 1946
[309] Obituary of wife, Catherine Losch, Utica Newspaper June 14, 1990

Arizona and in 1984 she returned to Utica. She was a member of Our Savior Lutheran Church, Temple Chapter #300 O.E.S., a past matron on the Imperial Court of Amaranth, and a member of the White Shrine.

Catherine M. Ulrich and Albert Lincoln (Red) Losch had the following child:

i.   Alvin D. Losch was born 29 September 1931 in Aberdeen, South Dakota and died 7 May 1950 in Utica, New York.[310] Alvin lived with his parents at 1118 Orchard St., Utica, New York at the time of his death. He was killed in an automobile accident. He enlisted in the Navy in 16 December 1948 and saw service in European waters. He had been employed at the Dairymen's League plant in North Utica and was a member of the Naval Reserve.

46. Walter W. Ulrich[4] (Anna M. Schmidt[3], John Jacob Schmidt[2], John Philip Schmidt[1]) was born 3 June 1904 in Utica, New York and died 11 December 1956 at 1118 Orchard Street, Utica, New York.[311] He married Elsie Manning in 1928. She was born in 1907 in New York State. She died in 1935. After the death of Elsie, Walter married Mary Ruth Bauer in 1946.[312] Walter was educated in Utica schools. He worked as a Western Union messenger. He then became a machinist with International Heater Co for 28 years and the as employed at the Utica Radiator Corporation. Walter W. Ulrich and Elsie Manning had one child who may still be living.

47. Kenneth J. Ulrich[4] (Anna M. Schmidt[3], John Jacob Schmidt[2], John Philip Schmidt[1]) was born 19 September 1912 in Utica, New York and died 24 January 1971 in St. Luke's Memorial Hospital, New Hartford, New York.[313] He married Josephine Szlachtowski 1 January 1934 in Rome, New York, the daughter of George Szlachtowski and Mary Mikoloska. She was born 12 April 1915 in Pennsylvania and died 26 October 1999 in Yorkville, New York.[314] Kenneth attended Utica schools and Utica Free Academy in Utica, New York. He had worked as the stockroom receiver for the International Heating and Air Condition Corporation in Utica, New York. He was a Lutheran and a member of the Quarter Century Club at International Heating. Kenneth J. Ulrich and Josephine Szlachtowski Ulrich had two children who may still be living.

48. Raymond A. Ulrich[4] (Anna M. Schmidt[3], John Jacob Schmidt[2], John Philip Schmidt[1]) was born 25 June 1915 in Utica, New York and died 10 November 1953 in St. Luke's Hospital, New Hartford, New York.[315] He married Anna Lorenz 12 January 1937 in Utica, New York, [316] the daughter of William Lorenz and Anna O'Rouke. She was born 6 March 1916 in Yonkers, New York and died 1 October 1999 in Masonic Home, Utica, New

---

[310] Obituary Utica Newspaper May 8, 1950
[311] Obituary Utica Newspaper December 12, 1956
[312] Marriage License Record, Utica, New York
[313] Social Security Death Index from Ancestry.com
[314] Obituary Utica Newspaper October 27, 1999
[315] Obituary Utica Newspaper November 11, 1953
[316] Obituary Utica Newspaper November 11, 1953

York.[317]Raymond died of injuries suffered in a hunting accident. Raymond attended Kernan School and Utica Free Academy in Utica, New York. He worked until 1946 for Scientific Welding Company, a firm owned by his father-in-law, William Lorenz. In 1946, he and Leibing formed the General Welding Company. He was a member of St. Joseph's Church, Utica, New York, and the Oneida Lake Association. He was active in hunting and fishing. Raymond A. Ulrich and Anna Lorenz Ulrich had three children who may still be living.

49. Maurice John Muthig Sr.[4] (Philomena (Minnie) M. Schmidt[3], John Jacob Schmidt[2], John Philip Schmidt[1]) was born 15 March 1900[318]and died in 1983 in New Jersey.[319] He married Alta Anderson 31 December 1919 in Philadelphia, Pennsylvania. She was born 17 May 1901 in Wilmington, Delaware and died 29 September 1920 in Philadelphia, Pennsylvania. Alta died very soon after childbirth. He married Emma Regan after 1929.

Maurice John Muthig Sr. and Alta Anderson had the following child:
105.   i.   Maurice John Muthig Jr was born 29 September 1920 in Philadelphia, Pennsylvania and died 6 August 1986 in Baltimore, Maryland. He was married 14 February 1942 in Philadelphia, Pennsylvania.[320]Maurice John Muthig Sr. and Emma Regan had one child who may still be living.

Photo of Maurice and Rosalie Muthig as children in the collection of Debbie Leach and used with permission.

50. Rosalie Muthig Minguez[4] (Philomena (Minnie) M. Schmidt[3], John Jacob Schmidt[2], John Philip Schmidt[1]) was born 5 September 1901 in Utica, New York.[321]She married Julius Minguez in 1920 in Philadelphia, Pennsylvania[322]He was born 21 December 1898 and died 20 April 1992 in Sarasota, Florida.[323]

Rosalie Muthig and Julius Minguez had the following children:
106.   i.   Dorothy Minguez Ziegler was born July 14, 1922 and died November 17, 2004 in Douglasville, Georgia.[324]
107.   ii.   Living Minguez

---

[317] Obituary Utica Newspaper October 2, 1999
[318] World War I draft registration from Ancestery.com
[319] Family information from Debbie Leach
[320] Family information from Debbie Leach
[321] Obituary probably from Philadelphia with no date
[322] World War I draft registration from Ancestery.com
[323] Social Security Death Index from Ancestry.com
[324] Social Security Death Index from Ancestry.com

iii.   Norman Minguez was born 18 August 1920 and died 8 August 1982.[325]

51. William G. Schmidt[4] (Frank Xavier Schmidt[3], John Jacob Schmidt[2], John Philip Schmidt[1]) was born 4 December 1904 in Boonville, New York and died 1 August 1937 in Rome, New York.[326]He married Helen Kaut in 1929. She was born in 1910.
William was involved in an accident which took 3 lives. William G. Schmidt and Helen Kaut had two children who may still be living.

52. Blanche L. Schmidt[4] (Frank Xavier Schmidt[3], John Jacob Schmidt[2], John Philip Schmidt[1]) was born 19 November 1906 in Boonville, New York and died 25 November 2001 in Eden Park Nursing Home, Utica, New York.[327]She married John E. Green 25 November 1925 in St. Patrick's Church, Utica New York, the son of Edward Green and Elizabeth Niermyer. He was born 9 October 1905 in Utica, New York and died 25 December 1954 in Utica, New York.[328]Blanche attended Kernan School in Utica, New York. She had been employed at General Electric Company and was a member of St. Paul's Church, Whitesboro and the Whitestown Senior Citizens. She had 20 grandchildren, 40 great grandchildren and one great-great granddaughter as indicated by her obituary. Blanche L. Schmidt and John E. Green had five children who may still be living.

53. Florence Schmidt[4] (Frank Xavier Schmidt[3], John Jacob Schmidt[2], John Philip Schmidt[1]) was born 1 November 1908 in Boonville, New York and died 27 September 2002 in the Martin Luther Nursing Home, Clinton, New York.[329] She married William J. Keck in 1930. She married Raymond W. Breen in 1957, the son of Thomas Breen and Lillian Utz. He was born 19 June 1927 in New Jersey and died 1 June 1982 in Utica, New York.[330] Florence Schmidt and William J. Keck had three children who may still be living.

54. Ruth Schmidt[4] (Frank Xavier Schmidt[3], John Jacob Schmidt[2], John Philip Schmidt[1]) was born 26 April 1910 in Utica, New York and died 23 September 1993 in Faxton Hospital, Utica, New York.[331]She married James Hughes who was the father of her children. After his death she married Charles Joslyn 29 August 1953. He was born 9 February 1924 in McConnellsville, New York and died 16 August 1992 in Rome Hospital, Rome, New York.[332]Ruth Schmidt and James Hughes had four children who may still be living.

---

[325] Family information from Debbie Leach
[326] Obituary Boonville, New York Newspaper August 2, 1937
[327] Obituary Utica Newspaper November 26, 2001
[328] Obituary Utica Newspaper December 26, 1954
[329] Obituary Utica Newspaper September 28, 2002
[330] Obituary Utica Newspaper June 2, 1982
[331] Obituary Utica Newspaper September 24, 1993
[332] Obituary Utica Newspaper August 17, 1992

55. Mildred Schmidt[4] (Frank Xavier Schmidt[3], John Jacob Schmidt[2], John Philip Schmidt[1]) was born 23 September 1912 and died 5 September 2001 in St. Elizabeth Hospital, Utica, New York.[333]She married George K. Pfiefer 12 May 1934 in St. Joseph's Church, Utica, New York. He was born 20 June 1912 in Utica, New York and died 26 April 1989 in Faxton Hospital, Utica, New York.[334]Mildred Schmidt and George K. Pfiefer had one child who may still be living.

56. Ethel Schmidt[4] (Frank Xavier Schmidt[3], John Jacob Schmidt[2], John Philip Schmidt[1]) was born 1 May 1914 in Utica, New York and died 30 September 2002 in Crossville, Tennessee.[335]She married Robert A. Moore 29 October 1932 in Albany Street Baptist parsonage, Utica, New York.[336]He was born 8 July 1910 and died 14 September 1991.[337] Ethel Schmidt and Robert A. Moore had two children who may still be living.

57. Frank X. Schmidt Jr[4](Frank Xavier Schmidt[3], John Jacob Schmidt[2], John Philip Schmidt[1]) was born 9 May 1915 in Utica, New York and died 5 May 1991 in St. Elizabeth Hospital, Utica, New York.[338]He married Marie Catinella in 1935 in St. Joseph's Church, Utica, New York, the daughter of Charles and Martha Catinella. She was born 6 December 1915 in Utica, New York and died 11 March 1998 in E.J. Noble Hospital, Alexandria Bay, New York.[339]Frank was educated in Utica, New York schools. Before his retirement Frank was employed by Alleghany Airlines. He was a member of St. Agnes Church, the Cornhill Senior Center, and the R.S.V.P. Frank has received many awards for his volunteer efforts with the Senior Centers over the years. He was a Navy veteran of World War II. His obituary indicated he had six grandchildren and eleven great-grandchildren. Frank X. Schmidt Jr. and Marie Catinella had two children who may still be living.

58. Carrie Schmidt[4] (Frank Xavier Schmidt[3], John Jacob Schmidt[2], John Philip Schmidt[1]) was born 16 April 1917 in Utica, New York and died 1 July 1990 in Utica, New York.[340] She married Peter Joseph Mullins 14 January 1943 in Scranton, Pennsylvania. He was born 26 April 1887 in New Jersey and died 26 May 1970 in Whitesboro, New York.[341] Carrie lived in Utica and was of Catholic faith. Carrie Schmidt and Peter Joseph Mullins had two children. There were no children listed in her obituary.

---

[333] Obituary Utica Newspaper September 6, 2001
[334] Obituary Utica Newspaper April 27, 1989
[335] Obituary Utica Newspaper October 1, 2002
[336] Wedding Announcement Utica Newspaper
[337] Social Security Death Index from Ancestry.com
[338] Obituary Utica Newspaper May 6, 1991
[339] Obituary Utica Newspaper March 12, 1998
[340] Obituary Utica Newspaper July 2, 1990
[341] Obituary Utica Newspaper May 27, 1970

59. Gertrude Schmidt[4] (John I. Schmidt[3], Joseph Smith[2], John Philip Schmidt[1]) was born 8 May 1897 in Utica, New York and died 13 February 1993 in Mohawk Valley Nursing Home, Ilion, New York.[342] She married John Murray Barnum in 1916. He was born in 11 Oct 1894[343] and died in 1950.[344] Gertrude was a self employed home care nurse for several years and at one time, managed the first A & P store in Ilion, New York. She was also employed in the lunchroom of several local schools. She attended the Ilion United Methodist Church, Ilion, New York.

Photo of Gertrude Schmidt, her son Arthur Barnum, her father John I. Schmidt and grandfather, Joseph Smith. Photo in the collection of Karen Schmidt and used with permission.

Gertrude Schmidt and John M. Barnum had the following children:

     i.   Arthur Barnum was born 4 July 1917 and died 12 January 2002 in Brewster, Massachusetts.[345]

     ii.   Living Barnum

     iii.   Living Barnum

60. Herbert J. Schmidt[4] (John I. Schmidt[3], Joseph Smith[2], John Philip Schmidt[1]) was born in 902 in Utica, New York and died 12 April 1982 in Faxton Hospital, Utica, New York.[346] He married Carolyn E. Williams in 1930 in Utica, New York, the daughter of William and Ettie Williams. She was born in 1908 in Deerfield, New York and died 4 June 1983.[347] Herbert was a Captain with the Utica Fire Department. He was a member of Our Lady of Lourdes Church. Herbert J. Schmidt and Carolyn E. Williams Schmidt had three children who may still be living.

Wedding Photo of Herbert J. Schmidt and Carolyn E. Williams in the collection of Karen Schmidt and used with permission.

61. Elizabeth P. Schmidt[4] (John I. Schmidt[3], Joseph Smith[2], John Philip Schmidt[1]) was born 20 August 1903 in Utica, New York and died 18 December 2001 in St. Joseph's Nursing Home, Utica, New

---

[342] Obituary Utica Newspaper February 14, 1943
[343] World War I draft registration from Ancestery.com
[344] Obituary Utica Newspaper of wife February 14, 1943
[345] Social Security Death Index from Ancestry.com
[346] Obituary Utica Newspaper April 13, 1982
[347] Obituary Utica Newspaper June 5, 1983

York.[348]She married Joseph P. O'Hare 8 June 1926 in Historic Old St. John's Church, Utica, New York.[349]He was born 25 June 1901 and he died 21 March 1991.[350]

Elizabeth P. Schmidt and Joseph P. O'Hare had the following children:

109. iii.   Living O'Hare

ii.   Paul Francis O'Hare was born in 1928[351]and died 3 February 1955 in Tokyo, Japan. [352]Paul was a Lieutenant in the Air Force and was killed in a collision of two jets. He graduated from Blessed Sacrament School and Utica Free Academy in Utica, New York.

110. iii.   Living O'Hare Palmer

62. Alfred Frederick Venn[4] (Wilhelmina Smith[3], Joseph Smith[2], John Philip Schmidt[1]) was born on 11 March 1898 in Oneida County, New York[353]and died 4 April 1973 in Homestead, Florida.[354]He married Genevieve Quinn 19 June 1919 in New York State, [355]the daughter of Robert Quinn and Loretta Christian. She was born 10 September 1901 in New York State and died 16 June 1988 in Homestead, Florida.[356]

Genevieve was raised in the Catholic faith. When she married Alfred Venn, she became a Methodist because Alfred's family was Methodist. She attended church regularly and her daughter, Vera remembers that they used to sit near Mary Cameron (Alfred's great-aunt who had come from England with his father, John c. 1890.) After Alfred's death, Genevieve married a man named Munson. Alfred Frederick Venn and Genevieve Quinn had four children who may still be living.

63. Olive Mae Schreppel[4](Mary J. Smith[3], Joseph Smith[2], John Philip Schmidt[1]) was born 14 September 1900 in Utica, New York and died 19 March 1990 in St. Elizabeth Hospital, Utica, New York.[357]She married George John Elsenbeck in 1920 in Utica, New York. He was born in 26 June 1895[358]in Utica, New York and died 27 August 1985 in Genesee Nursing Home, Utica, New York.[359]Olive lived on Valley Road in Oriskany, New York at the time of her death. She had been employed by the Globe Mill in Utica, New York and was of the Protestant faith. George received his education in the Utica schools. He was in the Naval Air Corps during World War I and was a member of the

---

[348] Obituary Utica Newspaper December 19, 2001
[349] Wedding Announcement Utica Newspaper June 9, 1926
[350] Social Security Death Index from Ancestry.com
[351] 1930 Utica, New York Census
[352] 1930 South Dakota Census
[353] Social Security Death Index from Ancestry.com
[354] Obituary Utica Newspaper April 5, 1973
[355] Family information from Diane Britting-Hayden
[356] Social Security Death Index from Ancestry.com
[357] Obituary Utica Newspaper March 20, 1990
[358] World War I draft registration from Ancestery.com
[359] Obituary Utica Newspaper August 27, 1985

American Legion Post #1113 in Whitestown, New York. He had been employed by the Bossert Manufacturing Company.

Olive Mae Schreppel and George John Elsenbeck had the following children:
     i.   Living Elsenbeck
114. ii.   Eugene K. Elsenbeck was born 14 July 1927 in Oriskany, New York and died 31 December 1993 in Clinton, New York.[360]He was married in December 1947 in Utica, New York.

64. William J. Schreppel[4](Mary J. Smith[3], Joseph Smith[2], John Philip Schmidt[1]) was born 2 July 1902 in Utica, New York and died 9 February 1977 in 9 West St., Whitesboro, New York.[361]He married Dorothy Harmon 29 August 1926 in Utica, New York, the daughter of Clarence F. Harmon and Helen Clouse. She was born 26 March 1905 in Utica, New York and died 24 June 1947 in Utica, New York.[362]After her death, William married Flossie Mae Shea in 1958 in White Plains, New York. William was educated in Utica, New York schools. He had been employed by the Village of Whitesboro, New York and was a school crossing guard at the time of his death. William J. Schreppel and Dorothy Harmon had four children who may still be living.

65. Mary Schreppel[4](Mary J. Smith[3], Joseph Smith[2], John Philip Schmidt[1]) was born 24 May 1904 in Utica, New York[363]and died 19 December 1971 in St. Elizabeth Hospital, Utica, New York.[364]She married Charles H. Paul in 1924 in Utica, New York. He was born 24 January 1894 in Utica, New York and died 12 January 1963 in St. Elizabeth Hospital, Utica, New York.[365]Mary was educated in Utica, New York schools. She had been employed for many years by the Globe Woolen Mills in Utica, New York and retired in 1944. She was a member of Trinity Lutheran Church and was also a member of the Parkway Senior Citizens and the Cornat at Adrean Terrace and the American Legion Auxiliary in Whitestown, New York. Charles had been educated in Utica, New York schools and had been employed for 32 years by the Bossert Corporation.   He was a member of the company's Quarter Century Club, St. Agnes Church and the Parkway Senior Citizens Center. Mary Schreppel and Charles H. Paul had three children who may still bc living.

66. John H. Schreppel[4] (Mary J. Smith[3], Joseph Smith[2], John Philip Schmidt[1]) was born 21 August 1906 and died 8 January 1992 in Ormond Beach, Florida[366]He married Ellen Henderson 21 December 1929 in Utica, New York, the daughter of Robert Henderson

[360] Obituary Utica Newspaper January 1, 1994
[361]Obituary Utica Newspaper February 10, 177
[362] Obituary Utica Newspaper June 25, 1947
[363] Family information from Charles Paul
[364] Obituary Utica Newspaper December 20, 1971
[365] Family information from Charles Paul
[366] Social Security Death Index from Ancestry.com

and Martha Manning. She was born 13 December 1907 in Hull, England and died 7 August 1985 in St. Luke's Memorial Hospital, Utica, New York.[367]John was a retired salesman for the West End Brewing Company. John H. Schreppel and Ellen Henderson had two children who may still be living.

67. Janet Louise Smith[4](Frederick John Smith[3], Joseph Smith[2], John Philip Schmidt[1]) was born 20 October 1911 in East Schuyler, New York and died 30 May 2000 in Rome Memorial Hospital, Rome, New York.[368]She married Armand Richard Bustos 3 July 1929. He was born 1 April 1907 in Los Angeles, California and died 29 September 1959 in Rome, New York.[369] She married George Burke 19 August 1961 in Rome, New York. He was born 14 August 1901[370] in Utica, New York and died 20 July 1970.[371] Janet was educated in Oriskany, New York schools. She had been employed at the former Rome State School in Rome, New York. She was a communicant of St. Mary's Church in Rome and a former member of the Alter Rosary Society. She had been a volunteer at the Rome Family Y and Rome Memorial Hospital. Janet Louise Smith and Armand Richard Bustos had two children who may still be living.

68. Joseph Arthur Smith[4] (Frederick John Smith[3], Joseph Smith[2], John Philip Schmidt[1]) was born 24 March 1913 and died 23 November 1983 in Jamul, California.[372]He married Irene Campbell 5 November 1934 in Plymouth, Michigan. He married Beverly Braham 2 June 1969 in California. Joseph Arthur Smith and Irene Campbell had four children who may still be living.

69. Elsie Joyce Smith[4](Frederick John Smith[3], Joseph Smith[2], John Philip Schmidt[1]) was born 13 January 1917 in Oriskany, New York and died 1 June 1974 in Rome Hospital, Rome, New York.[373]She married Fred Clarence Smith 3 September 1939. Elsie Joyce Smith and Fred Clarence Smith had eight children who may still be living.

70. Glennwood John Smith[4] (Francis Jacob Smith[3], Joseph Smith[2], John Philip Schmidt[1]) was born 10 March 1910 in Buffalo, New York and died 30 November 2003 in Levering, Emmet, Michigan.[374]He married Thelma Marguerite Tegge 29 August 1936 in Plymouth, Wayne, Michigan, [375]the daughter of William Tegge and Laura Belle. She was born 21

---

[367] Obituary Utica Newspaper August 8, 1985
[368] Obituary Rome, New York Newspaper May 31, 2000
[369] Family information from Jean Langford
[370] Social Security Death Index from Ancestry.com
[371] Family information from Jean Langford
[372] Social Security Death Index from Ancestry.com
[373] Obituary Rome, New York Newspaper June 2, 1974
[374] Social Security Death Index from Ancestry.com
[375] Family information from Karen Murdock

August 1916 in Detroit, Michigan and died 11 April 2003 in Levering, Emmet Michigan.[376]

Glennwood John Smith and Thelma Marguerite Tegge had the following children:

     i.   Linda Jean Smith was born 3 August 1944 in Plymouth, Wayne, Michigan and 13 August 2005 at 8425 E. Levering Road., Levering, Michigan.[377]

     ii.   Keith Glennwood Smith was born 29 January 1947 in Detroit, Michigan and died 20 October 2001 in Michigan.[378]

     iii.   Living Smith

71. Helen Rachel Humphrey[4](Eva Smith[3], Joseph Smith[2], John Philip Schmidt[1]) was born 7 January 1911 in Whitesboro, New York and died 1 April 2004 in the Eastern Star Home, Oriskany, New York.[379]She married Rowland Perry Martin 26 June 1929 in Oriskany, New York, the son of Chester Martin and Lena Rowlands. He was born 9 January 1905 in Rome, New York and died 16 March 1978 in Utica, New York.[380]
Helen Rachel Humphrey and Rowland Perry Martin had the following children:

     i.   William Chester Martin was born 2 June 1930 in Holland Patent, New York[381]and died in 1941.[382]

119.   ii   Living Martin

72. Hazel Eva Humphrey[4] (Eva Smith[3], Joseph Smith[2], John Philip Schmidt[1]) was born 6 August 1912.[383]She married Howard Frank Wooding 20 August 1929 in Whitestown, New York, son of Delbert Wooding and Mabel Walker. He was born 17 July 1911 in Oriskany, New York and died 20 June 1977 in St. Luke's Memorial Hospital, New Hartford, New York.[384]Howard owned and operated his own farm. He was also employed by Robert Burrows Trucking Company of Whitesboro, New York. He was an active baseball player in the Twilite League in the 1930's. He was a member of the Waterbury Memorial Presbyterian Church, and the Oriskany Lodge F. & A.M. No. 799. Hazel Eva Humphrey and Howard Frank Wooding had three children who may still be living.

73. Henry William Humphrey[4](Eva Smith[3], Joseph Smith[2], John Philip Schmidt[1]) was born 27 March 1914 in Whitesboro, New York and died 5 December 1993 in St. Luke's

---

[376] Social Security Death Index from Ancestry.com
[377] Family information from Karen Murdock
[378] Family information from Karen Murdock
[379] Social Security Death Index from Ancestry.com
[380] Obituary Utica Newspaper March 17, 1978
[381] Family information from Jean Langford
[382] Obituary of father, Rowland Martin, Utica Newspaper March 17, 1978
[383] Family information from Jean Langford
[384] Obituary Utica Newspaper June 21, 1977

Memorial Hospital, Utica, New York.[385]He married Flora Hebard 28 September 1940 in Whitesboro, New York, the daughter of Charles Hebard and Helen C. Burr. She was born 28 September 1917 in Whitesboro, New York and died 28 March 1990 in Utica, New York.[386]Henry was raised and educated in Oriskany, New York. He retired as the Food Service Manager of Marcy Psychiatric Center, Marcy, New York. He was a member of the Waterbury Memorial Presbyterian Church, a member and past master of Oriskany Lodge #799 F & AM, and a member of the Oriskany and Oneida County Historical Societies. Henry William Humphrey and Flora Hebard had two children who may still be living.

74. Mary Jessie Humphrey[4] (Eva Smith[3], Joseph Smith[2], John Philip Schmidt[1]) was born 17 May 1918 in Yorkville, New York and died 9 September 1997 in Hamilton, New York.[387]She married Arnold Jacob Leuenberger 14 February 1941 in Oriskany, New York, the son of Ernst Leuenberger and Rosa Jacob. He was born 13 April 1918 in Sentinel Butte, Golden Valley County, North Dakota and died 5 June 1994 in Vernon Center, New York.[388]Mary Jessie Humphrey and Arnold Jacob Leuenberger had three children who may still be living.

75. Raymond Smith Beil[4](Margaret Smith[3], Joseph Smith[2], John Philip Schmidt[1]) was born 7 February 1913 in Utica, New York and died 22 February 1988 in Presbyterian Home, New Hartford, New York.[389]He married Sue Vleck 11 July 1935 in Utica, New York. She died 17 July 1974 in Waterville, New York. Raymond lived in Waterville, New York most of his life. He was a custodian at Waterville Elementary School, Waterville, New York, retiring with 25 years of service. Prior to that, he worked for Devine Brothers and Savage Arms in Utica, New York. He was a member of the Waterville-Deansboro Lions Club. Raymond Smith Beil and Sue Vleck Beil had one child who may still be living.

76. Alma Louise Beil[4] (Margaret Smith[3], Joseph Smith[2], John Philip Schmidt[1]) was born 3 August 1914 in Utica, New York and died 20 June 1976 in New Hartford, New York.[390]She married Henry Francis Penner 10 November 1938 in St.

Wedding day photo of Alma Beil and Henry Penner from the collection of Judy Agedal and used with permission.

---

[385] Obituary Utica Newspaper December 6, 1993
[386] Social Security Death Index from Ancestry.com
[387] Social Security Death Index from Ancestry.com
[388] Social Security Death Index from Ancestry.com
[389] Obituary Utica Newspaper February 23, 1988
[390] Social Security Death Index from Ancestry.com

Joseph's Church, Utica, New York. He was born 2 November 1909 in Utica, New York and died 11 May 1975 in New Hartford, New York.[391]Alma was a member of St. Anthony of Padau Church in Chadwicks, New York. Henry was a postman in Utica, New York. Alma Louise Beil and Henry Francis Penner had one child who is still living.

78. Eugene F. McSweeney[4] (Anna Smith[3], Joseph Smith[2], John Philip Schmidt[1]) was born 7 October 1926 in Detroit, Michigan and died 10 July 1998 in Webster, Florida.[392] He married Irene in Detroit, Michigan. She was born on 11 September 1929 and died in September 1981 in Webster, Florida.[393]Eugene F. and Irene McSweeney had three children who may still be living.

79. Mildred Heneka[4] (Emma Shuemaker[3], Cornelia Schmidt[2], John Philip Schmidt[1]) was born in1907 in New York State[394] and died 28 July 1977 in St. Elizabeth Hospital, Utica, New York.[395]She married Otto Weber in 1926 in Utica, New York. He died in 1945.[396] She married Roy MacArthur in 1950 in Utica, New York, the son of Guy MacArthur and Charlotte Prosser. He was born 23 July 1917 in Oneida Castle, New York and died 26 August 1983 in Rome Hospital, Rome, New York.[397]Mildred received her education in Utica, New York schools and was a member of St. Joseph-St. Patrick's Church, Utica, New York. Mildred Heneka Weber and Otto Weber had three children who are still living.

Generation Five

80. George Marvin Bowman[5] (Susanna Etta Sifer[4], Mary Johanna Schmidt[3], John Jacob Schmidt[2], John Philip Schmidt[1]) was born 30 June 1917 in Utica, New York and died 19 March 1987 in Utica, New York.[398] He married Kathryn Lourdes McLoughlin 17 February 1940 in St. John's Church, New Hartford, New York, the daughter of Arthur McLoughlin and Dorothy Bryan. She was born in1921 in Utica, New York and died 9 April 1972 in Utica, New York.[399]He married Mildred Gaylord Wood Christ 29 July 1961 in Utica, New York.[400]She was born 2 June 1909 and died 9 August 1981 in Utica, New York.[401]George worked at General Electric in Utica, New York for several years

[391] Social Security Death Index from Ancestry.com
[392] Obituary Utica Newspaper July 11, 1998
[393] Social Security Death Index from Ancestry.com
[394] 1910 Utica, New York Census
[395] Obituary Utica Newspaper July 29, 1977
[396] Obituary Utica Newspaper of wife, Mildred, July 29, 1977
[397] Obituary Utica Newspaper August 27, 1983
[398] Obituary Utica Newspaper of George Bowman March 20, 298
[399] Obituary Utica Newspaper April 10, 1972
[400] Obituary Utica Newspaper of George Bowman March 20, 298
[401] Schuyler Corners Cemetery tombstone, Schuyler, New York

until his retirement. He was a member of the Maennerchor and the Lions Club in Utica, New York.

Children of George Marvin Bowman and Kathryn Lourdes McLoughlin Bowman are:

    i.   Living Bowman

    ii.   Deborah Bowman was born 24 November 1950 in Utica, New York and died 25 September 2003 in Camp Lejeune, North Carolina.[402]She was married twice and had two children who are still living.

George and his sister, Gertrude Bowman.

Photo in the author's collection.

83. Edmond D. Schmidt[5](Frederick U. Schmidt[4], Joseph Lee Schmidt[3], John Jacob Schmidt[2], John Philip Schmidt[1]) was born 20 December 1922 in Utica, New York and died 7 May 2004 in Rome, Oneida, New York.[403]He married Evelyn F. McGee 26 July 1942 in Stuttgart, Arkansas.[404]She was born 25 October 1922and died 4 January 1999.[405]He married Alberta Vollmer 14 February 2000.[406]She died in 2003. Edmond entered the Army Air Corps in 1941. He retired from the Air Force as a Chief Master Sergeant and Aircraft Maintenance Supervisor at Griffiss Air Force Base, Rome, New York in 1963. He was awarded the Good Conduct Medal with four Bronze Oak Leaf Clusters, American Defense Service Medal, American Campaign Medal, Asiatic-Pacific Campaign Medal, World War II Victor medal, Army of Occupation Medal, Air Force Longevity Service Award Ribbon, United Nations Service Medal and Distinguished Unit Award. He was then employed as Supervisor of the Maintenance and Reliability Programs at Mohawk Airlines and by the Rite Aid Distribution Center. Ed was an avid hunter, fisherman and outdoors man. He was a member and past president of the Rome Photo Club, Rome, New York.

Edmond D. Schmidt and Evelyn F. McGee had the following children:

    i.   Living Schmidt

    ii.   David L. Schmidt was born 6 December 1943 in Stuttgart, Arizona and died 15 December 2003 in St. Elizabeth Medical Center, Utica, New York.[407]David was a graduated from Rome Free Academy in1961. He received his BA degree from Brockport State in 1965 and his Masters degree from Syracuse University in 1992. He began his

---

[402] Program of funeral service given to me by her sister.
[403] Social Security Death Index from Ancestry.com
[404] Obituary Utica Newspaper July 27, 1942
[405] Social Security Death Index from Ancestry.com
[406] Obituary Utica Newspaper January 5, 1999
[407] Obituary Utica Newspaper December 16, 2003

career as a teacher at Parmalee School in the Rome School District, Rome, New York. He was the President of the Utica Teachers Association from 1973 to 1985. He was promoted to Assistant Superintendent of Schools in charge of Human Resources retiring in 1997.

  iii. Living Schmidt
  iv. Living Schmidt
  v.   Living Schmidt
  vi. Living Schmidt
  vii. Living Schmidt
  viii. Living Schmidt

84. Frances (Jane) Schmidt[5] (Frederick U. Schmidt[4], Joseph Lee Schmidt[3], John Jacob Schmidt[2], John Philip Schmidt[1]) was born 18 February 1925 in Utica, New York and died 19 July 2001 in Rome, New York.[408] She married Donald C. Wardell 18 April 1944 in Utica, New York, the son of George Wardell and Florence Starring. He was born 25 July 1923 in Russia Corners, New York and died 6 January 2000 in Rome, New York.[409] Frances (Jane) Schmidt and Donald C. Wardell had four children who may still be living.

85. Helen Schmidt[5] (Frederick U. Schmidt[4], Joseph Lee Schmidt[3], John Jacob Schmidt[2], John Philip Schmidt[1]) was born 18 December 1927 in Utica, New York and died 31 December 1990 in Crouse Irving Memorial Hospital, Syracuse, New York.[410] She married Joseph L. Theall 24 August 1954 in Westmoreland, New York. He was born 17 January 1929 and died 25 Dec 2006 in Rome, New York.[411] Helen Schmidt and Joseph L. Theall had eight children who may still be living.

86. Walter J. Schmidt Sr[5] (Frederick U. Schmidt[4], Joseph Lee Schmidt[3], John Jacob Schmidt[2], John Philip Schmidt[1]) was born 16 June 1937 in Utica, New York and died 31 December 1989 in Vernon Center, New York.[412] He married Laurena Bowen in January 1962 in St. Mark's Church, Clark Mills, New York. Walter attended Oriskany, New York schools and was a graduate of Mohawk Valley Community College, Utica, New York receiving his certificate in Police Science. He was employed as a machinist for the Oneida Molded Plastics County, Oneida, New York and was the former chief of Police of the Village of Clinton. He was of the Episcopal faith. Walter J. Schmidt Sr. and Laurena Bowen had six children who may still be living.

88. Norman L. Schmidt[5] (John Peter Schmidt[4], John Philippey Schmidt[3], John Jacob Schmidt[2], John Philip Schmidt[1]) was born 25 February 1937 in Utica, New York and died

---

[408] Obituary Rome, New York Newspaper July 20, 2001
[409] Obituary Utica Newspaper January 7, 2000
[410] Obituary Utica Newspaper January 1, 1991
[411] Social Security Death Index from Ancestry.com
[412] Obituary Utica Newspaper January 1, 1990

28 June 1998 in Oriskany, New York.[413]He was married 9 September 1961 in St. Mary's Church, Utica, New York.   Norman L. Schmidt and his wife had three children who are all living.

90. James H. Schmidt Jr.[5] (James Howard Schmidt[4], George E. Schmidt (Smith) Sr[3], John Jacob Schmidt[2], John Philip Schmidt[1]) was born 04 October 1919 in Utica, New York and died 18 December 1996 in Utica, New York.[414]He married Margaret M. Allen 30 April 1949 in St. Patrick's Church, Utica, New York, the daughter of Oliver Allen and Catherine Redmond. She was born 27 February 1925 in Prescott, Ontario, Canada and died 20 November 1990.[415]James served in the Army Air Corp during World War II.   He had been employed by Rome Air Development Center, Rome, New York and was a member of St. Peter's Church, Utica, New York. James H. Schmidt Jr. and Margaret M. Allen had three children who may still be living.

95. John E. Schmitt[5] (Margaret P. Uerz[4], Margaret (Maggie) Schmidt[3], John Jacob Schmidt[2], John Philip Schmidt[1]) was born in November 1921 and died 15 June 1977 in Utica, New York.[416]He married Eleanor Neuland in 1946 in Rochester, New York. She died in 1998. John attended Utica, New York schools and had worked for Kelsey Hayes, Whitesboro, New York. In 1968 he moved to San Francisco, California to work for the President Steamship Lines. He was an Army World War II veteran and a member of St. Joseph's-St. Patrick's Church and its Holy Name Society in Utica, New York. John E. Schmitt and Eleanor Neuland had six children who may still be living.

97. Fred C. Ulrich[5](Charles H. Ulrich[4], Anna M. Schmidt[3], John Jacob Schmidt[2], John Philip Schmidt[1]) was born 27 February 1928 in Utica, New York and died 11 July 2003 in Rome Memorial Hospital, Rome, New York.[417]He married Patricia Herring in 1946. He married Carol Tobin in 1976 in Scaunton, Virginia, the daughter of Walter and Carolyn Tobin. She was born 16 August 1929 in Utica, New York and died 11 December 2004 in Rome City Hospital, Rome, New York.[418]Fred was a graduate of Holland Patent High School, Holland Patent, New York and attended Utica College, Utica, New York. He served his country in the United States Army. Fred had been employed as a manager of a Ford dealership in Barneveld, New York for over twenty years. Most recently he was employed by Masda Corp, retiring in 1989.   Children of Fred C. Ulrich and Patricia Herring had two children who may still be living.

---

[413] Obituary Utica Newspaper June 29, 1998
[414] Obituary Utica Newspaper December 19, 1996
[415] Obituary Utica Newspaper November 21, 1990
[416] Obituary Utica Newspaper June 16, 1977
[417] Obituary Utica Newspaper July 12, 2003
[418] Obituary Utica Newspaper December 12, 2004

98. Elmer C. Ulrich[5](Charles H. Ulrich[4], Anna M. Schmidt[3], John Jacob Schmidt[2], John Philip Schmidt[1]) was born 22 August 1920 in Utica, New York and died 12 April 1984 in St. Luke's Hospital, New Hartford, New York.[419]He married Ethel S. Hart 20 July 1940 in Whitesboro, New York, the daughter of Elmer Hart and Luceil Behymer. She was born n 24 April 1921 in Town of Sullivan, New York and died 7 January 1985 in Whitesboro, New York.[420]Elmer C. Ulrich and Ethel S. Hart had three children who may still be living.

100. Robert G. Young[5] (Loretta M. Ulrich[4], Anna M. Schmidt[3], John Jacob Schmidt[2], John Philip Schmidt[1]) was born 1929 in Utica, New York. He died 25 November 1986 at Mullen Drive, Auburn, New York.[421]He was married and had lived in Auburn for 40 years. He was a communicant of St. Mary's Church, Auburn, New York and was employed at New York State Electric and Gas as a foreman in the line department. He was a member of the Quarter Century Club of the Gas and Electric and served with the United States Marines during the Korean War. He and his wife had one son who may still be living.

105. Maurice John Muthig Jr[5] (Maurice John Muthig Sr[4], Philomena (Minnie) M. Schmidt[3], John Jacob Schmidt[2], John Philip Schmidt[1]) was born 29 September 1920 in Philadelphia, Pennsylvania and died 6 August 1986 in Baltimore, Maryland. He was married 14 February 1942 in Philadelphia, Pennsylvania. Maurice John Muthig Jr. and his wife had two children who are still living.[422]

114. Eugene K. Elsenbeck[5] (Olive Mae Schreppel[4], Mary J. Smith[3], Joseph Smith[2], John Philip Schmidt[1]) was born 14 July 1927 in Oriskany, New York and died 31 December 1993 in Clinton, New York.[423]He was married in December 1947 in Utica, New York.

Eugene K. Elsenbeck his wife had the following children:

i.	Living Elsenbeck
ii.	Living Elsenbeck
iii.	Living Elsenbeck
iv.	Living Elsenbeck
v.	Living Elsenbeck
vi.	Living Elsenbeck
vii.	Living Elsenbeck
viii.	Kathleen Mae Elsenbeck was born 25 April 1951 in Utica, New York and

died 14 July 1987 in Roswell Park, Buffalo, New York.[424]She was married 6 May 1972

---

[419] Obituary Utica Newspaper April 13, 1984
[420] Obituary Utica Newspaper January 8, 1985
[421] Obituary Utica Newspaper November 26, 1986
[422] Family information from Debbie Leach
[423] Obituary Utica Newspaper January 1, 1993

in New York Mills, New York.   Kathleen received her education in New York Mills, New York schools. She had been employed at Utica Cutlery for many years. She attended Wolcott Presbyterian church in Oriskany, New York. She married Thomas E. Smoulcey and they had four children who may still be living.

Chapter Three

Descendants of Augustus Isaac Seifert

Generation One

1. Augustus Isaac Seifert[-1] was born *about* 1817 or 1818 in Bavaria, Germany and he died *about* 1884.[1]Augustus' first marriage was in Germany to a woman that was the mother of his son, Carl. No documentation has been found indicating what may have happened to Augustus' first wife and the family history begins with Augustus arriving in New York City on January 24, 1854 aboard the President Smidt.[2] He was 36 years old at the time and was accompanied by his first son, Carl, who was four and a half years old. Augustus emigrated from Bremen, Germany and was listed on the ship's manifest as a brewer from Walfushasen, Germany. August Seifert announced his emigration in the official newspaper "Intelligenzblatt Unterfranken". There is no more information in it except his name and place of residence, Walterhausen, Bavaria. The original newspaper is stored in the Haupstaatsarchiv in Munich. From 1840 to 1871 the emigrants had to publish their plan of emigration in the official newspaper. The creditors were able to announce their demands. The problem is that only about 50 % of the emigrants went this legal way by public announcement the other half went to America without any papers. In 1850 Walterhausen had a population of about 500 inhabitants.

Most likely Augustus traveled up the Hudson River from New York City and on the Erie Canal to Rome, New York eventually ending up in the Town of Ava, New York. Ava at that time had a large population of German immigrants. The Oneida County Court records indicate he filed a declaration of intent to become an American citizen on June 4, 1854 and listed Ava as his residence.

About 1855 Augustus married his second wife Catharina Gasser Preis. Perhaps he met her in Rome or Ava, New York as the 1855 Town of Lewis Census indicates they were

---

[1] Obituary of wife Utica Newspaper May 7, 1903
[2] Germans to America books

married. She was born in 1820 in Austria and died 6 May 1903 in New York Mills, New York.[3]

The 1855 Census in the Town of Lewis, New York lists the Seifert family with the spelling of Cifort. In the 1860 Town of Lewis Census, the family name was spelled Sifard and in 1870, it was spelled Lipher. In the 1880 Town of Lewis Census, the name was spelled yet another way "Seipher". It is important to remember that information in the census records were often recorded phonetically particularly the surnames. The census taker often encountered people of many ethnic backgrounds that spoke very little English or had heavy accents especially when recording information from recent immigrants. In addition, it was common 100 years ago for the census taker to use abbreviations to save time and paper and the old style writing of some letters in the alphabet looked similar to other letters. For instance sometimes "s" would look like a lower case "f" or "l". Census records can also include errors resulting from people lying in response to questions or incorrect information gathered from adjacent neighbors speaking on the immigrant's behalf. On February 13, 1860 at the Oneida County Court, Rome, New York Augustus Seifert renounced his allegiance to the King of Bavaria and became a naturalized citizen of the United States of America. Witnesses to the naturalization were Gustavus Hansman and Casper Westline both of Rome, New York.

Sometime between June 1854 and 1855, Augustus must have moved to the Town of Lewis as indicated in the 1855 Census. A map published in 1875 shows an A. Seifert living on what is now known as the Osceola Road just outside of the hamlet of West Leyden which was in the Town of Lewis. This may have been the location of the family homestead.

In the 1880 Town of Lewis Census, Augustus was listed with Catherine, Charles, George and Margaret and it stated he was born in Bayern, Germany. Further research revealed Bayern and Bavaria are one in the same. I have been unable to find documentation on Augustus' death. However, his wife's obituary indicated he died in 1884 and he was not listed in the 1892 Census that listed Catherine living with her son, George.

Catherina died of pneumonia at the home of Charles Darling at 7:00 p.m., 6 May 1903 in New York Mills, New York. In the 1880 census there was a Cornelius Darling age 27 living with the Seiferts in the Town of Lewis, New York and he was listed as a boarder. The 1870 Town of Lewis census shows the Darling family living next door to the Seiferts. I was unable to determine a connection between the Seiferts and the Darlings. Catherina's funeral took place from the home of her son, George Seifert, City Street, and St. Joseph's Church, both of Utica, New York.   Since Catherine's son Edward was born in Germany in May 1852, according to his obituary, she likely arrived in America

---

[3] Obituary Utica Newspaper May 7, 1903

between the summer of 1852 and the time the 1855 census were taken. According to the 1865 Town of Lewis Census, Catherine had 7 children (but only six were listed). I found later she had a daughter named Elizabeth from her first marriage that was not living with her in 1865. Elizabeth married Joseph Thoman and after his death married John Schwenk. However, the census record indicated that Catherine had been married three times.

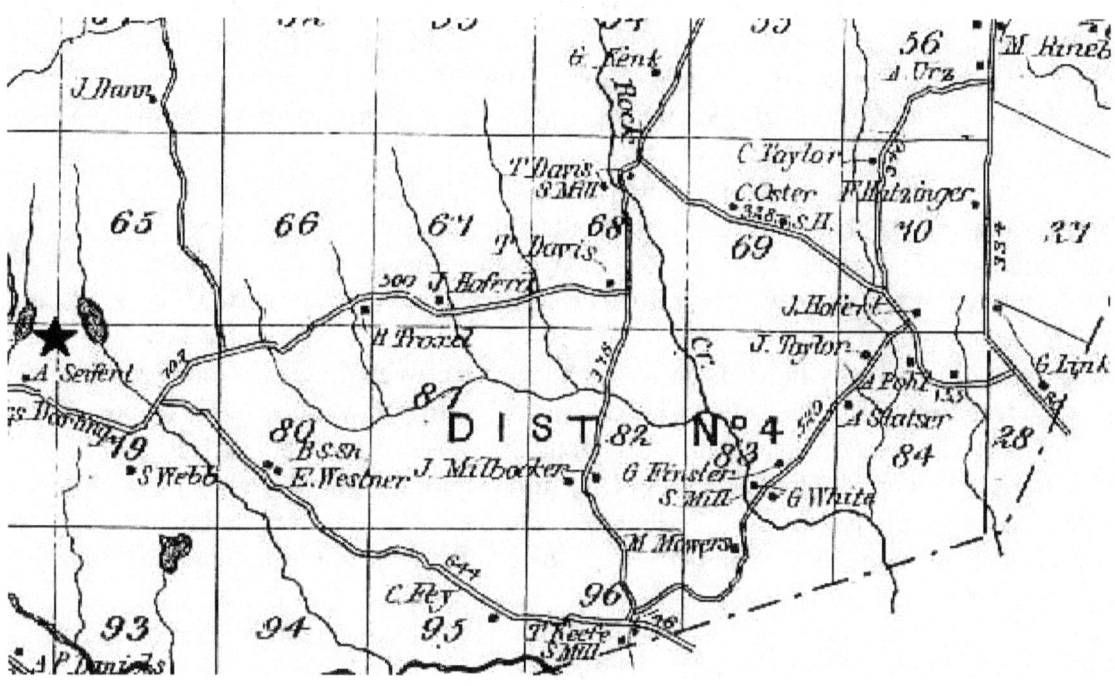

This is a portion of a Town of Lewis Map published in 1875 showing an A. Seifert residing on what is now known as the Osceola Road southwest of West Leyden, New York.

The Rome City Directory dated 1901-1902 indicated Catherine was living with her daughter, Margaret at 111 West Fox Street Rome, New York. Catherine's given German name was Cattarina or Catharina as indicated in her children's baptismal records in St. Michael's Church, Mohawk Hill, New York. It appears that her name was later Americanized to Catherine as shown in her obituary. Her surname had various spellings that included Gasser, Kafser, Gafser or Koiser. Gasser was listed on her daughter's death certificate. She was born in Austria or Germany, most likely near the border which was known to change from time to time during this time period. She came to America and then to Utica, New York as a young woman and eventually settled in West Leyden, New York where she lived until a few years before her death at which time she moved to Rome, New York to live with her daughter, Margaret. While in Utica, she was a member of St. Joseph's Church. She had 24 grandchildren and 3 great-grandchildren at the time of her death as indicated in her obituary.

Augustus Isaac Seifert and his first wife had the following child:

2.   i.   Charles August Seifert was born between 8 July 1847-1848 in Bavaria,[4] and died 26 March 1914 in Lee, New York.[5]

Augustus Isaac Seifert and Catharina Gasser Preis had the following children:

      i.   Maria (Mary) Seifert was born 11 January 1856 in West Leyden, New York. Maria was baptized in St. Michael's Church, Mohawk Hill, New York and her Godparents were Casper and Elizabetta Bohn.[6] The 1860 West Leyden, New York Census listed her as five years old. I believe she died young as she was not listed in the 1865 Census.

      ii.   Susanna (Susan) Seifert was born in January 1858 in West Leyden, New York. Susanna was baptized in St. Michael's Church, Mohawk Hill, New York and her Godparents were Joannes Heer and Susanna Herb.[7] The 1860 West Leyden, New York Census listed Susan as three years old and that her last name was Stafford.   She was not listed in subsequent census records.

3.   iii.   **George Sifer** was born 11 April 1861 in West Leyden, New York. George was baptized in Michael's Church, Mohawk Hill, New York and his Godparents were George Lenk and Sejus Resore[8] He died 23 January 1945 in Utica, New York.[9]

      iv.   John Seifert was born in December 1863 in Town of Lewis, New York. John was baptized in St. Michael's Church, Mohawk Hill, New York and his Godparents were Georgius Thomann and Barbara Schroeder.[10] John was not listed in any of the census after his baptismal record. He must have died young.

4.   v.   Margaret Seifert was born 16 April 1865 in Swancott Mills, Town of Lewis, New York and died 27 April 1925 in Rome, New York.

Generation Two

2. Charles August Seifert[2] (Augustus Isaac Seifert[-1]) was born 8 July 1847-1848 in Bavaria, Germany York.[11] He died 26 March 1914 in Lee, New York.[12] He married Emma

---

[4] Death Certificate of Charles August Seifert
[5] New York State Vital Records, Albany, New York
[6] FHC film of St. Michael's Church Records, Mohawk Hill, New York
[7] FHC film of St. Michael's Church Records, Mohawk Hill, New York
[8] FHC film of St. Michael's Church Records, Mohawk Hill, New York
[9] Obituary Utica Newspaper January 24, 1945
[10] FHC film of St. Michael's Church Records, Mohawk Hill, New York
[11] Death Certificate of Charles August Seifert
[12] New York State Vital Records, Albany, New York

G. Rivers 3 July 1884 in Delta, New York, the daughter of Abraham and Louise Rivers. She was born 15 June 1867 in Troy, New York and died 22 January 1947 in Oneida County Hospital, Rome, New York.[13] Charles was not a naturalized citizen. He would have obtained his citizenship under his father. He was unable to read or write. He died at his home in Lorena, New York after a four week illness. Ruth Seifert Fogg remembers visiting a grave as a child in the Point Rock Cemetery, Point Rock, New York. There was a wooden cross on this grave and she was told it was the grave of her grandfather, Charles Seifert. The wooden cross is now gone.

The 1860 Town of Lewis Census listed Charles' last name as Stafford even though he was living with his father and his father's name was spelled Sifard. This is another example of where the census taker may have misinterpreted what the informant said. In the 1870 Town of Lewis Census, Charles was listed as living on the farm of John Dunn and working as a day laborer on his farm. This farm was next door to his father's home and both of their last names were spelled Lipher instead of Seifert. He was 22 at the time and it states he was born in Germany. On October 16, 1878 Charles sold property to Gerrit-Hubert VanWagenen and Cornelia B., his wife. Charles Seifert sold land May 3, 1888 in the Town of Lewis, New York to Isaac Rivers for $150.[14]

In the 1900 Census Town of Lee, New York, Charles occupation was teamster. His name at this time was Sifer. He lived on West Lee Road, Lee, New York in 1910. His obituary said he was born in Lewis County, New York and resided there until 1 1/2 years ago when his health failed and he retired from active life. I believe he was born in Germany and his obituary was miswritten and should had said he lived in Lewis County instead of he was born in Lewis County. He attended Lee Center M.E. Church. His occupation was farming.

> ***Death notice in Rome newspaper of Emma Seifert, wife of Charles Seifert*** - *Funeral from home of granddaughter Mrs. Ivan Joanis, 414 N. George Street Rome, New York. The Rev. Kenneth Farnell, pastor of Lee Center Methodist Church officiated.*

Photo of Emma Rivers Seifert was in the collection of Suellen Brewster and is being used with permission.

Emma died of cerebral hemorrhage, cardiovascular disease, and diabetes mellitus. She had been hospitalized for five days prior to her death. She had been ailing for three

---

[13] Death Certificate of Charles August Seifert
[14] Lewis County Deed Records

years. Emma lived in the Point Rock vicinity in her earlier years. She had lived in Rome, New York since about 1914. She lived in Rome in various neighborhoods through 1941. In the 1915 Census she lived with four of her children, Burton, Mary, Lena, and Edward, at 302 W. Dominick Street Rome, New York. She was a member of the Point Rock Methodist Church. She lived at 117 West Fox Street Rome, New York at time of her death.

Charles August Seifert and Emma G. Rivers had the following children:

11.   i.   Burton C. Seifert was born 8 May 1885 in West Leyden, New York[15] and died 13 June 1956 in Rose Hospital, Rome, New York.[16]

          ii.   Mary (Minnie) Emma Seifert was born 4 May 1886 in Swancott Mills, New York and died 6 August 1943 in Rome Hospital, Rome, New York.[17]Mary never married and she lived with her mother her entire life. For 30 years prior to her death, she and her mother lived with a niece, Mrs. Ivan Joanis, 206 Liberty Street, Rome, New York. She was buried in the family plot at the Point Rock Cemetery, Point Rock, New York.[18]

Photo of Mary Seifert was in the collection of Suellen Brewster and is being used with permission.

12.   iii.   Susan Anna Seifert was born 28 October 1889 in Town of Lewis, New York and died 22 May 1963 in Buffalo, New York.[19]

13.   iv.   Lillian M. Seifert was born 19 August 1893 in Ava, New York[20] and died 23 June 1933 in Rome, New York.[21]

14.   v.   William Isaac Seifert was born 27 May 1899 in Point Rock, New York[22] and died 10 February 1962 in University Hospital, Ann Arbor, Michigan.[23]

          vi.   Lena Seifert was born 11 June 1902 in Point Rock, New York and died 28 December 1916 in Swancott Mills, New York.[24]Lena had been in failing health for several weeks and finally her physician advised that she be taken to a camp in the woods. Accordingly she went to a camp near Swancott's Mills where she was tenderly cared for by her sister and mother. Her nephew, William Caterham, remembers Lena as being deformed, but I do not know in what way.   Lena was a favorite with her many friends and possessed a bright and cheerful disposition which endeared her to all.

---

[15] Family information from Kari Fogg
[16] Obituary Rome, New York Newspaper June 14, 1956
[17] Obituary Rome, New York Newspaper August 7, 1943
[18] Obituary Rome, New York Newspaper August 7, 1943
[19] Family information from William Caterham
[20] Obituary Rome, New York Newspaper June 24, 1933
[21] New York State Vital Records, Albany, New York
[22] New York State Vital Records, Albany, New York
[23] Obituary in Ann Arbor Michigan Newspaper February 11, 1962
[24] Obituary Rome, New York Newspaper December 29, 1916

15.   vii.   Edwin Lyle Seifert was born 20 July 1904 in Point Rock or Lee Center, New York and died 8 September 1959 in Pasadena, California.[25]

viii.   Frederick Seifert was born about 1905 and died before the 1910 Census was taken. Frederick died in a "swinging" accident with a neighbor. Ruth Seifert-Fogg remembers her father William being opposed to any child being "swung by his arms". William may have witnessed this accident with his brother.

3. **George Sifer**[2](Augustus Isaac Seifert[-1]) was born 11 April 1861 in West Leyden, Lewis County, New York and he died 23 January 1945 in Utica, New York.[26] He married Mary Johanna Schmidt 7 June 1892 in Mary's Church, Prussian Settlement, West Leyden, New York.[27] She was the daughter of John Jacob Schmidt and Catherine Schroeder. She was born 8 November 1864 in West Leyden, New York and died 5 January 1958 in Utica, New York. For more on Mary Johanna Schmidt see Chapter Two.

This picture is the house in Ava, New York where Susanna Etta Sifer was born. On the porch are George Sifer and his wife, Mary. This picture was taken about 1931 and was in the author's collection.

George came to Utica, New York 4 April 1895 and went to work at the Kellogg Lumber Company where he worked for 47 years. The 1910 Utica, New York Census listed his occupation as a teamster working at a lumber yard. My mother, Gertrude Bowman, told me he delivered lumber by horse and wagon, occasionally stopping by his house so his grandchildren could see the horses.   In his elder years, he was the watchman for Kellogg Lumber. The Kellogg Lumber Company was located at 40-48 Seneca Street, Utica, New York. This was about a mile and a half walk for George to get to work. He lived in Ward 9 at 125 Hicks Street Utica, New York in 1900.   He was a member of Joseph's Church, Utica, New York.

---

[25] Family information from Shirley Kaelin
[26] Obituary Utica Newspaper January 24, 1945
[27] FHC film of St. Michael's Church Records, Mohawk Hill, New York

George Sifer and Mary Johanna Schmidt had the following children:

5.   i.   **Susanna Etta Sifer** was born 17 July 1893 in Ava, New York and died 20 June 1966 in Utica, New York.[28]

ii.   George John Sifer was born 18 April 1900 in Utica, New York and died 27 January 1958 in Utica, New York.[29] George was employed as an orderly at the Masonic Hospital and was a member of St. Joseph's Church, Utica, New York.

George and Mary Sifer in 1942
This picture taken on their 50th wedding anniversary
and was in the author's collection

4. Margaret Seifert[2] (Augustus Isaac Seifert[-1]) was born 16 April 1865 in Swancott Mills, New York. She died 27 April 1925 in Rome, New York. She married Isaac Rivers in 1882 in Delta, New York, the son of Abraham and Louisa Rivers. He was born 13 October 1859 in Swancott Mills, New York and died of nephritis 25 May 1931 in Rome, New York.[30]   At the time of her death, Margaret was living at 518 N. Jay Street Rome, New York and she was of the Presbyterian Faith. She died of paralysis and was buried in Lot 322 grave M in the Rome Cemetery, Rome, New York. Isaac lived in the Town of Lewis, New York in the 1880 Census with Nicholas Schrater and family. The 1910 Census said he was a house painter and lived at West Fox Street in Rome, New York. He lived at 518 North Jay Street, Rome, New York at the time of his death. His obituary indicated he was a paper hanger and a painter.

Photo of Margaret Seifert Rivers in the author's collection.

Margaret Seifert and Isaac Rivers had the following children:
6.   i.   Charles Jess Rivers was born 13 June 1882 in New York State[31] and died 27 December 1946 in Rome, New York.[32]

---

[28]   Obituary Utica Newspaper June 21, 1966
[29]   Obituary Utica Newspaper January 28, 1958
[30]   Obituary Rome Sentinel Newspaper May 26, 1931
[31]   World War I draft registration from Ancestery.com
[32]   Death notice in Rome, New York Newspaper, December 28, 1946

7.   ii.   Ada Rivers was born 30 May 1886 in Lewis County, New York and died 25 January 1965 in Rome, New York.[33]

8.   iii.   George R. Rivers was born 31 July 1888 in Lewis County, New York and died 3 April 1955 in Oneida County Hospital, Oneida, New York.[34]

9.   iv.   Lena Rivers was born in September 1891 in Swancott Mills, Lewis County, New York[35] and died 10 March 1971 in Rome Hospital, Rome, New York.[36].

10.   v.   Ida Rivers was born 25 December 1894 in Point Rock, New York[37] and died 3 February 1977 in Faxton Hospital, Utica, New York.[38]

Generation Three

5. Susanna Etta Sifer[3] (George Sifer[2,] Augustus Isaac Seifert[1]) was born 17 July 1893 in Ava, New York. Susanna was baptized in St. Michael's Church, Mohawk Hill, New York and Godparents were Michael Isenecker and Susanna Brady.[39] She died 20 June 1966 in Utica, New York.[40] She married George Francis Bowman 8 September 1916 in St. Joseph's Church, Utica, New York. He was the son of George Bowman and Rose Hahn. He was born 18 December 1891 in Jersey City, New Jersey[41] and died 8 January 1957 in Utica, New York.[42] For more on George Francis Bowman see Chapter Four.

Photo of Susanna Etta Sifer taken in 1910. She was 18 years old. Picture is in the author's collection.

Susanna "Etta" Sifer was my grandmother. I remember her as a very kind and caring person. She took care of her aging mother for many years that lived across the street. She would go over each morning and help her mother get up, get washed, get dressed and then would fix her breakfast. Etta, as she was called, would get on the Utica city bus and go to work at the Hearst Dress Shop in downtown Utica, New York. Her job at the store

[33] Obituary Rome, New York Newspaper January 26, 1965
[34] Obituary Rome, New York Newspaper April 4, 1955
[35] New York State Vital Records, Albany, New York
[36] Obituary Rome, New York Newspaper March 11, 1971
[37] Social Security Death Index from Ancestry.com
[38] Obituary Utica Newspaper February 4, 1977
[39] FHC film of St. Michael's Church Records, Mohawk Hill, New York
[40] Obituary Utica Newspaper June 21, 1966
[41] FHC Film 1403369, St. Patrick's Church Records, Jersey City, New Jersey
[42] Obituary Utica Newspaper January 9, 1957

was to do alterations on the dresses that customers would purchase. At lunch time, she would ride the bus back home and give her mother her lunch. When her workday was done, she would go home, have dinner with her husband and then go across the street to fix dinner for her mother and get her ready for bed and settled in for the night. She did this for years never varying from her routine. Her mother lived to be 92 years of age and outlived Etta's husband. According to the 1910 Utica, New York Census, Susanna worked as a strapper in a knitting mill. A strapper was a person who sewed cloth straps that take the place of eyelets and lacing in a garment.

Photo of Susanna Etta Sifer and George Bowman wedding party. Photo was in the author's collection.

The following wedding announcement was taken from Utica Daily Press September 7, 1916:

The marriage of Miss Susanna Sifer of 1108 Sunset Avenue, daughter of Mr. & Mrs. George Sifer, to George F. Bowman of 1107 Walnut Street took place at 9:00 a.m. in Street Joseph's Church, Rev. Phillip Friedman officiating. Thomas E. Ryan played the organ and the young ladies choir of the church sang the mass. The attendants of the bride were Miss Margaret Urtz, her cousin, as bridesmaid, and Miss Ida Rivers of Rome, another cousin, as maid of honor. Thomas Holland and John Swertfager attended the groom. The bride wore a gown of white moire, with georgette crepe trimmings, and wore a white veil trimmed with orange blossoms. She carried bride's roses. The bridesmaid was attired in pink taffeta with chiffon trimmings, and wore a wreath of pink roses. The maid of honor wore yellow taffeta, with white trimmings and a wreath of yellow roses. The couple left for a wedding trip to New York, Jersey City and Philadelphia, after a wedding breakfast at the home of the bride's parents. The groom is employed at the Savage arms plant and has many friends here. The bride was the guest of honor at variety showers held by Miss Emma Fehlner, Miss Margaret Bamberger and Miss Margaret Urtz. The couple will reside upon their return at 1106 Sunset Avenue, and many friends will wish them happiness.

Susanna Etta Sifer and George Francis Bowman had the following children:

16.   i.   George Marvin Bowman was born 30 June 1917 in Utica, New York. He died 19 March 1987 in Utica, New York.

    ii.   Living Bowman

6. Charles Jess Rivers[3] (Margaret Seifert[2], Augustus Isaac Seifert[1]) was born 13 June 1882 in New York State[43] and died 27 December 1946 in Rome, New York.[44] He married Mary Wall 6 November 1907 in the Town of Marcy, New York,[45] the daughter of Daniel Wall and Christine Miller. Mary was born 17 January 1885 in Northwood, New York and died 2 September 1958 at West Dominick Street Rome, New York[46] Mary Wall was educated in Northwood School and had resided in Rome, New York since her marriage. She was a member of the First Baptist Church, the Friendship Bible Class, the Helen Tuft Circle and Queen Esther Rebeckah Lodge.

This photo of Charles J. Rivers was in the collection of Suellen Brewster and is being used with permission.

Charles Jess Rivers and Mary Wall had the following children:

    i.   Clifford Rivers was born 3 July 1909 in Rome, New York and died 1 February 1999 in Rome Towers Apartments, Rome, New York.[47] Clifford served with the U.S. Army during World War II in the European Theater. Cliff had been employed for many years by the Utica Observer Dispatch retiring in 1965. He was a member of the First Baptist Church and the Rome Post Veterans of Foreign Wars. He never married.

    ii.   Howard W. Rivers was born in 1913 in Rome, New York and died 18 May 1962 in 1012 West Dominick Street, Rome, New York.[48] Howard had worked for Revere Copper and Brass for 20 years. He lived with his brother at the time of his death. His brother found him dead when he returned home one day. He was a member of the First Baptist Church in Rome, New York. Howard never married.

---

[43] World War I draft registration from Ancestery.com
[44] Death notice Rome, New York newspaper December 28, 1946
[45] Obituary Rome, New York Newspaper September 3, 1958
[46] Obituary Rome, New York Newspaper September 3, 1958
[47] Obituary Rome, New York Newspaper February 2, 1999
[48] Obituary Rome, New York Newspaper May 19, 1962

7. Ada Rivers[3] (Margaret Seifert[2], Augustus Isaac Seifert[1]) was born 30 May 1886 in Lewis County, New York and died 25 January 1965 in Rome, New York.[49] She married Frederick Sherwood 21 June 1905 in Rome, New York. He was born in 1880 and died 6 November 1928 in Rome, New York.[50] Ada went to Point Rock School in Point Rock, New York. She moved to Rome in 1902 and worked at Oneida County Hospital, Oneida New York. She lived at 117 West Fox Street Rome, New York at the time of her death.

Ada Rivers and Frederick Sherwood had the following children:

    i.   Gretta Mae Sherwood was born 19 October 1906 in Point Rock, New York and died 5 February 1987 in Betsy Ross Nursing Home, Rome, New York.[51] She married Louis H. Mabb 29 August 1936 in the First Methodist Church, Rome, New York.[52] Louis was born 22 September 1897 in Gloversville, New York and died 9 May 1962 in Rome, New York.[53] Gretta Mae Sherwood died after a long illness. She lived in Rome on Kriswood Drive and she did not have children.

18.   ii.   Stuart D. Sherwood was born 19 August 1908 in Rome, New York and died 26 April 1957 in Rome Hospital, Rome, New York.[54]

19.   iii.   Kenneth J. Sherwood was born 13 June 1912 in Rome, New York and died 13 August 1972 in Rose Hospital, Rome, New York.[55]

    iv.   Marion Sherwood was born 19 November 1918 in Rome, New York and died 10 November 1995 in Betsy Ross Nursing Home, Rome, New York.[56] She married Allan R. Stoddard 5 June 1943 in the First Baptist Church, Rome, New York. Alan was born 17 September 1917 in Westmoreland, New York, the son of Ray V. Stoddard and Villa Carr and died 31 October 1972 in Rome Hospital, Rome, New York.[57] Marion had worked at the Rome State School, Rome, New York. She lived at 5074   Brookfield Road, Lee Center, New York and she did not have children.

20.   v.   Helen Sherwood was born 28 January 1922 in Rome, New York and died 30 November 1978 in Rose Hospital, Rome, New York.[58]

8. George R. Rivers[3] (Margaret Seifert[2], Augustus Isaac Seifert[1]) was born 31 July 1888 in Lewis County, New York[59] and died 3 April 1955 in Oneida County Hospital, Oneida, New York.[60] He married Katherine in 1906 in Rome, New York. She was born in 1891

---

[49] Obituary Rome, New York Newspaper January 26, 1965

[50] Obituary Rome, New York Newspaper November 7, 1928

[51] Obituary Rome, New York Newspaper February 6, 1987

[52] Obituary Rome, New York Newspaper February 6, 1987

[53] Obituary Rome, New York Newspaper May 10, 1962

[54] Obituary Rome, New York Newspaper April 27, 1957

[55] Obituary Rome, New York Newspaper August 14, 1972

[56] Death certificate of Marion Sherwood

[57] Social Security Death Index from Ancestry.com

[58] Obituary Rome, New York Newspaper December 1, 1978

[59] World War I draft registration from Ancestery.com

[60] Obituary Rome, New York Newspaper April 4, 1955

in New York State.[61] Later he married Lulu C. Whitehead Keneflick in 1944 in Detroit, Michigan, daughter of John and Clara Whitehead. She was born 17 July 1883 in Kentucky and died 3 April 1955 in Oneida County Hospital, Oneida, New York.[62]George and his wife died the same day of natural causes just 3 hours and 25 minutes apart.   He had been seriously ill for three weeks and when she went to the hospital to visit him, she had a heart attack. The 1910 Rome New York Census said he had been married for two years and worked in a grocery store. George was a tool and die maker and was employed by the Rome Wire Company which was the predecessor to General Cable Corporation, Spargo Wire Company and the Chrysler Corporation in Detroit, Michigan.

George R. Rivers and Katherine had the following children:
21.   i.   Eleanor C. Rivers was born 29 July 1908 in New York State and died 19 July 2004 in Morrisville, New York.[63]She married LaVerne Minor.
     ii.   Living Rivers
     iii.   Living Rivers
     iv.   Living Rivers
     v.   Living Rivers

9. Lena Rivers[3] (Margaret Seifert[2],Augustus Isaac Seifert[1]) was born 16 September 1891 in Swancott Mills, New York[64]and died 10 March 1971 in Rome Hospital, Rome, New York.[65]She married Elmer Earl Gleasman Sr 1 June 1909 in the First Presbyterian Church, Rome, New York, the son of Charles Gleasman and Viola Neiss. He was born 22 October 1884 in New York State and died 27 September 1959 in Rome, New York.[66]

Lena Rivers and Elmer Earl Gleasman Sr had the following children:
22.   i.   Marvin E. Gleasman was born 2 December 1909 in Rome, New York and died 2 January 1971 in Rome, New York.[67]
23.   ii.   Elmer Earl Gleasman Jr was born November 1912 in Rome, New York and died 14 March 1971 in Rome Hospital, Rome, New York.[68]
24.   iii.   Arnold E. Gleasman was born 24 January 1915 in Rome, New York and died 31 December 1997 in Elizabeth Hospital, Utica, New York.[69]

10. Ida Rivers[3] (Margaret Seifert[2],Augustus Isaac Seifert[1]) was born 25 December 1894 in Point Rock, New York[70]and died 3 February 1977 in Faxton Hospital, Utica, New

[61] 1920 Rome, New York Census
[62] Obituary Rome, New York Newspaper April 4, 1955
[63] Social Security Death Index from Ancestry.com
[64] New York State Vital Records, Albany, New York
[65] Obituary Rome, New York Newspaper March 11, 1971
[66] Obituary Rome, New York Newspaper September 27, 1959
[67] Obituary Rome, New York Newspaper January 3, 1971
[68] Obituary Rome, New York Newspaper March 15, 1971
[69] Obituary Utica Newspaper January 1, 1998

York.[71] She married John M. Schwertfeger 29 April 1920 in St. Joseph's Church, Utica, New York, the son of John M. Schwertfeger and Margaret Weiss. He was born 21 July 1893 in Utica, New York and died 17 June 1960 in St. Luke's Memorial Hospital, New Hartford, New York.[72] John attended Joseph's School, Utica, New York. He was a member of St. Joseph's Church and it's Holy Name Society. For many years he owned and operated an electrical appliance store known as Belle Electric Company, on Lenox Avenue, Utica, New York. During World War II he was employed by Griffiss Air Force Base, Rome, New York. He belonged to the International Brotherhood of Electrical Workers Union.

Ida Rivers and John M. Schwertfeger had the following children:
25.   i.   Living Schwertfeger
26.   ii.   Patricia Schwertfeger was born 20 May 1933 in Utica, New York and died 27 May 1993 in Oklahoma City, Oklahoma.[73]

11. Burton C. Seifert[3] (Charles Seifert[2],Augustus Isaac Seifert[1]) was born 8 May 1885 in

West Leyden, New York and died 13 June 1956 in Rose Hospital, Rome, New York.[74] He married Bertha L. Finster 26 January 1910 and Josephine R. Back 28 July 1911 in Erie, PA. Josephine was born in 1894 in New York State[75] and died 4 January 1947.[76] Burton lived at 319 E. Bloomfield Street Rome, New York at time of his death had been ill for three weeks prior to his death. He had lived in Rome, New York for 33 years. Prior to that, he lived in Buffalo, New York. He had been employed by the Rome Cable Corporation and was a member of the Rome Moose Lodge and the Episcopal Church in Rome, New York.

Photo of Burton Charles Seifert in the collection of Marlene Pcolar and is being used with permission.

Burton C. Seifert and Bertha L. Finster had the following children:
27.   i.   Aletha I. Seifert was born 19 August 1910 in Rome, New York and died 21 March 1984 in Rome Hospital, Rome, New York.[77]

[70] Social Security Death Index from Ancestry.com
[71] Obituary Utica Newspaper February 4, 1977
[72] Obituary Utica Newspaper June 18, 1960
[73] Family information from Jeanne Miller
[74] Obituary Rome, New York Newspaper June 14, 1956
[75] 1930 Steuben, New York Census
[76] Obituary of Husband in the Rome, New York Newspaper June 14, 1956
[77] Obituary Rome, New York March 22, 1984

Burton C. Seifert and Josephine R. Back had the following children:

      i.   Infant Seifert was born 12 April 1928 in Westernville, New York and died 12 April 1928 in Westernville, New York.[78] This child was a stillborn.

12. Susan Anna Seifert[3] (Charles Seifert[2], Augustus Isaac Seifert[1]) was born 28 October 1889 in Town of Lewis, New York and died 22 May 1963 in Buffalo, New York.[79] She married Henry Caterham *about* 1910. He was born 5 July 1894 and died in 1944 in Buffalo, New York.[80] Susan lived in Rome, New York and later moved to Buffalo, New York where she remained until her death.

Susan Anna Seifert and Henry Caterham had the following children:

      i.   Stillborn Caterham.

      ii.   Maria Caterham died at the age of 3 when she fell off a porch and broke her neck. She was the second child born.[81]

28.   iii.   William H. Caterham was born 16 November 1922 in Buffalo, New York and died 20 October 2001 in Amherst, New York.[82]

29.   iv.   Living Caterham

This photo of Susan Seifert Caterham was in the collection of Suellen Brewster and is being used with permission.

13. Lillian M. Seifert[3] (Charles Seifert[2], Augustus Isaac Seifert[1]) was born 19 August 1893 in Ava, New York[83] and died 23 June 1933 in Rome, New York.[84] She married Edward Frank Swancott 26 June 1911 in Rome, New York, the son of Thomas W. Swancott and Lettie Fox. He was born 16 August 1888 in Lee Center, New York and died 20 May 1955 in Lee Center, New York.[85] Lillian died in Rome Hospital, Rome, New York of pneumonia. She had attended Lee Center M.E. Church. She lived on Main Street in Lee Center, New York to the east of the Methodist Church. Behind the house was the Swancott sawmill. Edward had been in the saw mill and lumber business practically all his life. He assisted his grandfather, David Swancott, and his father, in their extensive lumbering business in Swancott Mills, New York, later owning and operating his own

---

[78] Rome Cemetery Records
[79] Family information from Marjorie Majerowski
[80] Family information from Marjorie Majerowski
[81] Family information from Marjorie Majerowski
[82] Obituary Amhurst, New York newspaper October 21, 2001
[83] Ava, New York Town Records
[84] New York State Vital Records, Albany, New York
[85] Obituary Rome, New York May 21, 1955

business. He served as Superintendent of Highways for the Town of Lee, New York from 1934 to 1940, and was a former chief of the Lee Center Volunteer Fire Department.
He also was a member of the Lee Center Methodist Church.

Swancott Home, Lee Center, New York from the collection of Suellen Brewster and used with permission.

Lillian M. Seifert and Edward Frank Swancott had the following children:
30. i. Marjorie Elizabeth Swancott was born 24 August 1913 in New York State and died 28 November 1997 in Middle Tennessee Medical Center, Murfreesboro, Tennessee.[86]
31. ii. Living Swancott

Photo of Lillian Seifert Swancott from the collection of Suellen Brewster and used with permission.

14. William Isaac Seifert[3] (Charles Seifert[2], Augustus Isaac Seifert[1]) was born 27 May 1899 in Point Rock, New York[87] and died 10 February 1962 in University Hospital, Ann Arbor, Michigan.[88] He married Ethel Adella Kent 5 July 1918 in Rome, New York. She was born 10 May 1897 in the Town of Lee, New York and died in September 1982 in Lansing, Michigan.[89] William lived most of his adult life in Michigan.

Photo of William Isaac Seifert and his wife, Ethel from the collection of Ruth Fogg and used with permission.

William Isaac Seifert and Ethel Adella Kent had the following children:
32. i. Living Seifert
33. ii. Living Seifert
34. iii. Living Seifert
35. iv. Jane Helen Seifert was born September 1923 in Rome, New York and died 29 July 1984 in Lansing Michigan.[90]
36. v. Living Seifert

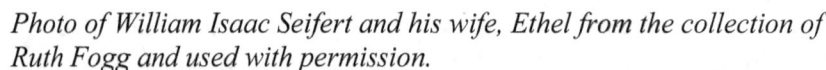

[86] Social Security Death Index from Ancestry.com
[87] New York State Vital Records, Albany, New York
[88] Obituary Ann Arbor, Michigan Newspaper February 11, 1962
[89] Social Security Death Index from Ancestry.com
[90] Social Security Death Index from Ancestry.com

37.   vi.   Living Seifert

38.   vii.   Betty Jo Seifert was born 18 January 1938 in Leslie, Michigan and died 23 August 1986 in Bradenton, Florida.[91]

15. Edwin Lyle Seifert[3] (Charles Seifert[2],Augustus Isaac Seifert[1]) was born 20 July 1904 in either Point Rock or Lee Center, New York[92]and died 8 September 1959 in Pasadena, California.[93]He married Dorothy Marguerete Joslyn *about* 1927, the daughter of Charles Elias Joslyn and Cora Belle Cooley. She was born 30 September 1909 in Vernon, New York and died 30 September 1974.[94]He married Julia Elizabeth (Betty) about 1933. Julia was born 15 May 1909 in New York State and died March 1978 in Van Nuys, Los Angeles, California.[95]Edwin, Betty and Shirley moved to Pasadena, California in July 1945. Edwin was a car salesman in Lansing, Michigan. In California he sold real estate for a while and then sold cars.

Edwin Lyle Seifert and Dorothy Marguerete Joslyn had the following child:

39.   i.   Shirley Seifert was born 2 February 1927 in Oneida, New York and died 18 Oct 2007 in Kingman, Arizona.[96]

Photo taken in 1951 of Edwin Lyle Seifert and his wife, Betty, from the collection of Suellen Brewster and used with permission.

Generation Four

16. George Marvin Bowman[4] (Susanna Etta Sifer[3], George Sifer[2], Augustus Isaac Seifert[1]) was born 30 June 1917 in Utica, New York and died 19 March 1987 in Utica, New York. For more on George Marvin Bowman, see Chapter Four.

George Marvin Bowman and Kathryn Lourdes McLoughlin had the following children:

40.   i.   Living Bowman

41.   ii.   Deborah Bowman was born 24 November 1950 in Utica, New York and died 25 September 2003 in Camp Lejeune, North Carolina.[97]She married twice. Both husbands are living and she had two children who are still living.

---

[91] Family information from Kari Fogg
[92] Family information from Shirley Kaelin
[93] California Death Index from Ancestry.com
[94] Family information from Shirley Kaelin
[95] California Death Index from Ancestry.com
[96] Social Security Death Index from Ancestry.com

18. Stuart D. Sherwood[4] (Ada Rivers[3], Margaret Seifert[2], Augustus Isaac Seifert[1]) was born
19 August 1908 in Rome, New York and died 26 April 1957 in Rome Hospital, Rome, New York.[98]He married Geraldine N. Roth 24 August 1929 in Toms River, New Jersey. She was born 28 October 1909.[99]

Stuart D. Sherwood and Geraldine N. Roth had the following children:
44.   i.   Living Sherwood
45.   ii.   Dale S. Sherwood was born 30 March 1935 in Rome, New York and died 25 March 2008 in New York State.[100]He was married 18 May 1957 in United Methodist Church, Lee, New York.[101]
46.   iii   Living Sherwood
           iv.   Living Sherwood

19. Kenneth J. Sherwood[4] (Ada Rivers[3], Margaret Seifert[2], Augustus Isaac Seifert[1]) was born 13 June 1912 in Rome, New York and died 13 August 1972 in Rose Hospital, Rome, New York.[102] He married Alcenia Martin in 1936 in Rome, New York. She died in 1967.[103]He married Dora (Dolly) Litz 17 June 1972 in Rome, New York. Kenneth was a truck driver for the highway department for 20 years. He was of the Baptist faith and a member of the American Federation of State, County and Municipal Employees, AFL-CIO. Alcenia Martin and Kenneth J. Sherwood divorced. They had six children all of whom are still living.

20. Helen Sherwood[4] (Ada Rivers[3], Margaret Seifert[2], Augustus Isaac Seifert[1]) was born 28 January 1922 in Rome, New York and died 30 November 1978 in Rose Hospital, Rome, New York.[104]She married Herbert F. Cutler 14 September 1940 in Rome, New York. She died 14 May 1964. Helen worked for Jet Cleaners and had lived at 307 W. Court Street Rome, New York at the time of her death. She had received her education at Rome Free Academy, Rome, New York.

Helen Sherwood and Herbert F. Cutler had the following children:
           i.   Living Cutler
           ii.   Living Cutler

---

[97] Prayer Card from funeral home in Camp Lejeune, North Carolina
[98] Obituary Rome, New York Newspaper April 27, 1957
[99] Birthdata.base.com
[100] Obituary Rome, New York Newspaper March 26, 2008
[101] Obituary Rome, New York Newspaper March 26, 2008
[102] Obituary Rome, New York Newspaper August 14, 1972
[103] Obituary of husbands in Rome, New York Newspaper August 14, 1972
[104] Obituary Rome, New York Newspaper December 1, 1978

iii.   William H. Cutler was born 8 September 1942 and died 8 January 1995 in Mount Airy, North Carolina.[105]

21. Eleanor C. Rivers[4] (George R. Rivers[3], Margaret Seifert[2], Augustus Isaac Seifert[1]) was born 29 July 1908 in New York State and died 19 July 2004 in Morrisville, New York[106]She married LeVerne Minor and lived in Chittenango, New York in 1955. Eleanor C. Rivers and LeVerne Minor had on child who is still living.

22. Marvin E. Gleasman[4] (Lena Rivers[3], Margaret Seifert[2], Augustus Isaac Seifert[1]) was born 2 December 1909 in Rome, New York and died 2 January 1971 in Rome, New York.[107]He married Mabel Northrup 12 May 1932 in Rome, New York, the daughter of Wesley Northrup and Cynthia Draper. She was born 10 April 1910 in Rome, New York and died 14 December 1985 at 2760 Lone Tree Road, Fallon, Nevada.[108]At one time Marvin owned Gleasman Oil of Rome, New York.

Marvin E. Gleasman and Mabel Northrup had the following children: living.
  i.   Living Gleasman
  ii.   Living Gleasman
  iii.   Living Gleasman
  iv.   Living Gleasman
47.   v.   Elizabeth Gleasman was born 21 October 1940 in Rome, New York and died 28 October 2003 in Rome Memorial Hospital, Rome, New York.[109]She was married 17 August 1962 in Zion Episcopal Church. She married a man named Hazlett.

23. Elmer Earl Gleasman Jr[4] (Lena Rivers[3], Margaret Seifert[2], Augustus Isaac Seifert[1]) was born 24 November 1912 in Rome, New York and died 14 March 1971 in Rome Hospital, Rome, New York.[110]He married Dorothy Seifert. She was born 25 November 1913 and died 20 October 2008 in Rome, New York.[111]Elmer Earl Gleasman Jr and Dorothy Seifert had two children, both of which are still living.

24. Arnold E. Gleasman[4] (Lena Rivers[3], Margaret Seifert[2], Augustus Isaac Seifert[1]) was born 24 January 1915 in Rome, New York and died 31 December 1997 in Elizabeth Hospital, Utica, New York.[112]He married Margaret Eva Thomas before 1933. She was born 9 January 1915.[113]He married Viola Podogrosi 6 September 1936 in Francis deSales

[105] Social Security Death Index from Ancestry.com
[106] Social Security Death Index from Ancestry.com
[107] Obituary Rome, New York Newspaper January 3, 1971
[108] Obituary Rome, New York Newspaper December 15, 1985
[109] Obituary Rome, New York Newspaper October 29, 2003
[110] Obituary Rome, New York Newspaper March 15, 1971
[111] Social Security Death Index from Ancestry.com
[112] Obituary Utica Newspaper January 1, 1998
[113] Family information from Kathleen Thomas

Church, Utica, New York. She was born 11 March 1914 in Holly, New York and died 17 September 2008 in East Springfield, New York.[114]Arnold had worked for Oneida Ltd. in Sherrill, New York and then for Hameline Dairy. He served in World War II.

Arnold E. Gleasman and Margaret Eva Thomas had the following child:
48.   i.   Richard Edward Gleasman was born 29 April 1933 and died 11 January 2003.[115]

Arnold E. Gleasman and Viola Podogrosi had the following children:
   i.   Living Gleasman
   ii.   Living Gleasman
   iii.   Living Gleasman
49.   iv.   Ann Gleasman was born 3 April 1948 in Utica, New York and died 12 October 2005 in Utica, New York.[116]

26. Patricia Schwertfeger[4] (Ida Rivers[3], Margaret Seifert[2], Augustus Isaac Seifert[1]) was born 20 May 1933 in Utica, New York and died 27 May 1993 in Oklahoma City, Oklahoma. She was married on 22 April 1961 in Utica, New York.[117]   Patricia Schwertfeger and her husband had three children who are still living.

27. Aletha I. Seifert[4] (Burton C. Seifert[3], Charles August Seifert[2], Augustus Isaac Seifert[1]) was born 19 August 1910 in Rome, New York and died 21 March 1984 in Rome Hospital, Rome, New York.[118]She married Ivan A. Joanis 16 January 1929 in St. Patrick's Church, Taberg, New York, the son of Frederick Joanis and Bertha Anderson. He was born 14 August 1909 in Washburn, Wisconsin and died 27 February 1990 in Rome Hospital, Rome, New York.[119]   Aletha graduated from Rome Free Academy. She was a member of St. Peter's Church, Rome, New York and a former member of the Women of the Moose. She had 18 grandchildren and 29 great-grandchildren at the time of her death as indicated in her obituary.   Aletha I. Seifert and Ivan A. Joanis had three children, all of whom are still living.

Photo of Aletha Seifert and her mother, Bertha L. Finster Seifert from the collection of Marlene Pcolar and used with permission

---

[114] Obituary Rome, New York Newspaper September 18, 2008
[115] Family information from Kathleen Thomas
[116] Obituary Utica Newspaper October 13, 2005
[117] Family information from Jeanne Miller
[118] Obituary Rome, New York Newspaper March 22, 1984
[119] Obituary Rome, New York Newspaper February 28, 1990

28. William H. Caterham[4] (Susan Anna Seifert[3], Charles August Seifert[2], Augustus Isaac Seifert[1]) was born 16 November 1922 in Buffalo, New York and died 20 October 2001 in Amherst, New York.[120] He married Evelyn Movalli 24 April 1948 in Buffalo, New York.   William was a graduate of Riverside High School and attended Bryant Stratton Business Institute and the University of Buffalo. He served in the Army Air Forces during World War II. He went to work in 1948 for his family's business, Con-O-Lite Burial Vault Company, and was   plant manager until the company was sold. From 1967 until his death, he was a sales representative for Frigid Fluid Company, which supplies embalming chemicals and sundries to upstate New York funeral directors. In the 1970's and early 1980's William also owned and operated two liquor stores, Kenwood Liquor Store on Elmwood

Photo of William H. Caterham from the collection of Suellen Brewster and used with permission.

Avenue in Kenmore, New York and Sheridan Park Liquor Store on Sheridan Drive in the Town of Tonowanda, New York. From 1974 until his death he also operated Frank Movalli and Associated, a cemetery monument and memorial dealership. He was a member of Gregory the Great Catholic Church in Amherst, New York. William H. Caterham and Evelyn Movalli had three children all of which are still living.

30. Marjorie Elizabeth Swancott[4] (Lillian M. Seifert[3], Charles August Seifert[2], Augustus Isaac Seifert[1]) was born 24 August 1913 in New York State and died 28 November 1997 in Middle Tennessee Medical Center, Murfreesboro, Tennessee.[121] She married Winfield Hodierne. He was born in 1909.[122] She had also been married George E. Grunner and Ken Fisher. She was married Harlen Robert Morey at the time of her death. Marjorie is buried in the Evergreen Cemetery in Lee Center, New York. Marjorie lived in Lee Center in 1933. The 1930 Census said she was the head of the household and her sister lived with her under the name of Swancott. She moved to Murfreesboro, Tennessee about 1976. Her obituary did not mention any children.

35. Jane Helen Seifert[4] (William Isaac Seifert[3], Charles August Seifert[2], Augustus Isaac Seifert[1]) was born 16 September 1923 in Rome, New York and died 29 July 1984 in Lansing, Michigan.[123] She married Rex Eugene Wood 4 April 1942 in at the home of her parents, Stockbridge, Michigan, the son of Arthur Wood and Blanche Wilbur. He was

[120] Obituary Amhurst, New York Newspaper October 21, 2001
[121] Obituary Rome, New York Newspaper November 29, 1997
[122] 1920 Rome, New York Census
[123] Family information from Kari Fogg

born 7 June 1921 in Leslie, Michigan and died 28 November 1975 in Lansing, Michigan.[124]Jane had been a member of Mt. Hope Presbyterian Church, Lansing, Michigan. Rex Eugene Wood had been a carpenter. He graduated from Leslie High School in 1941 and was a veteran of World War II, Army Infantry. Later he worked for Oldsmobile, Lansing, Michigan. Rex was in a very serious motorcycle accident in Lansing, Michigan about 1969. Jane Helen Seifert and Rex Eugene Wood had three children all of who may still be living.

38. Betty Jo Seifert[4] (William Isaac Seifert[3], Charles August Seifert[2], Augustus Isaac Seifert[1]) was born 18 January 1938 in Leslie, Michigan and died 23 August 1986 in Bradenton, Florida.[125]She was married 14 November 1954 in Brandon, Florida.[126]

39. Shirley Seifert[4] (Edwin Lyle Seifert[3], Charles August Seifert[2], Augustus Isaac Seifert[1]) was born 2 February 1927 in Oneida, New York[127]and died 18 October 2007 in Kingman, Arizona.[128] She married Alfred Joseph Kaelin 28 October 1946 in Pasadena, California, the son of Joseph Kaelin and Theresa Bussey. He was born 29 August 1925 in Rome, New York and died 22 October 1996 in Glendora, California.[129]Shirley moved to Lansing, Michigan after recovering from spinal meningitis after World War II. There she lived with her father and step-mother. She moved with them to California about 1948 where she met and married her husband Al Kaelin.

Al Kaelin was a Southern California and Arizona nurseryman. He graduated from Westmoreland High School, Westmoreland, New York and enlisted in the U.S. Navy as a radioman. He served aboard the USS El Dorado from 1943-1946. He was discharged in Southern California following the end of World War II. He met and married his wife, Shirley in Pasadena and they made their first home in Azusa. Mr. Kaelin started to work at Tuttle Brothers Nursery in Altadena. He attended night classes at Pasadena City College for four years and then went to work for Paul Gaines Nursery in Temple City, California where it did business at that location for over 25 years. In 1978 the nursery moved to LaVerne, California. When Mr. Gaines died, he willed his share of the nursery to Al. When Vida Huggs, Gaines' business partner died, she left her portion of the company to Al. He was active in the California Association of Nurserymen. After being located in LaVerne for three years, in 1981, Mr. Kaelin sold the nursery and retired near Kingman, Arizona. In 1986 he opened A & J Nursery only to close it down in 1992 for health reasons. In 1994 he and Shirley sold the acreage and moved into the city of Kingman, Arizona. It was in late 1995 when the family entered Mr. Kaelin into a nursing

---

[124] Family information from Kari Fogg
[125] Family information from Kari Fogg
[126] Family information from Kari Fogg
[127] Family information from Shirley Kaelin
[128] Social Security Death Index from Ancestry.com
[129] Family information from Shirley Kaelin

home in Glendora because of the dementia (previously diagnosed as Alzheimer's disease), where he died. He was married for 50 years and had four children, nine grandchildren and four great-grandchildren.

Chapter Four

Descendants of John Baumann Sr.

Generation One

1. John Baumann Sr[1] was born *about* 1826 in Saxony Germany and died about 1864. According to the family story, John left his family and never returned and his wife grieved herself to death. He married Martha (Martina Kohlhammer) about 1850. She was born *about* 1825 in Saxony, Germany and died 1 April 1868 in Utica, New York.[1] John Baumann came to Utica in 1853 as he was first listed in the 1853 Utica, New York City Directory as a cart man. At that time he was living at 23 S. Hamilton Street, Utica, New York.

The following is a death record on Martina Baumann taken from St. Joseph's Church Records, Utica, New York:

Translation of the above record: Martina Baumann, born Kohlhammer in the year 1868 on April 1, entered into the sacrament of death, Martina Kohlhammer, wife of Joannis Bauman, buried April 3, 1868 St. Joseph's Cemetery.

The 1855 Utica, New York Census, Ward Six indicates John Bouman was born in Germany. The 1860 Utica Census has his name spelled Bomann and states he was born

---

[1] St. Joseph's Church Death Records, Utica, New York

in Switzerland and was listed a laborer and was not a naturalized citizen. The 1865 Utica, New York Census indicates John's wife was a widow. In the 1870 Utica Census, the children were living by themselves with no parents at all and the oldest child was 18 years old. Their name was spelled Bauman. John's children were all baptized at St. Joseph's Church, Utica, New York and his name was as listed as Joannis Baumann.

The 1855 Utica Census listed Martha Bouman as born in Germany. This census also states she was not a naturalized citizen and had been living in Utica for four years. The 1860 Utica Census listed her name as Martina Bomann born in Switzerland. The 1865 Census lists her name as Marthina Bouman born in Germany and a widow. The variations in her place of birth could come from boarder changes in Europe during this period of time. No evidence has been found to determine if John and Martha came to America together or married after they arrived.

John Baumann Sr. and Martha (Martina) Kohlhammer had the following children:

2.   i.   Margaret Bowman was born 15 August 1851 in Utica, New York[2] and died 12 July 1921 in Utica, New York.[3]

3.   ii.   Mary Bowman was born 19 August 1853 in Utica, New York[4] and died 12 November 1932 in Utica, New York.[5]

4.   **iii.**   **George Bowman** was born 16 November 1856 in Utica, New York[6] and died 30 January 1898 in Jersey City, New Jersey.[7]

5.   iv.   John H. Bowman was born in February 1859 in Utica, New York[8] and died 27 December 1931 at 1216 Schuyler St., Utica, New York.[9]

Generation 2

2. Margaret Bowman[2] (John Baumann Sr.[1]) was born on 15 August 1851 in Utica, New York[10] and died 12 July 1921 in Utica, New York.[11] She married Jacob Wolff *about* 1872 in Utica, New York. He was born 1 August 1843 in Utica, New York[12] and died 20 January 1923 at 1317 Maple St., Utica, New York.[13]

---

[2] St. Joseph's Church Death Records, Utica, New York
[3] Forest Hill Cemetery Records, Utica, New York
[4] St. Joseph's Church Death Records, Utica, New York
[5] Obituary Utica Newspaper November 13, 1932
[6] St. Joseph's Church Death Records, Utica, New York
[7] New Jersey State Death Certificate
[8] 1900 Utica, New York Census, Ward Two
[9] Obituary Utica Newspaper December 28, 1931
[10] St. Joseph's Church Death Records, Utica, New York
[11] Forest Hill Cemetery Records, Utica, New York
[12] Obituary Utica Newspaper January 21, 1923
[13] Obituary Utica Newspaper January 21, 1923

The following is the baptismal record of Margaret Bowman taken from St. Joseph's Church records, Utica, New York:

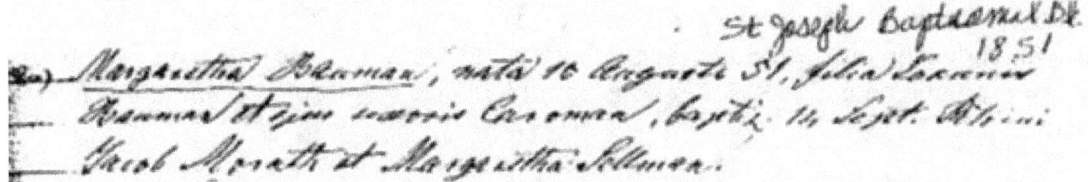

Translation of the above record: Margaretha Bauman, born August 15, 1861, daughter of Joannis Bauman and his wife Caroman, baptized September 14, 1851. Godparents were Jacob Morath and Margaretha Sellman.

Margaret was a member of St. Joseph's Church, Utica, New York and lived at 1002 Cleveland Avenue, Utica, New York at the time of her death. Jacob had worked at Utica Heater Company as a molder. He was a member of Zion's Lutheran Church, Utica, New York.

Margaret Bowman and Jacob Wolff had the following children:

6. i. Minneta (Minnie) Wolff was born 2 January 1873 in Utica, New York[14] and died 21 January 1960 in Utica, New York.[15]

7. ii. Ida Wolfe was born 24 January 1877 in Utica, New York and died 25 October 1955 in Utica, New York[16]

8. iii. Albert John Wolff was born 20 April 1880 in Utica, New York[17] and died 16 April 1954 in Rochester, New York.[18]

 iv. Cora L. Wolff was born 9 October 1882 in Utica, New York[19] and died 1 October 1971 in Genesee Nursing Home, Utica, New York.[20]She married Richard Watkins 29 October 1917, the son of Orville and Addie Watkins. He was born 20 January 1881 in Chittenango, New York and died 3 March 1959 in Utica, New York.[21] Cora was a seamstress for many years and was a member of the Old St. Luke's Episcopal Church, Utica, New York. Richard was employed by Niagara Mohawk Power Corporation as an operator in the gas department for 40 years. He lived in Utica most of his life and was a member of Dryer Memorial Methodist Church, Utica, New York.

9. v. Clarence Leonard Wolff was born 25 February 1885 in Utica, New York[22] and died 17 May 1953 in Rochester, New York.[23]

---

[14] Family information from Kate Hagan
[15] Obituary Utica Newspaper January 22, 1960
[16] Obituary Utica Newspaper October 26, 1955
[17] Family information from Kate Hagan
[18] Family information from Kate Hagan
[19] Family information from Diane Holland
[20] Family information from Diane Holland
[21] Obituary Utica Newspaper March 4, 1959
[22] Family information from Kate Hagan
[23] Obituary Utica Newspaper May 18, 1953

vi.   Leroy R. Wolff was born 27 May 1892 in Utica, New York[24]and died 15 November 1957 in Utica, New York.[25]Leroy married Nellie Evans 3 October 1918 in Utica, New York, the daughter of John Evans and Jennie Davis. She was born 7 November 1889 in Utica, New York and died 7 January 1950 in Utica, New York.[26] Leroy attended the old 19th Street School in Utica, New York. He was employed by the Partlow Corporation and was a communicant of St. Luke's Episcopal Church, Utica, New York.

3. Mary Bowman[2] (John Baumann Sr.[1]) was born 19 August 1853 in Utica, New York[27] and died 12 November 1932 in Utica, New York.[28]She married Leonard Kunkel in 1886 in Utica, New York, son of George Kunkel and Mary Kunkel. He was born 9 December 1857 in Coleman's Mills, New York[29]and died 30 March 1931 at 1212 Maple Street, Utica, New York.[30]Mary and Leonard were members of St. Joseph's Church, Utica, New York. Leonard lived most of his life in Utica and was employed for many years by the Department of Public Works.

The following is the baptismal record of Mary Bowman taken from St. Joseph's Church records, Utica, New York:

Translation of above record:
Maria Bauman born August 19, 1853, daughter of Joannis Bauman and his wife Martina Hamer. Baptized September 25, 1853. Godparents were Jacob Morath and his wife Catharina.

Mary Bowman and Leonard Kunkel had the following children:
i.   George H. Kunkel was born 1 December 1888 in Utica, New York[31]and died 22 December 1948 in Memorial Hospital, Utica, New York.[32]George was a First Company Quartermaster Corp World War I, Private. He was employed as a painter by

---

[24] Obituary Utica Newspaper November 16, 1957
[25] Obituary Utica Newspaper November 16, 1957
[26] Obituary Utica Newspaper January 8, 1950
[27] St. Joseph's Church Baptismal Records, Utica, New York
[28] Obituary Utica Newspaper November 13, 1932
[29] Obituary Utica Newspaper March 31, 1931
[30] Obituary Utica Newspaper March 31, 1931
[31] Obituary Utica Newspaper December 23, 1948
[32] Obituary Utica Newspaper December 23, 1948

Lionel Kempf, contractor and was a member of Painters Union 69, AFL, and a veteran of World War I. He was also a member of St. Joseph's Church.

      ii.   Nelson L. Kunkel was born 17 October 1893 in Utica, New York[33]and died 11 February 1970 in the Genesee Nursing Home, Utica, New York.[34]Nelson had attended Utica, New York schools and had worked as a self employed carpenter. He never married.

      iii.   Erma M. Kunkel was born 23 December 1895 in Utica, New York[35]and died 24 January 1969 in St. Luke's Memorial Hospital, New Hartford, New York.[36]She was married Edward Delavan VanSlyck 11 April 1936 in Rome, New York, the son of William H. VanSlyck and Mary A. Launt. He was born 14 December 1897 in Binghamton, New York and died 31 March 1957 in Utica, New York.[37]Erma attended Utica, New York Schools and was employed as a legal stenographer for the Leon Arthur law firm in Utica for many years. She retired in 1949.

4. George Bowman[2] (John Baumann Sr.[1]) was born 16 November 1856 in Utica, New York[38] and died 30 January 1898 in Jersey City, New Jersey.[39]He married Rose Hahn *about* 1878, the daughter of Augustus Hahn and Anna (Hannah) Grub. She was born 25 May 1854[40]and died 15 September 1892 at 150 Schuyler St. Utica, New York[41]of

Typhoid Malaria Fever. She was a member of the Zion's Lutheran Church, Utica, New York. After Rose's death, George married Bridget McArt 19 April 1894 in St. Patrick's Church, Jersey City, New Jersey. She was born April 1858 in Ireland[42]and died 26 February 1904 in Jersey City, New Jersey. She immigrated to America in 1879 from Ireland. The marriage of George Bowman and Bridget McArt was held at St. Patrick's Church, Jersey City, New Jersey. The witnesses were John Strangler and Ella McCabe. Father P. Hennessey was the officiating priest.[43]

Photo of George Bowman taken from the "Saturday Evening Post" in Utica, New York.

[33] World War I draft registration from Ancestery.com
[34] Obituary Utica Newspaper February 12, 1970
[35] Obituary Utica Newspaper January 25, 1965
[36] Obituary Utica Newspaper January 25, 1965
[37] Obituary Utica Newspaper April 1, 1957
[38] St. Joseph's Church Baptismal Records, Utica, New York
[39] New Jersey State Death Certificate
[40] New Forest Cemetery Records, Utica, New York
[41] New Forest Cemetery Records, Utica, New York
[42] 1900 Jersey City, New Jersey Census
[43] FHC Film 1403369, St. Patrick's Church Records, Jersey City, New Jersey

The 1880 Utica, New York Census showed George married to Rose and they had one child, David age 6 months. They lived on South Hamilton Street, Utica, New York and George's occupation was listed as an Iron Molder. Land records indicate that in 1883 August Hahn sold to George Bowman and his wife, property located on Hamilton Street, Utica, New York.

The following is the baptismal record of George Bowman taken from St. Joseph's Church records, Utica, New York:

Translation of above record: Georgius born Nov. 12, 1856, baptized December 26, 1856, legitimate son of Johannis Bauman and Martina Colammer. Godparents were Georgio Sellman and Margaretha Schram.

George Bowman and Rose Hahn had the following children:

    i.   David Bowman was born May 1880 in Utica, New York.[44] I do not think David lived to be very old as he was never listed in another census and his brothers never mentioned him.

    ii.   Edward Bowman was born June 1881 in Utica, New York[45] and died 29 October 1938 in Fort Plain, New York.[46] Edward never married.

Photo of Edward Bowman in the author's collection.

Utica Observer Dispatch, October 29, 1938:
A man found dead in a highway ditch between Nelliston and St. Johnsville this morning was believed to be Edward Bowman of Jersey City, New Jersey. Two of his brothers live in Utica. Believed to have been struck by a car operated by a hit and run driver while hitch-hiking to Utica to visit his brother Walter J. Bowman. Victim 58 years old had a cut on his head and bruises on his arms and hands. His clothes were torn and his false teeth were found lying near the body. Edward, who had been a frequent visitor to Utica, had sent his traveling bag to Utica after writing his brother that he would pay him a visit.

---

[44] 1880 Utica, New York Census
[45] 1900 Utica, New York Census
[46] New Forest Cemetery Records, Utica, New York

The American Railway Express receipt for the bag was found in the man's pocket and this, with the fact that the man had false teeth and had planned to visit Utica, led Utica relatives to believe that he was Edward Bowman. He had been unemployed for several years. Relatives expected to view the body during the day to make certain about the identification. The body was discovered at 8:15 a.m. by Francis O'Brien, St. Johnsville, driver of an oil truck. He stopped and investigated when he saw a hat lying on the shoulder of the highway. The body lay in a pool of water in the ditch. O'Brien notified Sheriff Gerald Nellis, Fonda, who began an investigation. A piece of some sort of vehicle was found nearby and this with injuries suffered by the man led the authorities to believe that he was a victim of a hit and run driver. Coroner Clark Congdon of Fort Plain was notified and he ordered the body removed in the Graves funeral parlors in Fort Plain for an autopsy. Besides the brother mentions, Mr. Bowman is survived by three other brothers, George Bowman, Utica, Thomas, Jersey City, Noble, Albany. Also a sister Viola, Jersey City. His body was interred November 1, 1938 in Utica, New York, New Forest Cemetery.

11.   iii.   Walter James Bowman was born 6 October 1883 in Syracuse, New York and died 4 November 1945 in Utica, New York.[47]

12.   iv.   Noble Philip Bowman was born 4 July 1886 in Utica, New York and died 18 October 1951 in Memorial Hospital, Albany, New York.[48]

13.   v.   Viola F. Bowman was born 14 August 1889 in Utica, New York and died 25 March 1970 in Albany, New York.

14.   vi.   **George Francis Bowman** was born 18 December 1891 in Jersey City, New Jersey[49] and died 8 January 1957 in Utica, New York.[50]

A photo of the Bowman children taken around 1915. From left to right in the back row are: Thomas, Noble, George, Walter. Viola and Edward are seated in the front row. Photo was in the author's collection.

[47] Obituary Utica Newspaper
[48] Family information from Virginia Krichbaum
[49] FHC Film 1403369, St. Patrick's Church Records, Jersey City, New Jersey
[50] Obituary Utica Newspaper January 9, 1957

George Bowman and Bridget McArt Bowman had the following children:

     i.   Anne Florence Baumann was born 28 February 1897 in Jersey City, New Jersey and died 18 May 1899 in Jersey City, New Jersey.[51]

10.   ii.   Thomas McArt Aloysius Bowman was born 31 August 1898 in Jersey City, New Jersey and died 22 July 1964 in Jersey City, New Jersey.[52]

5. John H. Bowman[2] (John Baumann Sr.[1]) was born in February 1859 in Utica, New York[53] and died 27 December 1931 in 1216 Schuyler St., Utica, New York.[54] He married Margaret Trester in 1881, the daughter of Peter and Margaret Trester. She was born 10 September 1860 in Utica, New York[55] and died 15 March 1937 at 1216 Schuyler Street. Utica, New York.[56] John had attended St. Joseph's School and was a member of St. Joseph's Church in Utica, New York. He had worked for Standard Oil Company for 23 years.

John H. Bowman and Margaret Trester had the following children:

     i.   George Lewis Bowman was born 21 November 1881 in Utica, New York[57] and died 29 January 1924 in Utica, New York.[58] George had been educated in Utica schools and was a member of St. Joseph Church. He did not have children.

16.   ii.   Hattie Bowman was born 13 July 1883 in Utica, New York[59] and died 22 January 1917 in Utica, New York.[60]

17.   iii.   Catherine Bowman was born 7 October 1885 in Utica, New York[61] and died 13 November 1941 at Evans Road, Marcy, New York.[62]

     iv.   Mary A. Bowman was born 6 April 1891 in Utica, New York[63] and died 6 April 1917 in Utica, New York.[64] Mary lived at 1216 Schuyler Street, Utica, New York at the time of her death. She was a member of St. Joseph's Church, Utica, New York.

17.   v.   Minnie Bowman was born in April 1894 in Utica, New York[65] and died 22 August 1917 at 1001 Walnut Street, Utica, New York.[66]

     vi.   John Edward Bowman was born 11 March 1894 in Utica, New York[67] and died 11 October 1942 in Marcy State Hospital, Marcy, New York.[68] John served in the US

---

[51] Holy Name Cemetery Records, Jersey City, New Jersey

[52] Family information from Virginia Krichbaum

[53] 1900 Utica, New York Census, Ward Two

[54] Obituary Utica Newspaper December 28, 1931

[55] Obituary Utica Newspaper March 15, 1937

[56] Obituary Utica Newspaper March 15, 1937

[57] World War I draft registration from Ancestery.com

[58] Obituary Utica Newspaper January 30, 1924

[59] Obituary Utica Newspaper January 23, 1917

[60] Obituary Utica Newspaper January 23, 1917

[61] New York State Vital Records

[62] Obituary Utica Newspaper November 14, 1941

[63] Obituary Utica Newspaper April 7, 1917

[64] Obituary Utica Newspaper April 7, 1917

[65] 1900 Utica, New York Census, Ward Two

[66] Obituary Utica Newspaper August 23, 1917

[67] World War I draft registration from Ancestery.com

Navy during WWI as a Seaman. He had attended St. Joseph's Church and School in Utica, New York and had worked for the Bossert Corporation for many years. John never married and was committed to the alyssum in Utica, New York.

18.   vii.   Margaret C. Bowman was born 12 December 1896 in Utica, New York[69] and died 6 April 1954 in 1216 Schuyler Street, Utica, New York.[70]

        viii.   Albert Bowman was born 17 July 1897 in Utica, New York[71] and died 21 September 1959 in Ogdensburg, New York[72] Albert attended Utica schools and was a member of St. Joseph's Church. He never married.

6.   Minneta (Minnie) Wolff [3](Margaret Bowman[2], John Baumann Sr[1]) was born 2 January 1873 in Utica, New York[73] and died 21 January 1960 in Utica, New York.[74] She married George Wesley Creaser 15 September 1897 in Utica, New York, the son of Thomas Creaser and Olivia Gorham. He was born 30 August 1869 in Plattsburg, New York[75] and died 2 December 1942 in Clinton, New York.[76] Later she married Charles Sidney Thayer in 1934. He was born 9 August 1877[77] and died in April 1966 in Whitesboro, New York.[78] Minnie is buried in Crown Hill Memorial Park, Kirkland, New York. She was educated in Utica, New York Schools and attended St. George's Episcopal Church, Chadwicks, New York.

Photo of Minneta Wolff, George Creaser and sons, Lester and Kenneth from the collection of Kate Hagan and used with permission.

Minneta (Minnie) Wolff and George Wesley Creaser had the following children:

19.   i.   Lester J. Creaser was born 27 August 1899 in New York State[79] and died 19 November 1955 in Ossining, New York.[80]

20.   ii.   Kenneth George Creaser was born 31 August 1904 in Utica, New York[81] and died 26 January 1982 in Faxton Hospital, Utica, New York.[82]

---

[68] Obituary Utica Newspaper October 12, 1942

[69] Obituary Utica Newspaper April 7, 1954

[70] Obituary Utica Newspaper April 7, 1954

[71] Obituary Utica Newspaper September 22, 1959

[72] Obituary Utica Newspaper September 22, 1959

[73] Family information from Kate Hagan

[74] Obituary Utica Newspaper January 22, 1960

[75] Obituary Utica Newspaper December 3, 1942

[76] Obituary Utica Newspaper December 3, 1942

[77] Family information from Kate Hagan

[78] Social Security Death Index from Ancestry.com

[79] Family information from Kate Hagan

[80] Family information from Kate Hagan

[81] Obituary Utica Newspaper January 26, 1982

[82] Obituary Utica Newspaper January 26, 1982

7. Ida Wolfe [3](Margaret Bowman[2], John Baumann Sr[1]) was born 24 January 1877 in Utica, New York and died 25 October 1955 in Utica, New York.[83] She married William David Tremblay 6 November 1906 in St. Joseph's Church, Utica, New York, [84]the son of John Tremblay. He was born 7 January 1879 in Canada[85]and died 4 January 1943 at Sunset Ave. Utica, New York.[86]

Ida Wolfe and William David Tremblay had the following child:

    i.   LaVere C. Tremblay was born 6 August 1907 in New York State[87] and died 9 March 1987 in Dallas, Texas.[88] He married Margaret Hayes 15 June 1932. She was born 1 Jul 1908 and died 9 Mar 2006.[89]

8. Albert John Wolff[3](Margaret Bowman[2], John Baumann Sr[1]) was born 20 April 1880 in Utica, New York[90]and died 16 April 1954 in Rochester, New York.[91] He married Isabelle 13 June 1904. She was born in 1881 in New York State.

Albert John Wolff and Isabelle had the following children:

21.   i.   Vivian Wolff was born 18 June 1905[92]and died 27 November 1985 in Rochester, New York.[93]

    ii.   Cleone V. Wolff was born 18 July 1908[94] and died 31 December 1987 in Rochester, New York.[95]She married Philip J. Siebold in 1927 and later married Mr. Prevost.

22.   iii.   Harold K. Wolff was born 21 September 1919[96]and died 30 January 1984 in Rochester, New York.[97]

9. Clarence Leonard Wolff[3](Margaret Bowman[2], John Baumann Sr[1]) was born 25 February 1885 in Utica, New York[98]and died 17 May 1953 in Rochester, New York.[99] He married Elizabeth Ann Ward 26 September 1913 in Collingwood, Simone, Canada,[100]

---

[83] Obituary Utica Newspaper October 26, 1955

[84] Wedding Announcement Utica Newspaper

[85] World War I draft registration from Ancestery.com

[86] Death Announcement Utica Newspaper January 5, 1943

[87] Social Security Death Index from Ancestry.com

[88] Social Security Death Index from Ancestry.com

[89] Social Security Death Index from Ancestry.com

[90] Family information from Kate Hagan

[91] Obituary Rochester, New York Newspaper April 17, 1954

[92] Social Security Death Index from Ancestry.com

[93] Obituary Rochester, New York Newspaper November 28, 1985

[94] Social Security Death Index from Ancestry.com

[95] Obituary Rochester, New York Newspaper January 1, 1988

[96] Social Security Death Index from Ancestry.com

[97] Obituary Rochester, New York Newspaper January 31, 1984

[98] Family information from Kate Hagan

[99] Obituary Rochester, New York Newspaper May 18, 1953

[100] Ontario, Canada Marriage Records from Ancestry.com

the daughter of James Ward and Elisa Adams. She was born in 1882 in Ontario, Canada and died 7 January 1950 in Rochester, New York.[101]

Clarence Leonard Wolff and Elizabeth Ann Ward had the following child:

23.   i.   Roy Leonard Wolff was born 11 July 1914 in Rochester, New York[102] and died 28 May 1994 in Lady Lake, Florida.[103]

10. Thomas McArt Aloysius Bowman[3](George Bowman[2], John Baumann Sr.[1]) was born 31 August 1898 in Jersey City, New Jersey and died 22 July 1964 in Jersey City, New Jersey.[104] Thomas was baptized in St. Patrick's Church, Jersey City, New Jersey; his godparents were Arthur Bowman and Mary McArt. The priest who baptized him was Father J.A. Keingh. He married Ethel Anderson 1 June 1927 in New York City, New York. She was born 27 September 1900 in New York City, New York[105] and died 15 June 1998 in Dover, Delaware.[106]

Thomas McArt Aloysius Bowman and Ethel Anderson had the following children:

        i.   Joseph Bowman was born 19 November 1929 in Greenville Hospital, Jersey City, New Jersey[107] and died 21 November 1929 in Jersey City, New Jersey.[108]

24.   ii.   Living Bowman

25.   iii.   Living Bowman

11. Walter James Bowman[3](George Bowman[2], John Baumann Sr.[1]) was born 6 October 1883 in Syracuse, New York and died 4 November 1945 in Utica, New York.[109] Walter was baptized in St. Patrick's Church, Jersey City, New Jersey and his godfather was Joseph Gordon.[110] The priest performing the baptismal was Father J.P. Shaheen. He married Mary T. Hage 12 June 1907 in St. Joseph's Church, Utica, New York, the daughter of John Hage and Ruttina Schafer. She was born 3 May 1884 in Utica, New York[111] and died 26 September 1972 in St. Luke's Hospital Memorial Hospital, New Hartford, New York.[112] Walter was employed as a polisher at the Savage Arms for 30 years. He was a member of St. Joseph's Church, Utica, New York. Mary attended Utica, New York schools. She lived in Utica and Whitesboro, New York most of her life, but

---

[101] Obituary Rochester, New York Newspaper January 8, 1950

[102] Family information from Diane Holland

[103] Social Security Death Index from Ancestry.com

[104] Family information from Tom Bowman

[105] Family information from Tom Bowman

[106] Family information from Tom Bowman

[107] Family information from Tom Bowman

[108] Family information from Tom Bowman

[109] Obituary Utica Newspaper November 5, 1945

[110] FHC Film #1403369 St. Patrick's Church, Jersey City, New Jersey

[111] Social Security Death Index from Ancestry.com

[112] Obituary Utica Newspaper September 27, 1972

the last two years she lived in Schenectady with her daughter, Evelyn. She was a member of St. Joseph's and St. Patrick's Church and St. Mary's Auxiliary of the Knights of St. John both in Utica, New York.

Photo of Walter James Bowman from the author's collection.

 Walter James Bowman and Mary T. Hage had the following children:

26.   i.   Walter John Bowman was born 30 November 1908 and died 9 May 1972 in Utica, New York. [113]

27.   ii.   Eleanor Bowman was born 26 July 1911 in Utica, New York and died 29 November 1977 in St. Luke's Hospital, Utica, New York.[114]

28.   iii.   Evelyn Anna Bowman was born 12 January 1915 in Utica, New York and died 25 February 2003 in Resurrection Nursing Home, Castleton, New York.[115]

12. Noble Philip Bowman[3] (George Bowman[2], John Baumann Sr.[1]) was born 4 July 1886 in Utica, New York and died 18 October 1951 in Memorial Hospital, Albany, New York. Noble was baptized James Noble on May 30, 1896 in St. Patrick's Church, Jersey City, New Jersey and his sponsor was Thomas Clark.[116] He married Clara Theresa Everhart on 22 May 1912 in St. John's Lutheran Church, Albany, New York. She was born 14 May 1887 in Albany, New York and died 16 November 1965 in Albany, New York.[117]

Photo of Noble Bowman, his wife Clara and his daughters, Bernice and Erma in the author's collection.

Noble Philip Bowman and Clara Theresa Everhart had the following children:

29.   i.   Bernice Carolyn Bowman was born 29 January 1914 in Albany, New York[118] and died September 17, 1985 in St. Peter's Hospital, Albany, New York.[119]

          ii.   Noble Richard Bowman was born 22 January 1916 in Albany, New York and died 16 June 1916 in Albany, New York.

          iii.   Living Bowman

30.   iv.   Living Bowman

---

[113] Obituary Utica Newspaper May 10, 1972
[114] Obituary Utica Newspaper November 30, 1977
[115] Obituary Utica Newspaper February 26, 2003
[116] FCH Film #1403369 St. Patrick's Church, Jersey City, New Jersey
[117] Family information from Virginia Krichbaum
[118] Family information from Virginia Krichbaum
[119] Family information from Virginia Krichbaum

13. Viola F. Bowman[3] (George Bowman[2], John Baumann Sr.[1]) was born 14 August 1889 in Utica, New York and died 25 March 1970 in Albany, New York. Viola was baptized Mary Viola 1 December 1895 at St. Patrick's Church, Jersey City, New Jersey and her sponsor was Mary Louise Clark.[120] The christening records said her date of birth was 6 August 1889. She married Henry Valet 3 July 1920 in Albany, New York.[121]He was born in 1881 in Germany.[122]

Photo of Viola F. Bowman in author's collection.

Viola F. Bowman Valet and Henry Valet had the following children:

31. i. Henry Andrew Valet was born 5 August 1921 in Albany, New York and died 21 February 1995 in Colonie, New York.[123]

32. ii. Edward George Valet was born 13 November 1922 in Albany, New York and died 25 May 1983 in Albany, New York.[124]

33. iii. Frederick George Valet was born 17 March 1926 and died 12 June 1991.[125]

  iv. Living Valet

34. v. Andrew Herman Valet was born 12 August 1932 in Albany, New York.[126]

14. George Francis Bowman[3] (George Bowman[2], John Baumann Sr.[1]) was born 18 December 1891 in Jersey City, New Jersey[127]and died 8 January 1957 in Utica, New York[128]George was baptized Joseph George on December 1, 1895 at St. Patrick's Church, Jersey City, New Jersey and his sponsor was Annie Clark.[129]He married Susanna Etta Sifer 8 September 1916 in St. Joseph's Church, Utica, New York, the daughter of

George Francis Bowman and Susanna Etta Sifer in 1915 about a year before they were married. Photo is in the author's collection.

---

[120] FCH Film #1403369 St. Patrick's Church, Jersey City, New Jersey

[121] Family information from Virginia Krichbaum

[122] 1930 Albany, New York Census, District 11

[123] Family information from Virginia Krichbaum

[124] Family information from Virginia Krichbaum

[125] Family information from Virginia Krichbaum

[126] Family information from Virginia Krichbaum

[127] FHC Film #143369 St. Patrick's Church, Jersey City, New Jersey

[128] Obituary Utica Newspaper January 9, 1957

[129] FCH Film #1403369 St. Patrick's Church, Jersey City, New Jersey

George Sifer and Mary Johanna Schmidt. She was born on 17 July 1893 in Ava, New York[130] and died 20 June 1966 in Utica, New York.[131] For more information on Susanna Etta Sifer, see Chapter Three.

The 1900 Jersey City, New Jersey Census placed George living with his stepmother in Jersey City, New Jersey. He was listed as Joseph and stated he was born in New Jersey. The 1910 Utica Census showed George living with this brother, Walter, in Utica, New York and said he was born in New York. In the 1920 and 1930 Census, he was married and living with his in-laws in Utica, New York and said he was born in New York. My mother always said there was a question as to where he was born as his mother died a few months after he was born and his father died when he was seven years old. My mother told me her father was in an orphanage for a period of time when he was a child. She does not know if he was in the orphanage in Utica or Jersey City.[132]

George "Baldy" Bowman was my grandfather and I remember him as being a lot of fun. In fact, when I was about three or four years old he took me to "The Barn" which was a local bar that he would frequent. He would put me up on the bar stool and I would say to the bartender "Give me a short one" and he would pour beer into a shot glass and give it to me. I also remember him calling my family "the farmers" because we had moved out of the city into the country. We were far from farmers, but that's the name he gave us.

I remember my grandfather having a garden and growing gladiolas. My mother tells the story that my grandfather sold these gladiolas to the people he worked with. She remembers almost every day in the summer; he would get on the city bus and with his bouquets of gladiolas and go into work. When he returned home, he gave my mother the money. She in turn gave it to her mother for safe keeping. My grandfather knew if he kept the money in his pocket he would spend it frivolously. He worked until he was 65 years of age, so he could collect the maximum in his Social Security. One week after he retired, he died of a massive heart attack. That was sad as he had so many plans for retirement.

Obituary taken from the Utica, New York newspaper January 9, 1957:

> *George F. Bowman, 65, of 226 North Genesee Street died unexpectedly in his home, Jan. 8, 1957, a week after he retired from the Bossert Division of the Rockwell Spring & Axle Co. Dr. Preston Clark, corner, said death was due to heart attack. Bowman was born in Utica, December 18, 1891, On Sept. 16, 1916, he married Etta Sifer in St. Joseph's Church. He was a member of St. Peter's Church. For the past 23 years he had been employed at the*

---

[130] Social Security Death Index from Ancestry.com
[131] Obituary Utica Newspaper June 21, 1966
[132] Verbal information from Gertrude Bowman Emery Weyneth

Bossert Division, retiring Jan. 1, 1957. Besides his wife he leaves a son, G. Marvin Bowman; a daughter, Mrs. Gordon Emery, Sauquoit; a brother Thomas, Jersey City, NJ; a sister Mrs. Violet Valet, Albany; four grandchildren and several nieces and nephews. The funeral will be held Friday morning from the Langdon Funeral Chapel, 630 Varick St., and from St. Peter's Church. Burial will be in St. Joseph's Cemetery.

George Francis Bowman and Susanna Etta Sifer had the following children:

35.   i.   George Marvin Bowman was born 30 June 1917 in Utica, New York and died 19 March 1987 in Utica, New York.[133]

36.   ii.   **Gertrude Marie Bowman**

15. Hattie Bowman[3] (John H. Bowman[2], John Baumann Sr.[1]) was born 13 July 1883 in Utica, New York[134]and died 22 January 1917 in Utica, New York.[135]She married Harry Dingman in November 1906 in St. Joseph's Rectory, Utica, New York, the son of Charles Dingman and Zenia Kettle. He was born in 1883 in Fort Plain, New York[136]and died 9 November 1975 in Bogyne Hospital, Syracuse, New York.[137] Hattie attended St. Joseph's School and was a member of St. Joseph's Church, Utica, New York. Harry had been employed as a retail sales clerk by Fort Plain stores. He also owned and operated a Fort Plain IGA store and later was employed by Beechnut of Canajoharie, retiring in 1955.

Hattie Bowman and Harry Dingman had the following child:

37.   i.   Cameta Dingman was born 20 January 1909 in Utica, New York[138]and died 23 October 1982 in St. Joseph's Hospital, Syracuse, New York.[139]

16. Catherine Bowman[3] (John H. Bowman[2], John Baumann Sr.[1]) was born 7 October 1885 in Utica, New York[140]and died 13 November 1941 in Evans Road, Marcy, New York.[141]She married William Edward Tournay in August 1916.[142]He was born 10 October 1887 in West Schuyler, New York.[143]Catherine had lived her entire life in Utica until the last two years, when she moved to Marcy, New York. She was a member of St. Joseph's Church, Utica, New York.

---

[133] Obituary Utica Newspaper March 20, 1987
[134] Obituary Utica Newspaper January 23, 1917
[135] Obituary Utica Newspaper January 23, 1917
[136] Obituary Utica Newspaper November 10, 1975
[137] Obituary Utica Newspaper November 10, 1975
[138] Social Security Death Index from Ancestry.com
[139] Obituary Utica Newspaper October 24, 1982
[140] New York State Vital Records
[141] Obituary Utica Newspaper November 14, 1941
[142] Obituary Utica Newspaper November 14, 1941
[143] World War I draft registration from Ancestery.com

Catherine Bowman and William Edward Tournay had the following children:
  i.   Edward Tournay was born in 1921.[144]
  ii.   Katherine Tournay was born in 1924.[145]

17. Minnie Bowman[3] (John H. Bowman[2], John Baumann Sr.[1]) was born in April 1894 in Utica, New York[146] and died 22 August 1917 at 1001 Walnut Street, Utica, New York.[147] She married Julius E. Breithaupt about 1911, the son of Julius Breithaupt and Emma Sittig. He was born 28 November 1883 in North Utica, New York[148] and died 6 May 1943 at Greatview Avenue, New Hartford, New York.[149] Minnie attended Utica schools and was a member of St. Joseph's Church, Utica, New York. For a number of years Julius operated the Geneto Electric Company. For 16 years prior to his death, he had lived in New Hartford, New York. He had also been employed as an electrician with the New York State Highway Department. He attended the Episcopal Church.

Minnie Bowman and Julius E. Breithaupt had the following child:
i.   Margaret E. Breithaupt was born 19 September 1916 in Utica, New York[150] and died 22 January 1978 at 6 Balsam Crescent, New Hartford, New York[151] She married Chester Kaleta in1938 in New Hartford, New York.[152] He was born 29 March 1916 and died in February 1973 in New Hartford, New York.[153] Margaret was not mentioned her father's obituary in 1943 or the 1930 Census. Margaret retired from Univac.

18. Margaret C. Bowman[3] (John H. Bowman[2], John Baumann Sr.[1]) was born 12 December 1896 in Utica, New York[154] and died 6 April 1954 in 1216 Schuyler St., Utica, New York.[155] She married Malvin A. Partello 10 November 1920 in St. Joseph's Church Rectory, Utica, New York.[156] He was born 13 May 1896 in Morehouseville, New York.[157] He died 1 December 1963 in St. Luke's Hospital Memorial Hospital, New Hartford, New York.[158] Margaret was a member of St. Joseph's Church, Utica, New York and its Alter Society. Malvin was a graduate of the College of the City of New York. He had been employed by the State Division of Naval Affairs. He served with Company B, 107th Infantry in World War I and received the Silver Star and the Purple Heart. He was commander of the Disabled American veterans of World War I and past commander of

---

[144] 1930 Utica, New York Census
[145] 1930 Utica, New York Census
[146] 1900 Utica, New York Census, Ward Two
[147] Obituary Utica Newspaper August 23, 1917
[148] Obituary Utica Newspaper May 7, 1943
[149] Obituary Utica Newspaper May 7, 1943
[150] Social Security Death Index from Ancestry.com
[151] Obituary Utica Newspaper January 23, 1978
[152] Obituary Utica Newspaper January 23, 1978
[153] Social Security Death Index from Ancestry.com
[154] Obituary Utica Newspaper April 7, 1954
[155] Obituary Utica Newspaper April 7, 1954
[156] Wedding Announcement, Utica Newspaper
[157] Social Security Death Index from Ancestry.com
[158] Social Security Death Index from Ancestry.com

the 27th Division Association., the Charles Adrean Post, the Utica Post of the American Legion and a member of the Civil Service Association of New York State.

Margaret C. Bowman and Malvin A. Partello had the following children:
  i.   Living Partello
  ii.   Living Partello.
  iii.   William G. Partello was born in 1926.[159]He was not mentioned in his father's obituary in 1963, so perhaps he was not alive at that time.

Generation Four

19. Lester J. Creaser[4] (Minneta (Minnie) Wolff[3], Margaret Bowman[2], John Baumann Sr.[1]) was born 27 August 1899 in New York State[160]and died 19 November 1955 in Ossining, New York.[161]He married Elizabeth Pattonin in 1925.

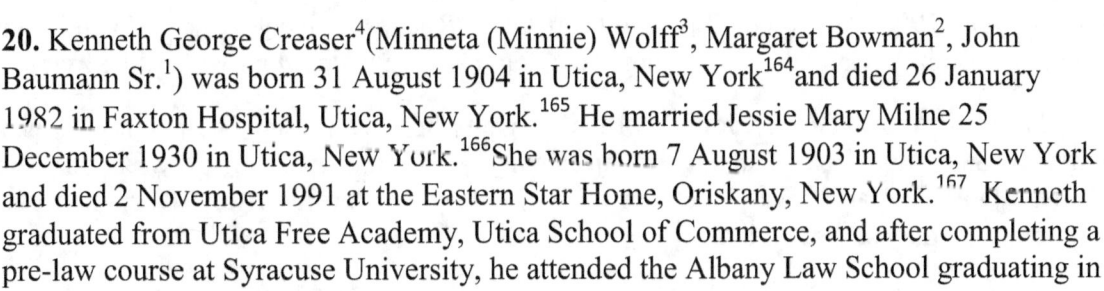

Lester J. Creaser and Elizabeth Patton had the following child:
  i.   Edward T. Creaser was born in 1929 in Massachusetts or New York[162] and died 6 June 1959 in W. Newton, Massachusetts.[163]He was a school teacher.

Photo of Lester J. Creaser from the collection of Kate Hagan and used with permission.

20. Kenneth George Creaser[4](Minneta (Minnie) Wolff[3], Margaret Bowman[2], John Baumann Sr.[1]) was born 31 August 1904 in Utica, New York[164]and died 26 January 1982 in Faxton Hospital, Utica, New York.[165] He married Jessie Mary Milne 25 December 1930 in Utica, New York.[166]She was born 7 August 1903 in Utica, New York and died 2 November 1991 at the Eastern Star Home, Oriskany, New York.[167] Kenneth graduated from Utica Free Academy, Utica School of Commerce, and after completing a pre-law course at Syracuse University, he attended the Albany Law School graduating in

---

[159] 1930 Utica, New York Census
[160] Family information from Kate Hagan
[161] Family information from Kate Hagan
[162] Family information from Kate Hagan
[163] Family information from Kate Hagan
[164] Obituary Utica Newspaper January 27, 1982
[165] Obituary Utica Newspaper January 27, 1982
[166] Obituary Utica Newspaper January 27, 1982
[167] Obituary Utica Newspaper November 3, 1991

1930. He practiced law in the Utica and Whitesboro area until his retirement in 1978. He was a member of the Whitesboro Presbyterian Church and served as a Trustee and Elder. For many years he was active in the Republican Party of the Town of Whitestown and the County of Oneida. He was an organizer of and the first President of the Whitestown Kiwanis in 1951. He was a member of Amicable Lodge No. 664, F & AM Ziyara Temple, Shrine Club of Greater Utica, Scottish Rite, and the Yahnundasis Golf Club.

Photo of Kenneth G. Creaser from the collection of Kate Hagan and used with permission.

Jessie graduated from Utica Free Academy and Oswego State Teacher's College. She was an elementary school teacher in the Utica and Whitesboro Central School Systems and for many years, taught kindergarten in the Yorkville and Harts Hill Elementary Schools. She was a member of the Whitesboro Presbyterian Church, Oriskany Chapter #524 O.E.S., Whitestown Genetaska Club, Whitestown Home Bureau, New York State and Whitesboro Teacher's Association, and was an avid doll collector, belonging to local doll clubs. Kenneth George Creaser and Jessie Mary Milne had one child who is still living.

Photo of Jessie Milne Creaser from the collection of Kate Hagan and used with permission.

21. Vivian Wolff[4] (Albert John Wolff[3], Margaret Bowman[2], John Baumann Sr.[1]) was born 18 June 1905[168] and died 27 November 1985 in Rochester, New York.[169] She married Thomas Moran. Vivian Wolff and Thomas Moran had one child who may still be living.

22. Harold K. Wolff[4] (Albert John Wolff[3], Margaret Bowman[2], John Baumann Sr.[1]) was born 21 September 1919[170] and died 30 January 1984 in Rochester, New York.[171] He married Doris.   Harold was a veteran of World War II. Harold K. and Doris had two children who may still be living.

23. Roy Leonard Wolff[4] (Clarence Leonard Wolff[3], Margaret Bowman[2], John Baumann Sr.[1]) was born 11 July 1914 in Rochester, New York[172] and died 28 May 1994 in Lady

---

[168] Social Security Death Index from Ancestry.com
[169] Obituary Rochester, New York Newspaper November 28, 1985
[170] Social Security Death Index from Ancestry.com
[171] Obituary Rochester, New York Newspaper January 31, 1984
[172] Social Security Death Index from Ancestry.com

Lake, Florida.[173]He married Joyce Roskrow Thomas 22 May 1947 in Rochester, New York.[174]She was born 8 January 1915 in Port Hope, Ontario, Canada[175]and died 17 June 1990 in Leesburg, Florida[176]Roy Leonard Wolff and Joyce Roskrow Thomas had four children who may still be living.

26. Walter John Bowman[4] (Walter James Bowman[3], George Bowman[2], John Baumann Sr.[1]) was born 30 November 1908 and died 9 May 1972 in Utica, New York[177]Walter was married three times. He first married Stella, then he married Jennie and lastly he married Carolyn A. Hubbard in 1967 in Utica, New York, the daughter of Charles A. Hubbard and Catherine Lowery. She was born 7 March 1937 in Utica, New York and died 27 September 2004 in St. Joseph's Nursing Home, Utica, New York.[178]Walter John Bowman and Carolyn A. Hubbard had five children who may still be living.

Photo of Walter John Bowman and his Uncle George Francis Bowman from the author's collection.

27. Eleanor Bowman[4] (Walter James Bowman[3], George Bowman[2], John Baumann Sr.[1]) was born 26 July 1911 in Utica, New York. She died 29 November 1977 in St. Luke's Hospital, Utica, New York. She married Laurence T. Manch 25 August 1930, the son of Anthony and Mary Manch. He was born 25 January 1909 in Keene, New Hampshire [179] and died 6 November 1946 in Utica, New York.[180]Eleanor later married Anthony Cimino in 1949. Eleanor was educated at St. Joseph's School and Utica Free Academy in Utica, New York. For many years she was employed by the Utica Knitting Company. She was a member of St. Joseph-St. Patrick's Church, Utica, New York. Eleanor Bowman and Laurence T. Manch had one child who may still be living.

28. Evelyn Anna Bowman[4] (Walter James Bowman[3], George Bowman[2], John Baumann Sr.[1]) was born 12 January 1915 in Utica, New York. She died 25 February 2003 at the Resurrection Nursing Home, Castleton, New York.[181] She married Arnold Christian Rieben 1 September 1930 in St. Joseph's Church, Utica, New York, the son of Christian Rieben and Rosa Louise Ludy.

---

[173] Social Security Death Index from Ancestry.com
[174] Family information from Diane Holland
[175] Family information from Diane Holland
[176] Social Security Death Index from Ancestry.com
[177] Obituary Utica Newspaper May 10, 1972
[178] Obituary Utica Newspaper September 28, 2004
[179] Obituary Utica Newspaper November 7, 1946
[180] Obituary Utica Newspaper November 7, 1946
[181] Obituary Utica Newspaper February 26, 2003

He was born 16 December 1908 in New York City and died 6 April 1986 in Castleton, New York.[182]She was raised in Utica, New York and moved to Castleton in 1974. Evelyn was a communicant of Sacred Heart Church in Castleton, New York. Evelyn Anna Bowman and Arnold Christian Rieben had one child who is still living.

Photo of Evelyn Bowman taken in 1941 from the author's collection.

29. Bernice Carolyn Bowman[4] (Noble Philip Bowman[3], George Bowman[2], John Baumann Sr.[1]) was born 29 January 1914 in Albany, New York and died[183] September 17, 1985 in St. Peter's Hospital, Albany, New York.[184]She married Roland Archie Allen 27 April 1935 in St. John's Lutheran Church, Albany, New York.[185] He was born 19 September 1909 in Nova Scotia, Canada and died 20 November 1968 in Albany, New York.

Bernice Carolyn Bowman and Roland Archie Allen adopted the following children:
> i.   Living Allen
> ii.   Mary Linda Allen was born 27 July 1950 and died 5 August 1995.[186]

31. Henry Andrew Valet[4] (Viola F. Bowman[3], George Bowman[2], John Baumann Sr.[1]) was born 5 August 1921 in Albany, New York and died 21 February 1995 in Colonie, New York.[187]He married Helen Pricilla Preusser 15 January 1949.[188]She was born 18 September 1928.[189]Henry Andrew Valet and Helen Pricilla Preusser had five children who may still be living.

32. Edward George Valet[4] (Viola F. Bowman[3], George Bowman[2], John Baumann Sr.[1]) was born 13 November 1922 in Albany, New York and died 25 May 1983.[190]He married Alma Gokey 11 January 1950.[191] She was born 4 March 1930.[192] Edward George Valet and Alma Gokey had two children who may still be living.

33. Frederick George Valet[4] (Viola F. Bowman[3], George Bowman[2], John Baumann Sr.[1]) was born 17 March 1926 and died 12 June 1991.[193]He married Jean Ellen Whittle in 1945

[182] Obituary Utica Newspaper April 9, 1986
[183] Family information from Virginia Kirchbaum
[184] Family information from Virginia Kirchbaum
[185] Family information from Virginia Kirchbaum
[186] Family information from Virginia Kirchbaum
[187] Family information from Virginia Kirchbaum
[188] Family information from Virginia Kirchbaum
[189] Family information from Virginia Kirchbaum
[190] Family information from Virginia Kirchbaum
[191] Family information from Virginia Kirchbaum
[192] Family information from Virginia Kirchbaum
[193] Family information from Virginia Kirchbaum

in England. He later married Elaine Connors in Troy, New York. She was born in 1932 and died 1 November 1998.[194]

Frederick George Valet and Jean Ellen Whittle had the following children:
  i.   Living Valet
  ii.   Frederick H. Valet was born 24 December 1948 in Albany, New York, and died 29 August 1997 in Georgia.[195]He was married in 1977 in California.[196]
  iii.   Living Valet
Frederick George Valet and Elaine Connors had two children who are still living.

35. George Marvin Bowman[4] (George Francis Bowman[3], George Bowman[2], John Baumann Sr.[1]) was born 30 June 1917 in Utica, New York and died 9 March 1987 in Utica, New York.[197]He married Kathryn Lourdes McLoughlin 17 February 1940 in St. John's Church, New Hartford, New York, the daughter of Arthur McLoughlin and Dorothy Bryan. She was born in 1921 in Utica, New York and died 9 April 1972 in Utica, New York.[198] He later married Mildred Gaylord Wood Christ 29 July 1961 in Utica, New York.[199]She was born 2 June 1909 and died 9 August 1981 in Utica, New York.[200] George worked at GE for several years until his retirement.

George Marvin Bowman and Kathryn Lourdes McLoughlin had the following children:
  i.   Living Bowman
  ii.   Deborah Bowman was born 24 November 1950 in Utica, New York and died 25 September 2003 in Camp Lejeune, North Carolina.[201]She married twice and had two living children by the first husband.

George Marvin Bowman and his sister, Gertrude Marie.
Photo in the author's collection.

36. Gertrude Marie Bowman[4] (George Francis Bowman[3], George Bowman[2], John Baumann Sr.[1]) was born 14 January 1920 in Utica, New York. Gertrude was baptized in St. Joseph's Church, Utica, New York and her godparents were Gertrude Servatius and Herbert Schmidt. She married Gordon Charles Emery 26 April 1941 in St. Joseph's

---

[194] Family information from Virginia Kirchbaum
[195] Family information from Catherine Valet
[196] Family information from Virginia Kirchbaum
[197] Obituary Utica Newspaper March 10, 1987
[198] Obituary Utica Newspaper April 10, 1972
[199] Wedding Announcement Utica Newspaper
[200] Schuyler Corners Cemetery, Schuyler, New York
[201] Funeral Service Program

Church, Utica, New York,[202] the son of Alcide F. Emery and Mary Agnes Foote. He was born 29 March 1915 in Utica, New York[203] and died 9 October 1981 in Utica, New York.[204] After Gordon's death, Gertrude married Howard E. Weyneth 1 August 1987 in St. Patrick's Church, Clayville, New York,[205] the son of Leigh Weyneth and Ina Myers. Howard was born 30 January 1917 in Seneca Castle, New York[206] and died 13 April 2004 in Blake Hospital, Bradenton, Florida.[207] Gertrude is still living at the time of the writing of this book. She is my mother and has given permission to list her in this book. She worked for Chicago Pneumatic for several years, retiring in 1974 and now lives in Bradenton, Florida.

Gordon C. Emery served in the United States Navy during World War II. He worked for Chicago Pneumatic Tool Company for many years retiring in 1973. He lived in Bradenton, Florida and Sauquoit, New York until his death.

The following wedding announcement was appeared in the Utica, New York newspaper:

Announcement has been made of the marriage of Miss Gertrude Marie Bowman, daughter of Mr. and Mrs. George F. Bowman, 231 N. Genesee Street and Gordon C. Emery, son of Mr. and Mrs. Alcide Emery, 1131 Downer Ave. The ceremony took place April 26 in St. Joseph's Church with the Rev. Gabrial Kohlbrenner officiating. Miss Bernadine Caldwell was the maid of honor, and Harold Emery, brother of the bridegroom, the best man. The ushers were Marvin Bowman, brother of the bride, and DeWitt Harmon. The bride wore a princess style gown of white slipper satin and a fingertip veil caught with orange blossoms. She carried a bouquet of white roses. The maid of honor wore a princess style gown of pink slipper satin with matching tiara and veil. She carried a bouquet of pink roses. A wedding breakfast was served in the home of the bride followed by a reception. The couple will live in Schenectady where the bridegroom is connected to the General Electric Company.

Wedding photo of Gertrude Marie Bowman in the author's collection.

---

[202] Wedding Announcement Utica Newspaper
[203] Social Security Death Index from Ancestry.com
[204] Obituary Utica Newspaper October 10, 1981
[205] Family information from Gertrude Bowman
[206] Social Security Death Index from Ancestry.com
[207] Obituary Bradenton, Florida Newspaper April 14, 2004

Howard E. Weyneth was a salesman for Metropolitan Insurance for 40 years. He had been a member of the American Legion and Seneca Lake Yacht Club in Geneva, NY. He was an Army Air Force veteran of World War II and received the Victory Medal and the Good Conduct Medal. He had 15 grandchildren and 6 great grandchildren at the time of his death.

Gertrude Bowman (still living) and Gordon Charles Emery are my parents and I have decided to list with permission my mother, my sister and myself in this book.

      i.   **Karen Susanne Emery** married Martin Jay Dwyer in 1968 and has one daughter, two grandsons and two step grandsons.

      ii.   Gaile Joyce Emery married Michael John Shimon in 1979 and has one daughter and one grandson.

37. Cameta Dingman[4] (Hattie Bowman[3], John H. Bowman[2], John Baumann Sr.[1]) was born 20 January 1909 in Utica, New York[208] and died 23 October 1982 in St .Joseph's Hospital, Syracuse, New York.[209] She married Leroy Wendell Richardson. Cameta had lived in Syracuse for 40 years. She was a member of the Onondaga Hill United Methodist Church. Cameta Dingman and Leroy Wendell Richardson had two children who may still be living.

---

[208] Social Security Death Index from Ancestry.com
[209] Obituary Utica Newspaper October 24, 1982

Stories Meme told me!

Gertrude was named "Meme" by her first grandchild. She was interviewed in November 2008 and these are the stories she told.

Gertrude Marie Bowman

I was born, Gertrude Marie Bowman, on January 14, 1920 at 1106 Sunset Avenue, Utica, New York. I was named after my godmother, Gertrude Servatius.

My parents, George Francis Bowman and Susanna Etta Sifer met through my mother's girlfriend. Her girlfriend invited my mother to meet her new boyfriend. Apparently he liked my mother better than his new girlfriend as they began dating after that and he became my father.

Photo of Gertrude Bowman 1920 in the author's collection.

Childhood

When I was 21 months old, my brother, Marvin, and I came down with polio. At that time, homes with polio patients were quarantined because of the polio. Before I had polio, I could talk and walk, but after I recovered, I had difficulty talking for a period of time. The words just would not come out right. My brother, at age four, had a more severe case of polio than I did. His speech was not affected, but one of his legs was almost useless and he had to have a back and leg brace. Our mother rubbed both of our legs several times a day with olive oil which she kept warm on the back of the stove. She would take us to the clinic, where and she was told she was doing a wonderful job with her kids. Many of the kids contacting polio would never walk again. Marvin was able to walk, but always had a limp.

I remember always having running water and electricity. My chores as a young child included making my bed and dusting for my grandmother. My mother made all of my dresses and once a year my grandmother would buy me a dress and that would be my best dress for the year. I learned to knit and embroidery from my grandmother. The first thing I embroidered was a butterfly and I was very proud of my accomplishment. In fact, I rode my bicycle down the street waving the embroidered butterfly.

I roller skated every Saturday morning with my friend Lawrence, who was my age. I couldn't pronounce Lawrence so I called him "Nawnie". He went to the public school and I was going to a Catholic school. The Catholic schools didn't have kindergarten, so I went with Lawrence to the public school occasionally.

I liked to read books such as the Bobsey twins, and enjoyed going to the library to pick out other books to read. I sewed clothes for my dolls and played with them. I had a box that my father put string across and I hung the doll clothes in the make shift doll closet. The little closet was full of clothes. My grandmother helped me with my sewing.

Photo of Gertrude and Marvin about 1927 in the author's collection.

My best friend was Jane Smithers. Jane's mother was not a very neat housekeeper. We would go to Jane's house and raise cane by jumping on the beds, etc. It never bothered Jane's mother. We played store in their dining room by turning the chairs and the table over. We had a great time. One time, Jane's little brother Buddy told the rag man that he could take the mattress that his mother had airing out on the front porch. His mother came out on the porch just in time to save the mattress from the rag man.

My father taught my brother and me how to swim. We went to Nine Mile Creek and went swimming there.

Down on the Farm

My most memorable times were when my family, including my grandparents, lived on the farm in Maynard, New York. I was 10 years old at the time. We raised chickens and had a dog named King. They delivered eggs to Faxton Hospital and many other locations in the City of Utica. My grandparents bought the farm when my grandfather retired. They lived downstairs in the house and we lived upstairs.

Photo of the chicken farm in Maynard, New York taken in 1931 in the author's collection.

My Father

When I was born, my father, George Francis Bowman, worked at the Globe Mill in Utica. He worked there until it closed down. He was out of work for a while in the early 1930's. When the family lived on the farm, he worked for Wheel Works in Utica and rode his bike to work. I think he may have gotten laid off and was out of work again eventually being hired by Bossert's in Utica. He worked there until he retired in December 1956. He had a garden and raised vegetables and gladiolus. The family nicknamed him the "Gladiolus King". He must have gone bald very young as I do not remember him with hair. The family called him "Baldy". My most vivid image of my father was when he would get mad at Marvin and me, take off his belt as if he was going to whip us and end up making us laugh.

My Mother

My mother, Etta Sifer, went to work in the mill after we moved from the farm to North Genesee Street. Sometime after 1940, she went to work at the Hurst Dress Shop on Genesee Street in Utica, New York. She worked there as an alteration lady until she became ill in 1966.

Photo of George Francis Bowman and Susanna Etta Sifer about 1915 in the author's collection

My Grandparents

I loved my grandparents "they were everything to me". I went to their house on Saturdays and clean for my grandmother and bake for my grandfather. My grandfather would say "I like the food that Gertie's cooks". He especially liked my apple kuchen. He worked for the Kellogg Lumber Company delivering lumber by horse and wagon. When he would stop by the house, I would look out the window and feel sorry for the horses because they did not have a hat and coat on. Occasionally my grandfather would take my brother and me for a ride in the wagon. He worked seven days a week and would have to be at work early in the morning.

Photo of George and Mary Sifer about 1944 in the author's collection.

My grandmother was a beautiful seamstress sewing for many of the wealthy people in Utica making wedding gowns and fancy dresses. She had a sewing room in her apartment where she did her sewing. She would stay up until two in the morning sewing. Before my grandmother was married, she was a governess for two children at the Park Avenue home of George L. Roberts, a nephew of Ellis H. Roberts, then U.S. Treasurer. She traveled considerably with the Roberts' family, spending summers in the Catskills. She later spent three years in Kansas City working as a dressmaker.

Family

My parents spent their evenings with Marvin and me. One favorite pass time was when my father would set up a boxing ring by wrapping rope around chairs. Then my brother and I would get in the ring and try to knock each other down. It was lots of fun. The family got a radio when I was a young girl. I remember sitting in front of the radio with Marvin and listening to Santa Claus.

Sunday mornings the family would go to church together at St. Joseph's Church in Utica and in the afternoon, we would enjoy a nice Sunday dinner.

My family went to a camp in Morehouseville. My mother asked my brother and me to go out and pick blueberries. I did not want to pick blueberries, so I said to my brother. "I've got an idea! We can fill the buckets half full with dirt and then pick blueberries and put them on top and it won't take us so long." When we returned with the buckets full, our mother dumped the blueberries out in the sink and all the dirt came out too. She was not very happy with Marvin and me.

Photo of Marvin and Gertrude about 1926 in the author's collection.

Relatives

Aunt Mary and Uncle Walt were one of my favorite relatives. My father would take me and my brother to their house every Sunday morning after church. In the summer he would pull us in the cart and in the winter he would pull us in a sleigh. We would play the player piano singing "Bye Bye Blackbird" having a wonderful time. Aunt Mary and Uncle Walt would come to my home every Friday night and they would play cards and talk politics. I particularly remember them discussing Social Security.

Often in the summer I traveled to Albany to visit my cousins, Irma, Bernice and Virginia. Their father, Noble Bowman, worked for the railroad as a conductor, so I would ride the train to Albany with him. I would normally spend about two weeks with them in the summer loving every minute of the stay.

Holidays

My family spent Christmas and holidays with my grandparents. I remember Thanksgiving when my grandmother would bring out the good china and all the good food we would have. One Christmas I remember receiving a doll from my parents and the doll carriage from my grandparents. In the carriage there was also a wrist watch from my Uncle George. When I saw the watch I said to my grandmother "Oh, Grandma I got a witch watch and it ticks."

Photo of the family Christmas tree in the author's collection.

At Easter, Easter baskets were hidden in my grandmother's house. We would have a big Easter dinner together.

On the Fourth of July my brother and I had small firecrackers. Aunt Midge, Uncle Noble, Irma, Bernice and Virginia would come from Albany for the weekend. We would all sit out on the porch and set off firecrackers. Then we would all go to Aunt Mary's and Uncle Walt's and celebrate at their house.

I remember birthdays being celebrated with my grandparents. My mother always made a cake, and we would have cake and ice cream and open presents in my grandmother's home.

I remember going to family reunions for the Seifert family in West Leyden, New York. We played games which included three legged race, etc.

School Days

I didn't really like school very much. I went to St. Joseph's School through eighth grade and to Utica Free Academy for high school. I had to walk to school unless I was lucky, someone's father would give me a ride. I was very sick in my first year of high school and ended up with an infection in my mouth causing me to lose my front tooth. My favorite teacher, Mrs. George, came to visit me at my home while I was out sick. I was active in the Knights of St. John's Drill Team as a teenager.

Photo of Gertrude while active in the Knights of St. John's Drill Team in the author's collection.

My contribution

I contributed to the family income by babysitting after I graduated from Utica Free Academy. Earning $12 a week, I gave all but a dollar to my mother. Later I went to work for Divine Brothers in Utica until I married and moved to Schenectady.

The Funny Five

When I was a freshman in high school, I and four other girls organized the "Funny Five". We called ourselves that because every time we got together all we did was laugh and have fun. The girls were Bernie Caldwell, Frannie Angier, Jeanne Schwertfeger and Theresa Heidelberger. When we were 16 years old, we had a card party to raise money so we could go to Jeanne's parent's camp at Sylvan Beach for a week in the summer.

Following a meeting to discuss what we would have to eat, two of the girls went to the store and ordered the food. My Uncle George went over to the store to pick up the order. When we arrived at the camp and looked in the bags, it was not the food we ordered. My Uncle had picked up the wrong order. We laughed and laughed and cooked the food we had. The group stayed to together until the girls all got married. Later on in life when the girls were all widows we reunited and started meeting for lunch. That went on for several years, and at this time Jeanne and I are the only two still alive.

Photo of "The Funny Five" taken about 1935 in the author's collection.

How I met Gordon Emery

I went with my girlfriend, Tess to where Tess's boyfriend, Ray, was playing basketball. Gordon was on the same team. He asked someone about me. The next Saturday evening, I went roller skating with my girlfriend, Bernie. Gordon was there but not roller skating. He came over to see me and offered to take me home. When I got home, I told my mother, "Oh Mom, I just met this wonderful guy". My mother asked a little bit about him. She was not happy because she had never heard me rave about anyone before and she was worried that this would be the one, and it was. After that we began to date. One evening when we went out, before we went into the restaurant, Gordon asked me to marry him. He told me we couldn't get married right away because he didn't have job. He gave me an engagement ring the following Christmas. He went to a school to learn to be a mechanic and actually didn't have a job when we got married, but soon after he got hired by General Electric in Schenectady.

We were married April 26, 1941 and went to Niagara Falls for our honeymoon. Gordon borrowed his father's car and off we went. We stayed with my cousin, Evelyn and Arnie Rieben as they were living in the Niagara Falls area at the time.

Shortly after we were married, World War II broke out and Gordon enlisted in the United States Navy. I took him to Albany where he was inducted into the Navy. While we were waiting we were standing under a ledge of a building and all of a sudden a pigeon from above pooped right on Gordon's head. We decided right there and then that he would remain safe during the war; it worked as he was never sent out of the country. While he was in boot camp I went back to Utica to stay with my parents. Gordon called one day to tell me he would be going through New York City on the train and there would be a two hour layover. So I immediately made arrangements to meet him there, packed a bag of clothes including several pair of shoes and got on the train arriving in New York City only to discover he was not there. I called my father back in Utica and learned Gordon called him to tell him there had been a change and his layover was in Philadelphia instead of New York. I was very disappointed and got the next train back to Utica. My uncle

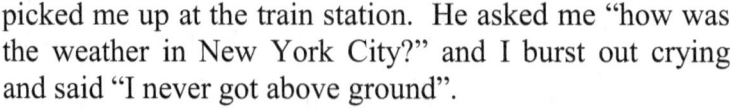

picked me up at the train station. He asked me "how was the weather in New York City?" and I burst out crying and said "I never got above ground".

Photo of Gordon Charles Emery in 1944 in the author's collection.

In January of 1945 Gordon was sent to San Diego with the understanding that his unit would be deployed. After he arrived in San Diego, he found out he would be staying in the States for a while, so he called me and I went out to join him. Wearing my muskrat coat, I left Utica, New

York in early January 1945 in below zero temperatures. My mother was sobbing at the train station. I rode the train to Chicago where I had to change trains and train stations. I met a couple of sailors on the train who offered to help me get there and I boarded the train to Los Angeles. It took five days to get there. When I arrived in Los Angeles, I discovered the next train to San Diego was full and they were only letting service men and their families on. I could get on a train the following morning, so I spent the night in the Los Angeles train station. Meanwhile Gordon was waiting for me in San Diego. When I did not get off the last train, he slept in the train station all night waiting for me while I was sleeping in the Los Angeles train station. The next morning I was able to get the first train out, which again was full, but they let me sit on my suitcase. Finally I arrived in San Diego where it was 80 degrees so I was carrying my muskrat coat. Gordon looked at me and said "Gee, you look like hell". We found a room to live in and had a

memorable time in San Diego. Throughout the remainder of our 40 years together, I remember Gordon saying every time we had a big snow storm "Gertrude why did we ever leave San Diego?" I have to admit I wondered that myself some times. I worked in the airplane factory during our stay in San Diego. After the war ended in 1945, Gordon was discharged from the Navy and we boarded the train back to Utica, New York on Christmas Day 1945.

Gertrude and Gordon in California.
Photo in the author's collection

Gordon and I had 40 years together and raised two daughters. We lived in Sauquoit, New York for most of our married years. We retired and spent our winters in Bradenton, Florida.

Chapter Five

Descendants of Augustus Hahn

Generation One

1. Augustus Hahn[1] was born 15 January 1825 in Hanover, Germany[1] and died 4 May 1908 in Deerfield, New York.[2] He married Anna (Hannah) Grub in 1851 in St. Paul's Church in Fort Plain, New York.[3] She was born in 1828 in Hanover, Germany and died 5 December 1874 in Deerfield, New York.[4] After the death of Anna, Augustus married Maria Menning (Minung) 6 September 1878 in Utica, New York. The witnesses for the marriage of Augustus Hahn and Maria Menning (Minung) were J. Schaefer and W. Geiersbach. She was born in 1824 in Würtemberg, Germany and died in 1884. After her death, he married Caroline Ketchener (Kirchner) Bauer in 1888 in Utica, New York. She was born 1 December 1832 in Prussia, Germany[5] and died 10 October 1902 at 223 Mohawk Street, Utica, New York.[6] Caroline was born in Germany and came to this country at the age of 10. She married in Albany and later moved to Utica, New York where her first husband died. She lived in the house on Mohawk Street for over 30 years. She was a member of St. Paul's Lutheran Church. She had 48 grandchildren at the time of her death. The 1860 Deerfield, New York Census states Augustus and his wife were both born in Hannover, Germany and his name was spelled Hann. The 1870 Utica, New York Census spelled his name Auguste Hahn and stated he was born in Prussia.

Photo of August Hahn in his later years in the author's collection.

---

[1] Death Certificate of Augustus Hahn
[2] Death Certificate of Augustus Hahn
[3] Civil War Records of Augustus Hahn
[4] Tombstone in First Baptist Cemetery, Utica, New York
[5] Obituary Utica Newspaper October 11, 1902
[6] Obituary Utica Newspaper October 11, 1902

August learned the trade of plasterer in Germany and went into the German military service. In 1848 he escaped from Germany and came to America settling in Utica, New York. He worked at his trade here and also as a stone mason. He was self employed most of his life. He was a member of the German Rifle Co., Post John F. McQuade, G.A.R. In 1883 August sold property to George Bowman and his wife in the amount of $450. The property was listed on Hamilton Street in Utica, New York (40' frontage and 100' deep.) Returning from the civil war, Augustus settled in Deerfield, New York and lived there until 1884 at which time he moved to Mohawk Street in Utica, New York.

The naturalization record found on Augustus Hahn showed a Declaration of Intent on October 1, 1852 with the Naturalization being October 25, 1854.

Civil War Journey

Augustus enlisted in the Civil War at Deerfield, New York to serve three years, on August 29, 1862 in Company F of the 146th Regiment of New York Volunteers commanded by Captain Sweet. He was enlisted as a Private at the age of 37 years old.

On May 5, 1864 Augustus was taken capture during action at Wilderness, Virginia and was held at the Andersonville Prison in Georgia for ten months. He was also in a prison in Florence, North Carolina for a period of time. He was paroled from possession of the

enemy at N.E.Ferry, North Carolina Feb 26, 1865 and reported at Camp Parole, Annapolis, Maryland on March 12, 1865. He was furloughed March 17, 1865 for 30 days and returned May 2, 1865 at which time he was sent to Camp Distribution, Alexandria, Virginia May 9, 1865. He was hospitalized from June 29 to July 4, 1865 in the Regimental Division Hospital with the diagnosis of a hernia for which he was fitted for a truss. This hospital was a field hospital.

He mustered out with his company near Alexandria, Virginia on July 16, 1865. His personal description was five feet five and a half inches tall, dark complexion and dark hair, eyes brown. [7]

Photo of August Hahn in his Civil War Uniform in the author's collection.

---

[7] Civil War Records of August Hahn

Augustus died at the home of his daughter, Mrs. John Eisenhuth in Deerfield, New York. His death certificate said he died of old age with general breaking down. Augustus' Civil War records indicated his wife Anna's name as Hanah Grap or Grop.

Augustus Hahn and Anna (Hannah) Grub had the following children:

2.   i.   Antoinette Hahn was born 20 May 1852 in Utica, New York[8]and died 25 May 1924 at 341 South Street, Utica, New York.[9]

3.   ii.   **Rose Hahn** was born 25 May 1854[10] and died 15 September 1892 at 150 Schuyler St. Utica, New York.[11]

4.   iii.   Catharine Hahn was born 24 April 1858 in Utica, New York[12]and died 31 January 1918 in Peoria, Illinois.[13]

5.   iv.   Elizabeth Katherine Hahn was born 22 September 1862 in Deerfield, New York and died 2 January 1935 in Utica, New York.[14]

This picture was given to me along with many other photos of the Hahn family which leads me to believe they could be Hahn sisters. The girl seated looks a lot like Viola Bowman so perhaps she is Rose Hahn.

Generation Two

2. Antoinette Hahn[2] (Augustus Hahn[1]) was born 20 May 1852 in Utica, New York[15]and died 25 May 1924 at 341 South Street, Utica, New York.[16] She married William F. M. Geiersback 1 January 1874 in Utica, New York, the son of Christian and Catherine Geiersback.[17]He was born 13 April 1853 in Utica, New York and died 2 February 1885 in Deerfield, New York. After the death of William, Antoinette married Michael McManus in 1893 in Utica, New York. He died in 1911. Antoinette was a member of St. Paul's Lutheran Church, Utica, New York

---

[8] Obituary Utica Newspaper May 26, 1924
[9] Obituary Utica Newspaper May 26, 1924
[10] New Forest Cemetery Records, Utica, New York
[11] New Forest Cemetery Records, Utica, New York
[12] Death Certificate of Catharine Hahn Looft
[13] Death Certificate of Catharine Hahn Looft
[14] Obituary Utica Newspaper January 3, 1935
[15] Obituary Utica Newspaper May 26, 1924
[16] Obituary Utica Newspaper May 26, 1924
[17] Records at the Oneida County Historical Society

Antoinette Hahn and William F. M. Geiersback had the following children:

6.   i.   William A. Geiersbach was born 28 April 1874 in Deerfield, New York and died 13 March 1926 in Syracuse, New York.[18]

7.   ii.   Rosanna Geiersbach was born 11 April 1876 in Utica, New York[19] and died 5 April 1939 in Utica, New York.[20]

Photo of Antoinette Hahn in the author's collection.

iii.   Antoinette Geiersback was born in 1878 in Utica, New York[21] and died 7 January 1948 in Rome Hospital, Rome, New York[22] She married Richard Droye 8 October 1924 in Utica, New York. He was born in 1877 in Prussia, Germany[23] and died 31 July 1962 in Utica, New York.[24] Antoinette lived at 706 First St., Rome, New York at the time of her death. She was a member of St. Paul's Lutheran Church, Utica, New York.

iv.   Henry Geiersback was born in 1878.[25]

v.   Matilda Geiersbach was born 18 February 1880 in Utica, New York and died 1 November 1960 in St. Luke's Hospital, New Hartford, New York.[26] Matilda lived at 621 Plant Street, Utica, New York and worked as a seamstress. She was last employed by Mansky & Son Furriers. She was a member of the Church of the Redeemer and the United Lutheran Church Women in Utica, New York. She never married.

3. Rose Hahn[2] (Augustus Hahn[1]) was born 25 May 1854[27] and died 15 September 1892 in 150 Schuyler St. Utica, New York of Typhoid Malaria Fever.[28] She married George Bowman *about* 1878, the son of John Baumann Sr. and Martha (Martina) Kohlhammer. He was born 16 November 1856 in Utica, New York[29] and died 30 January 1898 in Jersey City, New Jersey.[30] Rose lived at 150 Schuyler Street, Utica, New York at time of her

---

[18] Obituary Utica Newspaper March 14, 1926
[19] Obituary Utica Newspaper April 6, 1939
[20] Obituary Utica Newspaper April 6, 1939
[21] Obituary Utica Newspaper January 8, 1948
[22] Obituary Utica Newspaper January 8, 1948
[23] 1925 Utica, New York Census, Ward 10
[24] Death Announcement Utica Newspaper August 1, 1962
[25] 1880 Utica, New York Census
[26] Obituary Utica Newspaper November 2, 1960
[27] New Forest Cemetery Records, Utica, New York
[28] New Forest Cemetery Records, Utica, New York
[29] St. Joseph's Church Baptismal Records, Utica, New York
[30] Death Certificate from New Jersey on George Bowman

death and was a member of the Zion's Lutheran Church, Utica, New York. The 1880 Census stated George was married to Rose and they had one child, David age 6 months. They lived on South Hamilton Street in Utica, New York and George's occupation was an Iron Molder.

Rose Hahn and George Bowman had the following children:

        i.   David Bowman was born in May 1880 in Utica, New York.[31] It could be David did not live to be very old as the brothers never mentioned him nor was he mentioned in another census.

        ii.   Edward Bowman was born in June 1881 in Utica, New York[32] and died 29 October 1938 in Fort Plain, New York.[33]

8.   iii.   Walter James Bowman was born 6 October 1883 in Syracuse, New York and died 4 November 1945 in Utica, New York.[34]

9.   iv.   Noble Philip Bowman was born 4 July 1886 in Utica, New York and died 18 October 1951 in Memorial Hospital, Albany, New York.[35]

10.   v.   Viola F. Bowman was born 14 August 1889 in Utica, New York and died 25 March 1970 in Albany, New York.[36]

11.   **vi.**   **George Francis Bowman** was born 18 December 1891 in Jersey City, New Jersey[37] and died 8 January 1957 in Utica, New York.[38]

4. Catharine Hahn[2] (Augustus Hahn[1]) was born 24 April 1858 in Utica, New York[39] and died 31 January 1918 in Peoria, Illinois.[40] She married Frederick P. Looft in 1882 in Utica, New York. He was born 25 December 1851 in Germany (Denmark)[41] and died 8 March 1932 in St. Francis Hospital, Peoria, Illinois.[42] Frederick's death certificate said he died of Pulmonary infarction. He had under gone an operation on March 12, 1932 for gangrenous appendicitis. Fred lived at W. Wilcox Avenue in Peoria, Illinois 2nd ward in the 1920 Census. His death certificate said he had been a carpenter and a self employed contractor.

Photo of Frederick P. Looft in the author's collection.

---

[31] 1880 Utica, New York Census
[32] 1900 Jersey City, New Jersey Census
[33] New Forest Cemetery Records, Utica, New York
[34] Obituary Utica Newspaper November 5, 1945
[35] Family information from Virginia Krichbaum
[36] Family information from Virginia Krichbaum
[37] Family History Center Film 14303369, St. Patrick's Church, Jersey City, New Jersey
[38] Obituary Utica Newspaper January 9, 1957
[39] Death Certificate on Catherine Hahn Looft
[40] Death Certificate on Catherine Hahn Looft
[41] Death Certificate of Frederick Looft from Peoria, Illinois
[42] Death Certificate of Frederick Looft from Peoria, Illinois

Catharine Hahn and Frederick P. Looft had the following children:

      i.   Elizabeth (Lizzie) Looft was born in 1884 in Illinois[43]and died 11 January 1957 in Methodist Hospital, Peoria, Illinois.[44]Elizabeth married George W. Gibbons. He was born 20 Feb 1881 in Illinois. Elizabeth and George lived in the Logan, Illinois Township in 1920.

Photo of Elizabeth Looft in the author's collection.

      ii.   Laura Looft was born 12 November 1886 in Peoria, Illinois[45]and died 25 December 1966 in Proctor Hospital, Peoria, Illinois.[46]Laura lived in Peoria all her life and had lived with her sister, Jessie E. Look, for the last three years of her live. She never married.

12.   iii.   Charles W. Looft was born 27 February 1890 in Illinois[47]and died 19 July 1958.[48]

      iv.   Martha (Mattie) Looft was born 4 March 1893 in Peoria, Illinois[49]and died 7 January 1952 in Peoria, Illinois.[50] She married Howard R. Lonsdale in 1922 in Peoria, Illinois. He was born 25 Dec 1894 in Pottstown, Illinois.[51]The 1930 Peoria, Illinois Census indicated Mattie was a widow.

Photo of Martha Looft in the author's collection.

      v.   George Henry Looft was born 25 January 1896 in Peoria, Illinois[52]and died 25 June 1916 in St. Francis Hospital, Peoria, Illinois of a hemorrhage of the brain due to injuries received in a motorcycle accident.[53]George never married.

---

[43] Obituary Peoria, Illinois Newspaper January 2, 1957
[44] Obituary Peoria, Illinois Newspaper January 2, 1957
[45] Obituary Peoria, Illinois Newspaper December 26, 1966
[46] Obituary Peoria, Illinois Newspaper December 26, 1966
[47] World War I draft registration from Ancestery.com
[48] Obituary of Ethel Looft in the Peoria, Illinois Newspaper May 4, 1988
[49] Springdale Cemetery Records, Peoria, Illinois
[50] Springdale Cemetery Records, Peoria, Illinois
[51] World War I draft registration from Ancestery.com
[52] Death Certificate from Peoria, Illinois on George Henry Looft
[53] Death Certificate from Peoria, Illinois on George Henry Looft

vi.   Jessie Looft was born 20 August 1901 in Peoria, Illinois[54] and died 27 March 1974 at Ward Road, Limestone Township, Illinois.[55] Jessie married Arthur Funk who was born 15 October 1891 in Peoria, Illinois.[56] She later married Enno E. Look 25 Oct 1962 in Peoria, Illinois.   Jessie was a tester for Peoria Milk Testing Laboratory for about ten years, retiring in 1963. She was survived by her husband, a stepdaughter, Mrs. Leona Mulvaney of Mapleton and a stepson, Raymond Look of Peoria.

5. Elizabeth Katherine Hahn[2] (Augustus Hahn[1]) was born 22 September 1862 in Deerfield, New York and died 2 January 1935 in Utica, New York.[57] She married John J. Eisenhuth 22 May 1883 in Utica, New York.[58] He was born 23 August 1860 in Utica, New York[59] and died 29 December 1934 in Utica, New York.[60] Elizabeth died of stomach cancer having been ill for some time. She and her husband died within a few days of each other. Elizabeth died at her home on Herkimer Road, Utica, New York. She was a member of the Church of the Redeemer and the Ladies Auxiliary, Order of Railway Conductors and Bacon Women's Relief Corps 24. John was born in Utica but his parents came from Germany. He was educated in St. Joseph's School, Utica, New York. In 1892 he went to work for the D.L. & W. Railroad and had been in its employ ever since. He worked as a brakeman and then as a switching engine in the yard. Later he went on the road and eventually became a conductor, first on freight trains and then on passenger trains. February 12, 1923 he was made conductor on the milk train which runs between Utica and Binghamton and in 1926 he retired. He was a member of Kincald Division, Order of Railway Conductors, and he was also a member of the Railroad Veterans Association. He was a lifelong member of St. Joseph's Church, Utica, New York.

Photo of Elizabeth Hahn and the children are her daughter, Lillian, and her nephew, George Bowman in the author's collection.

---

54 Obituary Peoria, Illinois Newspaper March 28, 1974
55 Obituary Peoria, Illinois Newspaper March 28, 1974
56 World War I draft registration from Ancestery.com
57 Obituary Utica Newspaper January 3, 1935
58 50th Wedding Anniversary Announcement Utica Newspaper
59 Obituary Utica Newspaper December 30, 1934
60 Obituary Utica Newspaper December 30, 1934

Elizabeth Katherine Hahn and John J. Eisenhuth had the following children:

i.   Frederick George Eisenhuth was born 4 April 1884 in Utica, New York[61] and died 29 June 1971 in St. Luke's Memorial Hospital, Utica, New York.[62] He married Amelia Ann Wandres 8 May 1918.[63] Amelia was born in 1877 in Utica, New York and died February 2, 1935.[64] Following the death of Amelia, Fred married Bertha M. Fuber 5 November 1935.[65] She was born in 1897 in Berne, Switzerland and died 4 November 1971 in Utica, New York.[66] Fred operated the Ideal Engineering Company on First Street in Utica for several years. He was a member of Trinity Lutheran Church, Liberty Lodge F&AM, the Utica Commandery Knights Templar and the Universal Council of Engineers.

Photo of Frederick George Eisenhuth in the author's collection.

ii.   Emma E. Eisenhuth was born 14 December 1887 in Utica, New York,[67] and died 21 July 1982 in St. Luke's Memorial Hospital, Utica, New York.[68] She married John C. Moore 28 September 1916 at the home of her parents, Utica, New York.[69] John was born 8 February 1889 in Cherry Valley, New York[70] and died 4 August 1965 at 105 Wells Place, Utica, New York. [71] Emma attended Utica, New York schools and was a member of Our Savior Lutheran Church and was a Charter Member of the North Utica Senior Citizens. She also served as a Republican Inspector of the 3rd District of the 17th Ward for many years. She did not have children.

Photo of Emma E. Eisenhuth's Wedding in the author's collection.

---

[61] Obituary Utica Newspaper June 30, 1971
[62] Obituary Utica Newspaper June 30, 1971
[63] Obituary Utica Newspaper June 30, 1971
[64] Obituary Utica Newspaper February 3, 1935
[65] Obituary Utica Newspaper November 6, 1971
[66] Obituary Utica Newspaper November 6, 1971
[67] Obituary Utica Newspaper July 22, 1982
[68] Obituary Utica Newspaper July 22, 1982
[69] Wedding Announcement Utica Newspaper
[70] World War I draft registration from Ancestery.com
[71] Obituary Utica Newspaper August 5, 1965

13. iii. Mary Barbara (Mayme) Eisenhuth was born 20 January 1890 in Utica, New York[72] and died 2 June 1971 in St. Luke's Memorial Hospital, Utica, New York.[73]

iv. John William Eisenhuth was born 29 April 1894 in Utica, New York,[74] and died June 1894 in Utica, New York.[75]

14. v. Lillian Adeline Eisenhuth was born 26 September 1896 in Utica, New York[76] and died 8 November 1982 in Utica, New York.[77]

Generation Three

6. William A. Geiersbach[3] (Antoinette Hahn[2], Augustus Hahn[1]) was born 28 April 1874 in Deerfield, New York[78] and died 13 March 1926 in Syracuse, New York.[79] He married Catherine Brammer in 1897. She was born in 1870 in New York State.[80] William had been a sheet metal worker and at one time owned the Ornamental Iron Work at 72 Hotel Street, Utica, New York.

William A. and Catherine Geiersbach had the following children:

15. i. Viola M. Geiersbach was born 12 February 1898 in New York State[81] and died 27 March 1981 in Chula Vista, San Diego, California.[82]

16. ii. May C. Geiersbach was born 7 May 1899[83] and died January 1974 in Syracuse, New York.[84]

17. iii. Edna A. Geiersbach Ward was born 23 December 1900 in Utica, New York[85] and died 22 December 1992 in Crouse Irving Memorial Hospital, Syracuse, New York.[86]

iv. William M. Geiersbach was born 4 August 1902 in Utica, New York[87] and died 15 February 1976 in San Diego, California.[88]

7. Rosanna Geiersbach[3] (Antoinette Hahn[2], Augustus Hahn[1]) was born 11 April 1876 in Utica, New York[89] and died 5 April 1939 in Utica, New York.[90] She married Fred C.

---

[72] Obituary Utica Newspaper June 3, 1971
[73] Obituary Utica Newspaper June 3, 1971
[74] Information taken from the family bible
[75] Information taken from the family bible
[76] Obituary Utica Newspaper November 9, 1982
[77] Obituary Utica Newspaper November 9, 1982
[78] Obituary Utica Newspaper March 14, 1926
[79] Obituary Utica Newspaper March 14, 1926
[80] 1910 Deerfield, New York Census
[81] California Death Index from Ancestry.com
[82] Obituary Utica Newspaper March 28, 1981
[83] Social Security Death Index from Ancestry.com
[84] Social Security Death Index from Ancestry.com
[85] Birth Announcement from Utica Newspaper
[86] Obituary Utica Newspaper December 23, 1992
[87] New York State Vital Records
[88] California Death Index from Ancestry.com

Schimmel 16 July 1912 in Utica, New York. He was born 19 September 1864[91]and died 6 November 1939 in Utica, New York.[92]Rosanna lived in Utica all her life. She was a member of St. Paul's Lutheran Church. She had four grandchildren at the time of her death. Fred enlisted as a private in Company L., 26th Regiment, U.S. Volunteers, July 20, 1899, and served in the Philippines during the Spanish American War. He received an honorable discharge when the company was mustered out of service in San Francisco May 13, 1901. He was a member of E.H. Liscum-O. Ross Wheeler Camp 33, United Spanish American War Veterans.

Rosanna Geiersbach had the following child:

      i.   Julia Schimmel was born in 26 June 1902 and died in July 1969 in Indian Lake, New York.[93]Julie lived in Indian Lake in 1939 and was married to Frank Philo.[94]

Rosanna Geiersbach and Fred C. Schimmel had the following child:

      ii.   Helen Schimmel was born 17 September 1914 and died 29 April 1994 in Utica, New York.[95]She married George E. Joslin. He was born 19 February 1916 and died 7 June 1992 in Utica, New York.[96]Helen lived in Rochester, New York in 1939. Helen and George had four children three of whom may still be living.

8. Walter James Bowman[3] (Rose Hahn[2], Augustus Hahn[1]) was born 6 October 1883 in Syracuse, New York. He died 4 November 1945 in Utica, New York.[97]He married Mary T. Hage 12 June 1907 in St. Joseph's Church, Utica, New York, the daughter of John Hage and Ruttina Schafer. She was born 3 May 1884 in Utica, New York[98]and died 26 September 1972 in St. Luke's Hospital Memorial Hospital, New Hartford, New York.[99]For more information on Walter Bowman see Chapter Four.

---

[89] Obituary Utica Newspaper April 6, 1939

[90] Obituary Utica Newspaper April 6, 1939

[91] Obituary Utica Newspaper November 7, 1939

[92] Obituary Utica Newspaper November 7, 1939

[93] Social Security Death Index from Ancestry.com

[94] Obituary of her step father, Fred C. Schimmel Utica Newspaper November 7, 1939

[95] Social Security Death Index from Ancestry.com

[96] Social Security Death Index from Ancestry.com

[97] Obituary Utica Newspaper November 5, 1945

[98] Social Security Death Index from Ancestry.com

[99] Obituary Utica Newspaper September 27, 1972

Walter James Bowman and Mary T. Hage had the following children:

18.   i.   Walter John Bowman was born 30 November 1908 and died 9 May 1972 in Utica, New York.[100]

19.   ii.   Eleanor Bowman was born 26 July 1911 in Utica, New York and died 29 November 1977 in St. Luke's Hospital, Utica, New York[101]

20.   iii.   Evelyn Anna Bowman was born 12 January 1915 in Utica, New York and died 25 February 2003 in Resurrection Nursing Home, Castleton, New York.[102]

9. Noble Philip Bowman[3] (Rose Hahn[2], Augustus Hahn[1]) was born 4 July 1886 in Utica, New York and died 18 October 1951 in Memorial Hospital, Albany, New York.[103]He married Clara Theresa Everhart 22 May 1912 in St. John's Lutheran Church, Albany, New York.[104]She was born 14 May 1887 in Albany, New York and died 16 November 1965 in Albany, New York.[105]For more information on Noble Bowman, see Chapter Four.

Children of Noble Philip Bowman and Clara Theresa Everhart are:

21.   i.   Bernice Carolyn Bowman was born 29 January 1914 in Albany, New York[106] and died September 17, 1985 in St Peter's Hospital, Albany, New York.[107]

        ii.   Noble Richard Bowman was born 22 January 1916 in Albany, New York, and died 16 June 1916 in Albany, New York.[108]

        iii.   Living Bowman

22.   iv.   Living Bowman

10. Viola F. Bowman[3] (Rose Hahn[2], Augustus Hahn[1]) was born 14 August 1889 in Utica, New York and died 25 March 1970 in Albany, New York. She married Henry Valet 3 July 1920 in Albany, New York.[109]He was born in 1886 in Germany.[110]For more information on Viola Bowman, see Chapter Four.

Viola F. Bowman and Henry Valet had the following children:

23.   i.   Henry Andrew Valet was born 5 August 1921 in Albany, New York and died 21 February 1995 in Colonie, New York.[111]

---

[100] Obituary Utica Newspaper May 10, 1972
[101] Obituary Utica Newspaper November 30, 1977
[102] Obituary Utica Newspaper February 26, 2003
[103] Family information from Virginia Krichbaum
[104] Family information from Virginia Krichbaum
[105] Family information from Virginia Krichbaum
[106] Family information from Virginia Krichbaum
[107] Family information from Virginia Krichbaum
[108] Family information from Virginia Krichbaum
[109] Family information from Virginia Krichbaum
[110] World War I draft registration from Ancestery.com
[111] Social Security Death Index from Ancestry.com

**24.   ii.   **Edward George Valet was born 13 November 1922 in Albany, New York and died 25 May 1983.

**25.   iii.   **Frederick George Valet was born 17 March 1926 and died 12 June 1991.[112]

iv.   Living Valet

**26.   v.   **Living Valet

11. George Francis Bowman[3] (Rose Hahn[2], Augustus Hahn[1])[43] was born 18 December 1891 in Jersey City, New Jersey[113]and died 8 January 1957 in Utica, New York.[114] He married Susanna Etta Sifer 8 September 1916 in St. Joseph's Church, Utica, New York, the daughter of George Sifer and Mary Johanna Schmidt. She was born 17 July 1893 in Ava, New York[115]and died 20 June 1966 in Utica, New York.[116]For more information on George Bowman, see Chapter Four.

George Francis Bowman and Susanna Etta Sifer had the following children:

**27.   i.   **George Marvin Bowman was born 30 June 1917 in Utica, New York and died 19 March 1987 in Utica, New York.[117]

28.   ii.   Gertrude Bowman Emery Weyneth. For more information on Gertrude, see Chapter Four.

12. Charles W. Looft[3] (Catharine Hahn[2], Augustus Hahn[1]) was born 27 February 1890 in Illinois[118]and died 19 July 1958.[119]He married Ethel M. McQuown 31 March 1915 in Peoria, the daughter of Charles A. McQuown and Hester Ann Tyson. She was born 5 July 1892 in Elmwood, Illinois[120]and died 3 May 1988 in Methodist Medical Center, Peoria, Illinois.[121]The 1920 Peoria, Illinois Census indicated Charles was a carpenter and lived on Bell Avenue in Peoria.

Photo of Charles W. Looft in the author's collection.

---

[112] Family information from Virginia Krichbaum
[113] Family History Center Film 14303369, St. Patrick's Church, Jersey City, New Jersey
[114] Obituary Utica Newspaper January 9, 1957
[115] Social Security Death Index from Ancestry.com
[116] Obituary Utica Newspaper June 21, 1966
[117] Obituary Utica Newspaper March 20, 1987
[118] World War I draft registration from Ancestery.com
[119] Obituary of wife, Ethel M. Looft, Peoria, Illinois Newspaper May 4, 1988
[120] Obituary Peoria, Illinois Newspaper May 4, 1988
[121] Obituary Peoria, Illinois Newspaper May 4, 1988

Charles W. Looft and Ethel M. McQuown had the following children:

    i.   Betty Looft died at birth.

    ii.   Living Looft

29.   iii.   JoAnn Looft was born 28 March 1934 in Peoria, Illinois and died 9 April 2002 in Peoria, Illinois.[122] She was married 24 October 1985.

13. Mary Barbara (Mayme) Eisenhuth[3] (Elizabeth Katherine Hahn[2], Augustus Hahn[1]) was born 20 January 1890 in Utica, New York[123] and died 2 June 1971 in St. Luke's Memorial Hospital, Utica, New York.[124] She married Herbert Frederick Dewhurst 12 April 1924 in Utica, New York.[125] He was born 18 May 1887 in Willowvale, New York[126] and died in 1941 in Utica, New York.[127] Mary was employed for over fifteen years by the Doyle-Knower Co, retiring in 1958. She was a member of St. Paul's Episcopal Church and the North Utica Senior Citizens Club.

Mary Barbara Eisenhuth. Photo in the author's collection.

Mary Barbara (Mayme) Eisenhuth and Herbert Frederick Dewhurst had the following children:

    i.   Emma Dewhurst

    ii.   Fred Dewhurst

30.   iii.   Mary Jane Dewhurst was born 25 March 1925 in Utica, New York[128] and died 20 February 2001 in North Utica, New York.[129]

14. Lillian Adeline Eisenhuth[3] (Elizabeth Katherine Hahn[2], Augustus Hahn[1]) was born 26 September 1896 in Utica, New York[130] and died 8 November 1982 in Utica, New York.[131] She married William Tobias Knittel 17 February 1919, the son of Frank F. Knittel and Rose Ginty Canning.

[122] Obituary Peoria, Illinois Newspaper April 10, 2002

[123] Obituary Utica Newspaper June 3, 1971

[124] Obituary Utica Newspaper June 3, 1971

[125] Obituary Utica Newspaper June 3, 1971

[126] World War I draft registration from Ancestery.com

[127] Obituary of wife, Mary Dewhurst, Utica Newspaper June 3, 1971

[128] Obituary Utica Newspaper February 21, 2001

[129] Obituary Utica Newspaper February 21, 2001

[130] Obituary Utica Newspaper November 9, 1982

[131] Obituary Utica Newspaper November 9, 1982

He was born 20 March 1893 in Utica, New York[132]and died 5 January 1942 in Chadwicks, New York.[133]After William's death, Lillian married James Joseph Creedon 12 September 1942 in St. Peter's Church, Utica, New York,[134] the son of John Creedon and Catherine Crowley. He was born 23 May 1895 in Little Falls, New York[135]and died 8 February 1960 in St. Luke's Memorial Hospital, New Hartford, New York.[136]Lillian died at Broadacres in Utica, New York. She was a member of St. Paul's Episcopal Church, Utica, New York. William Knittel had been employed at Broadacres and had served in World War I in the United States Navy. Lillian Adeline Eisenhuth and William Tobias Knittel had one child who is still living.

Photo of Lillian Adeline Eisenhuth in the author's collection.

James Creeden attended Little Falls, New York schools. He was a veteran of World War I, serving in France, where he was wounded and was awarded a Purple Heart medal. He was adjutant of Chapter 138, DAV and a member of St. Peter's Church, Utica, New York. He was a plumbing and heating contractor for many years and later was employed by the Horrocks-Ibbotson Co., until his retirement.

Generation 4

15. Viola M. Geiersbach[4] (William A. Geiersbach[3], Antoinette Hahn[2], Augustus Hahn[1]) was born 12 February 1898 in New York State[137]and died 27 March 1981 in Chula Vista, San Diego, California.[138]She married Victor O. Gauthier 6 September 1918 in St. Paul's Church Rectory, Whitesboro, New York.[139]He was born in 1898. Viola had lived in Mattydale, California and was previously employed by Prestolite Company., retiring in 1961 after 31 years of service. She was a former communicant of St. Margaret's Catholic Church and a member of the Third Ward Men's Club Auxiliary.

---

[132] Obituary Utica Newspaper January 6, 1942
[133] Obituary Utica Newspaper January 6, 1942
[134] Wedding Announcement, Utica Newspaper
[135] Obituary Utica Newspaper February 9, 1960
[136] Obituary Utica Newspaper February 9, 1960
[137] California Death Index from Ancestry.com
[138] Obituary Utica Newspaper March 28, 1981
[139] Wedding Announcement Utica Newspaper

Viola M. Geiersbach and Victor O. Gauthier had the following child:

  i. Arthur Phillip Gauthier was born 24 February 1919 in New York State[140]and died 6 February 1989 in San Diego, California.[141]

16. May C. Geiersbach[4] (William A. Geiersbach[3], Antoinette Hahn[2], Augustus Hahn[1]) was born 7 May 1899[142]and died in January 1974 in Syracuse, New York.[143] She married Edward A. Vanalstine in 1923. He was born 18 December 1899 in Syracuse, New York[144]and died 18 December 1991 in Syracuse, New York.[145]Edward retired after 40 years as a custodian and a crossing guard with Bessie B. Riordan School in Mattydale. He was the town constable for Mattydale until 1932 when he was appointed as a special deputy by the Onondaga County Sheriff's Department. He was a member of Calvary United Methodist Church, Mattydale and the Mattydale Volunteer Fire Department. He boxed in the Golden Gloves as a youth under the ring name of "Kid Davis". He served with the Army's 1st Combat Engineers in France during World War I and was the last surviving charter member of Mattydale Post 3146, Veterans of Foreign Wars, where he was a former commander and Chaplin. He was a life member of the Disabled American Veterans and a member of the Masonic War Veterans. May C. Geiersbach and Edward A. Vanalstine have six children who may still be living.

17. Edna A. Geiersbach[4] (William A. Geiersbach[3], Antoinette Hahn[2], Augustus Hahn[1]) was born 23 December 1900 in Utica, New York[146]and died 22 December 1992 in Crouse Irving Memorial Hospital, Syracuse, New York[147]She married James R. Ward in 1923. He was born in 1901.[148]Edna was a native of Utica and had lived in Constantia, New York for 42 years. She was a punch press operator with the former Easy Washer Company of Syracuse. She was a member of St. Bernadett's Church. At the time of her death, she had ten grandchildren, 24 great-grandchildren and six great-great-grandchildren. Edna A. Geiersbach Ward and James R. Ward had three children who may still be living.

18. Walter John Bowman[4] (Walter James Bowman[3], Rose Hahn[2], Augustus Hahn[1]) was born 30 November 1908 and died 9 May 1972 in Utica, New York.[149]Walter was married three times. The first wife was named Stella and the second wife was named Jennie. In 1967 he married Carolyn A. Hubbard in Utica, New York, the daughter of Charles A.

---

[140] California Death Index from Ancestry.com
[141] California Death Index from Ancestry.com
[142] Social Security Death Index from Ancestry.com
[143] Social Security Death Index from Ancestry.com
[144] Social Security Death Index from Ancestry.com
[145] Social Security Death Index from Ancestry.com
[146] Obituary Utica Newspaper December 23, 1992
[147] Obituary Utica Newspaper December 23, 1992
[148] 1930 Syracuse, New York Census
[149] Obituary Utica Newspaper May 10, 1972

Hubbard and Catherine Lowery. She was born 7 March 1937 in Utica, New York[150]and died 27 September 2004 in St. Joseph's Nursing Home, Utica, New York.[151]Walter John Bowman and Carolyn A. Hubbard had five children who may still be living.

19. Eleanor Bowman[4] (Walter James Bowman[3], Rose Hahn[2], Augustus Hahn[1]) was born 26 July 1911 in Utica, New York and died 29 November 1977 in St. Luke's Hospital, Utica, New York.[152]She married Laurence T. Manch 25 August 1930, the son of Anthony and Mary Manch. He was born 25 January 1909 in Keene, New Hampshire[153] and died 6 November 1946 in Utica, New York.[154]After the death of Laurence, Eleanor married Anthony Cimino in 1949. Eleanor was educated at St. Joseph's School and Utica Free Academy, Utica, New York.   For many years she was employed at the Utica Knitting Company. She was a member of St. Joseph-St. Patrick's Church, Utica, New York. Lawrence was a member of St. Joseph's Church and was employed as a sales representative by Sunshine Dairies. Eleanor Bowman and Laurence T. Manch had one child who may still be living.

20. Evelyn Anna Bowman[4] (Walter James Bowman[3], Rose Hahn[2], Augustus Hahn[1]) was born 12 January 1915 in Utica, New York and died 25 February 2003 in Resurrection Nursing Home, Castleton, New York.[155]She married Arnold Christian Rieben 1 September 1930 in St. Joseph's Church, Utica, New York, the son of Christian Rieben and Rosa Louise Ludy. He was born 16 December 1908 in New York City and died 6 April 1986 in Castleton, New York.[156]Evelyn was a communicant of Sacred Heart Church in Castleton. New York. She was raised in Utica, New York and moved to Castleton in 1974. Evelyn Anna Bowman and Arnold Christian Rieben had one child who is still living.

21. Bernice Carolyn Bowman[4] (Noble Philip Bowman[3], Rose Hahn[2], Augustus Hahn[1]) was born 29 January 1914 in Albany, New York[157]and died September 17, 1985.[158]She married Roland Archie Allen 27 April 1935 in St. John's Lutheran Church, Albany, New York. He was born 19 September 1909 in Nova Scotia and died 20 November 1968 in Albany, New York.

---

[150] Obituary Utica Newspaper September 28, 2004
[151] Obituary Utica Newspaper September 28, 2004
[152] Obituary Utica Newspaper November 30, 1977
[153] Obituary Utica Newspaper November 7, 1946
[154] Obituary Utica Newspaper November 7, 1946
[155] Obituary Utica Newspaper February 26, 2003
[156] Obituary Utica Newspaper April 8, 1986
[157] Family information from Virginia Krichbaum
[158] Family information from Virginia Krichbaum

Bernice Carolyn Bowman Allen and Roland Archie Allen adopted two children:
  i.   Living Allen
  ii.   Mary Linda Allen was born 27 July 1950 and died5 August 1995.

23. Henry Andrew Valet[4] (Viola F. Bowman[3], Rose Hahn[2], Augustus Hahn[1]) was born 5 August 1921 in Albany, New York and died 21 February 1995 in Colonie, New York.[159] He was married 5 January 1949. Henry Andrew Valet and his wife had five children who may still be living.

24. Edward George Valet[4] (Viola F. Bowman[3], Rose Hahn[2], Augustus Hahn[1]) was born 13 November 1922 in Albany, New York and died 25 May 1983.[160]He was married 11 January 1950. Edward George Valet and his wife had two children who may still be living.

25. Frederick George Valet[4] (Viola F. Bowman[3], Rose Hahn[2], Augustus Hahn[1]) was born 17 March 1926 and died on 12 June 1991.[161]He married Jean Ellen Whittle in 1945 in England. He later married Elaine Connors in Troy, New York. She was born in 1932 and died 1 November 1998.

Frederick George Valet and Jean Ellen Whittle had the following children:
  i.   Living Valet
42.   ii.   Frederick H. Valet was born 24 December 1948 in Albany, New York and died 29 August 1997 in Georgia.[162] He was married in 1977 in California.
43.   iii.   Living Valet

Frederick George Valet and Elaine Connors had two children who are still living.

27. George Marvin Bowman[4] (George Francis Bowman[3], Rose Hahn[2], Augustus Hahn[1]) was born 30 June 1917 in Utica, New York and died 19 March 1987 in Utica, New York.[163]He married Kathryn Lourdes McLoughlin 17 February 1940 in St. John's Church, New Hartford, New York, the daughter of Arthur McLoughlin and Dorothy Bryan. She was born in 1921 in Utica, New York[164]and died 9 April 1972 in Utica, New York.[165] He later married Mildred Gaylord Wood Christ 29 July 1961 in Utica, New York.[166]She was born 2 June 1909 and died 9 August 1981 in Utica, New York.[167]

---

[159] Family information from Virginia Krichbaum
[160] Family information from Virginia Krichbaum
[161] Family information from Virginia Krichbaum
[162] Family information from Catherine Valet
[163] Obituary Utica Newspaper Mach 20, 1987
[164] Obituary Utica Newspaper April 10, 1972
[165] Obituary Utica Newspaper April 10, 1972
[166] Wedding Announcement Utica Newspaper
[167] Schuyler Corners Cemetery, Schuyler, New York

Children of George Marvin Bowman and Kathryn Lourdes McLoughlin are:

49.   i.   Living Bowman

50.   ii.   Deborah Bowman was born 24 November 1950 in Utica, New York and died 25 September 2003 in Camp Lejeune, North Carolina.[168] She was married 23 January 1971 in Utica, New York and married again later on. She and her first husband had two children who are still living.

29. JoAnn Looft[4] (Charles W. Looft[3], Catharine Hahn[2], Augustus Hahn[1]) was born 28 March 1934 in Peoria, Illinois and died 9 April 2002 in Peoria, Illinois.[169]She was married three times. The first time was 18 January 1952, the second time was in February 1965 and the third time was 24 October 1985. JoAnn Looft and her first husband had three children who are still living.

30. Mary Jane Dewhurst[4] (Mary Barbara (Mayme) Eisenhuth[3], Elizabeth Katherine Hahn[2], Augustus Hahn[1]) was born 25 March 1925 in Utica, New York[170]and died 20 February 2001 in North Utica, New York.[171]She married Clyde P. Starbird 31 January 1948 in St. Paul's Episcopal Church, Utica, New York. He was born in 1916 in Bowdoin, Maine[172]and died 23 August 1970 in St. Luke's Memorial Hospital, New Hartford, New York[173]Mary Jane was raised and educated in Utica, New York and was a graduate of

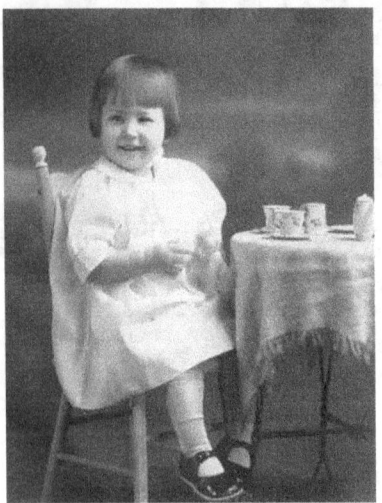

Utica Free Academy. She and Clyde were members of St Paul's Episcopal Church, serving as church organist for over 50 years. For a number of years she also taught private piano lessons. She was a member of the Marcy Senior Citizens, the Utica Maennerchor, and the Order of the Eastern Star. Clyde served in the Navy during World War II. He had been employed for over 23 years at the Utica Typewriter Co. Mary Jane Dewhurst and Clyde P. Starbird had one child who is still living.

Photo of Mary Jane Dewhurst at about three years old in the author's collection.

---

[168] Funeral program from Funeral Home in Camp Lejeune, North Carolina
[169] Obituary Peoria, Illinois Newspaper April 10, 2002
[170] Obituary Utica Newspaper February 21, 2001
[171] Obituary Utica Newspaper February 21, 2001
[172] Obituary Utica Newspaper August 24, 1970
[173] Obituary Utica Newspaper August 24, 1970

INDEX

This index lists all people mentioned in the book. There are also two ships listed in the index under "Ships".

In some cases the spelling of surnames are different between the parents and the children. For instance: Baumann and Bowman and Schroeder and Schrader and Seifert and Sifer. Also, the name Urtz is spelled Urtz, Uerz, Uertz and Urz.

Women are listed under their maiden names and married names. Women's maiden names are in ( ); their married names are in [ ].

Individuals with unknown surnames are listed at the beginning of the index.

Julia (Seifen), 10
Margaret [Sins], 30
Lintney, Lavina [Urtz], 28
Litz, Dora or Dolly [Sherwood], 138
Loftus, Esther C. [Dwyer], 60
Lonsdale
Howard, 182
Martha or Mattie (Looft), 182
Looft
Betty, 189
Catherine (Hahn), 179, 181, 182
Charles W., 182, 188
Elizabeth or Lizzie [Gibbons], 182
Ethel M. (McQuown), 188
George Henry, 182
Frederick P., 181, 182
Jessie [Funk] [Look], 182, 183
JoAnn, 189, 194
Laura, 182
Living, 189
Martha or Mattie [Lonsdale], 182
Look
Enno E., 183
Jessie (Looft) [Funk], 182, 183
Mrs. Leona [Mulvaney], 183
Raymond, 183
Lorenz
Anna [Ulrich], 105, 106
Anna (O'Rourke), 105
William, 105
Losch
Albert, 104
Albert Lincoln (Red), 104, 105
Alvin D., 105
Bertha (Miller), 104
Catherine M. (Ulrich), 84, 104, 105
Dewey W., 104
Lowery, Catherine [Hubbard], 163, 192
Ludy, Rosa Louise [Rieben], 163, 192

-M-

Mabb
Greta Mae (Sherwood), 132
Louis H., 132
MacArthur
Charlotte (Prosser), 115
Guy, 115

Mildred (Heneka) [Weber], 94, 115
Roy, 94, 115
Mainwaring, Gladys [Chadwick], 49
Manch
Anthony, 163, 187
Eleanor (Bowman) [Cimino], 156, 163, 187, 187
Laurence T., 163, 187
Mary, 163, 187
Manning
Elsie [Ulrich], 105
Martha [Henderson], 112
Martin
Alcenia [Sherwood], 138
Chester, 113
Helen [Humphrey], 91, 113
James, 43
Lena (Rowlands), 113
Living, 113
Mary (Burdick), 43
Roland Perry, 113
Rosemary (Schrader), 43
Victor Levi, 43
William Chester, 113
Massa, Maria [Colacicco], 62
Mathew
Margaret [Schroeder], 6, 7
Rosina, 7
Mathis, Anna Mary, 53
Mattee, Casper, 6
Mattles, Franciscus Anton, 77
McArt
Bridget (Bowman), 149
Mary, 155
McCabe, Ella, 149
McCann, Katherine [Cole], 35
McCorduck
Ada P. [Thomann], 37, 54, 55
Donald R., 55
George A., 54, 55
George E., 55
Robert, 55
McCracken
Dolores [Schrader], 63
Frederick, 63
Marie (Peterson), 63
McGee
Eileen E. (Corcoran), 65
Evelyn F. [Schmidt], 116
Florence (Sentiff), 23, 45
Franklin, 45
Franklin J., 45
John, 45
Joseph Warren, 45, 65

Living, 65
Mary (Oberst), 45
Vincent Edward, 65
McGuley, Ethel [Cook], 58
McLaughlin
Arthur, 115, 165, 193
Dorothy (Bryan), 115, 165, 193
Katherine [Bowman], 95, 115, 116, 137, 165, 193, 194
McMahon
Blanche Mary [Wright] (Uertz), 28, 47
James E., 47
James E. Jr., 47
James E. Sr., 47
Mary (Wengert), 47
McManus
Antoinette (Hahn) [Geiersbach], 179, 180
Michael, 179
McQuown
Charles A., 188
Ethel M. [Looft], 188
Hester Ann (Tyson), 188
McSweeney
Anna (Smith), 75, 76, 93
Eugene, 93, 115
Irene (?), 93, 115
John Francis, 93
Lois Jean, 93
Menning or Minung
Maria [Hahn], 177
Messmer
Adelaid, 25
Anna (Sentiff), 8, 25
George, 25
Irene, 25
Mikoloska, Mary [Szlachtowksi], 105
Miller
Bertha [Losch], 104
Christine [Wall], 131
Milne, Jessie Mary [Creaser], 161, 162
Minguez
Dorothy [Ziegler], 106
Julius, 106
Living, 106
Norman, 107
Rosalie (Muthig), 85, 106
Minor
Eleanor C. (Rivers), 133,139
LaVerne, 133,139
Mirkes